2394217-1
6/11/8

C0-ATX-277

The Phonological Enterprise

The Phonological Enterprise

MARK HALE AND CHARLES REISS

OXFORD
UNIVERSITY PRESS

OXFORD

UNIVERSITY PRESS

Great Clarendon Street, Oxford OX2 6DP

Oxford University Press is a department of the University of Oxford.
It furthers the University's objective of excellence in research, scholarship,
and education by publishing worldwide in

Oxford New York

Auckland Cape Town Dar es Salaam Hong Kong Karachi
Kuala Lumpur Madrid Melbourne Mexico City Nairobi
New Delhi Shanghai Taipei Toronto

With offices in

Argentina Austria Brazil Chile Czech Republic France Greece
Guatemala Hungary Italy Japan Poland Portugal Singapore
South Korea Switzerland Thailand Turkey Ukraine Vietnam

Oxford is a registered trade mark of Oxford University Press
in the UK and in certain other countries

Published in the United States
by Oxford University Press Inc., New York

© Mark Hale and Charles Reiss 2008

The moral rights of the authors have been asserted
Database right Oxford University Press (maker)

First published 2008

All rights reserved. No part of this publication may be reproduced,
stored in a retrieval system, or transmitted, in any form or by any means,
without the prior permission in writing of Oxford University Press,
or as expressly permitted by law, or under terms agreed with the appropriate
reprographics rights organization. Enquiries concerning reproduction
outside the scope of the above should be sent to the Rights Department,
Oxford University Press, at the address above

You must not circulate this book in any other binding or cover
and you must impose the same condition on any acquirer

British Library Cataloguing in Publication Data

Data available

Library of Congress Cataloging in Publication Data

Data available

Typeset by SPI Publisher Services, Pondicherry, India
Printed in Great Britain
on acid-free paper by
Biddles Ltd., King's Lynn, Norfolk

ISBN 978–0–19–953396–1 (hbk.)
ISBN 978–0–19–953397–8 (pbk.)

1 3 5 7 9 10 8 6 4 2

Contents

Preface

This book is an application to phonological theory of the biolinguistic perspective advocated by Chomsky (2005). Our discussion ranges over the three kinds of factor that determine the set of attainable I-languages: genetic endowment specific to language, linguistic experience, and extralinguistic considerations. With respect to the first factor, we argue for the logical necessity of a discrete, innately available system for phonological representation and computation. With respect to the second factor, we make proposals concerning the differences among languages with respect to attained segment inventories and rules. Finally, we discuss the nature of language change and the performance systems, factors that fall outside of the Human Language Faculty as a mental organ, but which nonetheless play a role in determining what phonological mental grammars, phonological I-languages, are attainable. Our intention, in both our criticisms and our positive suggestions, is to convince phonologists that taking the biolinguistic perspective seriously leads to more satisfying explanatory models in their field. There is much to be gained both by recognizing where current work diverges from the biolinguistic perspective (in our opinion, to its detriment), and by making explicit widespread, but implicit, biolinguistic assumptions.

Much of the material in this book has been in development for over ten years, and has been presented orally or in print in various forms. We stubbornly maintain that many of our arguments have not been adequately addressed, and in fact we take a comment from Prince and Tesar (1999) that we are "swimming against the tide" of current phonological research as an unintended compliment. We are not so deluded as to believe that we have solved the many difficult questions of phonological computation and acquisition that are discussed in the literature, but we are confident that we do raise serious objections to much of the logic, empirical claims, and methodology advocated by working phonologists.

It is often said that Optimality Theory (OT) has become the dominant paradigm in phonological theorizing since its advent in the mid 1990s. In our view—with theories of constraints including overtly functionalist work that explicitly aims to model behavior; phonetically "grounded" models that aim to soften the line between competence and performance; pseudo-formalist, markedness dependent approaches that belie a closeted functionalism; and finally, mathematically interesting work based on idealisms that preclude the possibility of any eventual relevance to human language—the OT label does not identify a coherent research community.

The situation is no less dire if we turn from the nature of the constraints to models of the computational system. Stochastic ranking and variable ranking have wrought havoc with the notion of an OT grammar as a strict ranking of conflictings constraints. Recent work in Stratal Optimality Theory and Harmonic Serialism has abandoned the two-level approach that was such an important aspect of early OT anti-derivational rhetoric. It is time to examine the foundations of the phonological enterprise.

In our exploration of the phonological literature, we came to realize that many issues that we objected to in Optimality Theory were in fact inherited from earlier generative models of phonology, especially with respect to markedness and acquisition; so our book is not to be read as a call to return to what phonologists were doing 15 or 25 years ago. We hope to encourage new ways both of understanding the goals of phonological theorizing and of finding results in the field.

We are grateful to many of our students and to audiences at many conferences through the years, particularly the Manchester Phonology Workshop and the Montreal–Ottawa–Toronto Phonology Workshop. We appreciate, especially, several linguists who encouraged us by engaging in criticism of our work and participating in sometimes vigorous discussion and debate through the years, including Bill Idsardi, Bert Vaux, Glyne Piggott, Morris Halle, David Odden, and Abby Cohn. Their input has certainly sharpened our thinking and our presentation, and we hope that they will continue to offer constructive criticism.

We thank Anna Maria di Sciullo for encouraging and supporting our work for many years in the context of several major research projects that she has led, with funding from the Social Sciences and Humanities Research Council of Canada and other agencies. Our own grants from the Council are also gratefully acknowledged.

Our largest debt is to Madelyn Kissock. In some sections we present research which was 'officially' jointly undertaken with her, but her influence extends to our thinking throughout the book.

Mark Hale and Charles Reiss

Concordia University, Montreal
June 2007

List of figures

For the errors of definitions multiply themselves according as the reckoning proceeds, and lead men into absurdities, which at last they see, but cannot avoid, without reckoning anew from the beginning.

Hobbes, *Leviathan*, Chapter IV: "Of Speech"

1

Introduction

1.1 Socrates' Problem

Chomsky, inspired by Russell, often makes reference to Plato's Problem, roughly: "How is it that we come to know so much (as humans) given the limited and unstructured nature of experience?" In this book we are concerned instead with what we dub Socrates' Problem, in recognition of our own uncertainty about the most fundamental issues in phonology: "How is it that we are sure of so little (as scientists), given the fact that we spend so much time (and, unlike Socrates, make so much money) trying to figure things out?" Socrates was considered wise precisely because he recognized the extent of his ignorance. In emulation of Socrates, we will perhaps mistakenly (in the opinion of some, clearly so) adopt the position that we are not alone in the unfathomable depths of ignorance, and that the field as a whole can only benefit from the re-examination of fundamental issues that we invite the reader to undertake with us.

This book is about the phonological component of the human language faculty. It is not about sound patterns or data sets. We will attempt to show in this book that there is already too much data-fitting in the phonological literature, and too little concern with a more fundamental task: constructing insightful, logically coherent theories. In an attempt to address this problem, we will structure this book around the analysis of two extremely simple data sets and the issues that must be addressed in analyzing them. Our discussion will lead us to foundational issues in phonology, linguistics, and cognitive science, including questions of the form and acquisition of knowledge.

1.2 What is Universal Grammar a theory of?

Before introducing the data, we want to set forth our view of the empirical domain for which Universal Grammar (UG) is responsible. First, we take it as uncontroversial that humans have some kind of language faculty, or set of interacting faculties, that we will conveniently refer to as "the language faculty". There is no reason to believe that our pens or our dogs have a similar set of faculties, although our dogs clearly have some of the capacities that are necessary for the existence of a language faculty, e.g. capacities for memory and symbolic representation. Once we accept the existence of a language faculty, it is also uncontroversial that this faculty has an initial state, before any experience with a particular language. Under this view Universal Grammar, the theory of this initial state, is a topic of study, not a hypothesis.

The question then arises as to what data constitute evidence for the nature of UG, and how this data should be used in theory construction. For example, should the theory of UG attempt to model an initial state that can account for all and only the attested languages of the world? This seems to us to be obviously wrong, since the set of attested languages, languages for which descriptions are available, is just an arbitrary subset of existing human languages, a set whose membership depends on accidents of history, including the whims of graduate student advisors, missionaries, and funding agencies. A more reasonable idea is that UG should be concerned with any possibly attestable human language, e.g. our neighbor's idiolect of "English", or the "Japanese" dialect spoken by someone in two hundred years.

It also seems clear that one could define computational systems which operate over linguistic representations which we do not want UG to be concerned with. For example, there is no evidence that the language faculty makes reference to prime numbers, so we do not want to build into UG the power to express rules lengthening vowels in prime-numbered syllables. Similarly, there seem to be no languages that reverse word order to form interrogative sentences, although such a language is trivial to describe.

The language faculty, *qua* computational system, is embedded in actual humans. Particular languages arise through the interaction of the language faculty with experience, but this experience is mediated by the organism's input systems. Therefore, while the computational possibilities allowed by the language faculty in its initial state define an upper bound on the set of attestable languages, this is not the sole limitation on that set. The input systems further restrict the set of languages which can come into being in the world. We argue here that yet another "filter" on the set of attestable languages is the nature of language change. It may be the case that the phonology *can* generate alternations describable as "p → s /_ r",[1] but it may also be the case that the conjunction of diachronic events necessary to lead to such a grammar

---

[1] We will assume, purely for the purpose of discussion, that this is indeed the case in what immediately follows. The matter is an empirical one and this particular example could easily be replaced by any of an (infinite) set of others without affecting the overall point.

is of vanishingly low probability, and thus such grammars are unattested and, practically speaking, unattestable.

It follows from the fact that grammars are learned, and that the details of individual grammars encode in some respects the details of their ancestors (see Hale 2007), that UG, as a theory of the computational system, will necessarily make it possible to describe languages for which we could never find direct evidence. UG must be a theory of what is humanly computable *using the language faculty*.

(1)   ATTESTED $\subset$ ATTESTABLE $\subset$ HUMANLY COMPUTABLE $\subset$ STATABLE
  a. Attested: Cree-type grammars, English-type grammars, French-type grammars
  b. Attestable: "Japanese" in 200 years, Joe's "English"
 ⤳c. Humanly computable: p $\rightarrow$ s / __ r
  d. Statable: V $\rightarrow$ V: in prime numbered syllables: paka$_2$nu$_3$tipa$_5$fose$_7$ $\rightarrow$ paka:nu:tipa:fose:

We offer here three simple arguments in support of the position that (1c) best describes the purview of UG, providing more sophisticated support for this position in the remainder of this book.

As a first argument, imagine that the human auditory system changed in such a way that high-frequency noise was no longer audible to humans. It would no longer be possible to acquire languages with fricatives like [s] or [ʃ]. The absence of fricatives would be completely explicable in terms of the changes in auditory perception, and it would be unnecessary, and also implausible, to propose that the representational capacities of the human language faculty changed in exact lockstep with the changes in audition, so as not to allow the representation of fricatives.[2] If we accept this thought experiment, it appears to follow that there is no reason to assume that the *current* state of the language faculty duplicates exactly the restrictions imposed by the input and output systems with which it interfaces.[3] Grammars are partly learned. The human transducers and performance systems presumably allow a human to "learn" a large number of formal, computational systems, some of which represent "grammars", some of which do not. That is, it is not the case that everything that our performance systems, broadly construed, can deal with is linguistic. There is, however, no reason to believe—indeed, it would be quite surprising if it were the case—that these systems did not also limit the set

---

[2] A similar thought experiment, but from the production side, is presented in Ch. 8.

[3] The thought experiment can be made more extreme and more concrete by considering the fact that a congenitally deaf set of parents may have hearing children whose language faculties are no different from those of children of hearing parents.

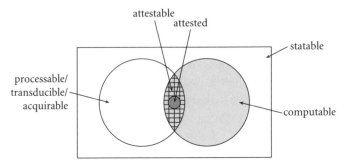

attestable
attested
statable
processable/
transducible/
acquirable
computable

FIGURE 1.1 Attested, attestable, computable, processable, and statable grammars

of attestable languages beyond the (upper) limits determined by the initial state of the acquirer, i.e. UG (sometimes, in an aquisition context, labeled S_0). That is, just as some representations are tractable for our processors, but not computationally tractable for a grammar, some representations are presumably computationally tractable for a grammar, but not tractable for our processors. This can be represented as in Figure 1.1 (see Reiss 2007 for further elaboration).

Second, note that this argument parallels a more familiar one. A generative grammar generates an unbounded number of sentences, and an unbounded number of those sentences are of unbounded length. Sentences over a certain length are not attestable because of the limits of human attention, human patience, human lifespans, etc. Just as the limits of human performance systems are recognized in our models of individual grammars, they must be recognized in our model of general grammar—some computationally possible systems may be unattestable. Universal Grammar must model all the attestable languages and then some.

Our third argument utilizes a particular phonological theory, but should be accessible even to those unfamiliar with the details. The theory of stress computation developed by Halle and Idsardi (1995) is mathematically explicit, elegant, and has a wide empirical coverage. We know that all theories in all domains are ultimately incomplete or otherwise flawed, but let us suppose that the Halle–Idsardi model is the best theory of stress we have. In this model, syllables are projected onto a metrical grid, generating in the first instance grid lines of asterisks, each of which corresponds to a syllable. For example, in the simplest case a four-syllable word will project a grid line of this form: ****.

In this model, a further step in computing stress is the insertion of boundary markers, "(" and ")", which group asterisks into feet. One type of boundary insertion rule is the Edge-Marking Rule, which is determined on a language-specific basis within a range defined by three parameters. The rule may insert a Left or Right parenthesis to the Left or Right of the Left- or Rightmost asterisk. We can thus characterize the essential elements of a given system by specifying a triplet of values for an "Edge:" parameter, each value ranging over the set {L,R}. "Edge:RLR" thus is to be read "insert a right parenthesis (the first R) to the left (the L) of the rightmost (the second R) asterisk." There are thus eight possible combinations of parameter settings, with eight distinct effects on a string of asterisks:

(2)   Halle–Idsardi Edge-Marking Rules
    a.   Edge:RRR   ****)   Insert a R parenthesis to the R of the R-most*
    b.   Edge:RLR   ***)*   Insert a R parenthesis to the L of the R-most *
    c.   Edge:RRL   *)***   Insert a R parenthesis to the R of the L-most *
    d.   ?Edge:RLL   )****   etc.
    e.   Edge:LLL   (****
    f.   Edge:LRL   *(***
    g.   Edge:LLR   ***(*
    h.   ?Edge:LRR   ****(

Note that Edge-Marking Rules (2d) and (2h) are marked with a question mark. This denotes the fact that no conceivable data could indicate to the linguist that a language has such a version of the Edge-Marking Rule for word-level stress. For the same reason, no child equipped with a Halle–Idsardi-type stress computation module in its phonology would ever find evidence to set the Edge-Marking Rule as either (2d) or (2h). Inserting parentheses in those ways has no effect on the grouping of asterisks, and thus can play no role in stress computation.

Should the language faculty contain explicit statements that (2d) and (2h) are not possible Edge-Marking Rules? Clearly not, since such statements would serve no purpose. A learner will never posit (2d) or (2h), whether or not the innate knowledge of stress computation contains, say, constraints like *RRL and *LLR. It follows from our position that if neuroscience advanced to the point where we could program specific grammars into human brains, then (2d) and (2h) would be computable by the human language faculty. The absence of such rules from the set of attested and attestable (in the absence of neural programming) languages is a fact about how specific languages are learned. It is not a fact about the cognitive architecture (Pylyshyn 1984) of the language faculty.

Chomsky (1957) points out that there is no straightforward way to restrict a generative grammar to sentences of a predefined length. In other words, the assumption of an unbounded set of sentences including ones of arbitrary length actually makes it possible to construct a *simpler* model. The same considerations hold for the stress example just discussed. In the case of sentence length, we can appeal to performance factors and the nature of corpora to explain the absence of sentences over some defined length in a given corpus. Similarly, we can adduce learnability considerations to explain the absence of certain combinations of independent parameters of the Halle–Idsardi stress model. These absences need not arise from restrictions encoded in mental grammars (instantiated in individuals), or even in our models, since the empirical data never arise that motivate positing such a restriction. Such restrictions thus can never be empirically relevant to either the learner or the scientist. The absence of certain combinations of parameter settings is accidental from a grammatical perspective.

We return to such metatheoretical issues throughout the book. However, we now turn to discussion of two simple data sets to illustrate Socrates' Problem—the fact that even when confronted with the most basic phonological facts, tremendous uncertainty exists as to how an analysis should proceed.

1.3 Some simple data: Georgian laterals

Consider a simple case of allophonic patterning such as the distribution of light and dark laterals in Georgian (Robins and Waterson 1952). The light [l] occurs only before front vowels and the dark [ɫ] occurs elsewhere. The language has five vowels [i,e,u,o,a], so we have several options concerning how to formulate the relevant rule. Let's consider two of them. We could formulate a rule like (3a) such that /ɫ/ > [l] before non-low front vowels, or, since there are no low front vowels, we can formulate a rule like (3b) which lacks any specification as to the height of the triggering vowels.

(3)   Georgian lateral fronting
- Vowels: [i,e,u,o,a]
- /ɫ/ → [l] before i and e

a. $\begin{bmatrix} +\text{lateral} \\ +\text{son} \\ \vdots \end{bmatrix} \rightarrow [-\text{back}]$ before $\begin{bmatrix} -\text{back} \\ +\text{ATR} \\ -\text{low} \\ -\text{round} \end{bmatrix}$

OR

b. $\begin{bmatrix} +\text{lateral} \\ +\text{son} \\ \vdots \end{bmatrix} \rightarrow [-\text{back}]$ before $\begin{bmatrix} -\text{back} \end{bmatrix}$

No language-internal evidence would bear on the matter of selecting the correct formulation of the rule, since the only front vowels in the language are non-low. In other words, the rules are extensionally equivalent. Despite the fact that we tend to teach beginning students that the second rule is better, since it is more concise, we will argue that the first is the better solution. In the course of this book, we hope to convince you that you should care which answer is closer to the correct one, and that justifying this claim is not as hopeless an enterprise as it may have seemed in the past.

1.4 Some more simple data: Catalan consonant alternations

Consider the following alternations based on well-known and widely discussed data from Catalan. For the time being, we will restrict discussion to these forms, although more data will be provided as the discussion progresses.

(4)   Catalan adjectives

masc.	fem.	gloss
sɛk	sɛkə	'dry'
sek	seɣə	'blind'

The vowels [e] and [ɛ] are contrastive in some dialects of Catalan, but are irrelevant to our discussion—we represent a dialect that distinguishes the vowels merely as an aid to keeping the lexical items distinct in our discussion. What we are interested in is the fact that the stem-final consonants are identical in the masculine forms, but different in the (suffixed) feminine forms.

This is just about the simplest kind of phonological data set one could imagine, one that is typically given to first-semester phonology students. We will argue, however, that it is far from obvious how such data should be analyzed, and that providing a thoughtful solution to this problem raises a tremendous number of difficult issues. Many of these issues have been raised in the past, but to our minds they have not been satisfactorily resolved.

Here are seven possible approaches to our mini-dataset:

(5)   Approaches to the Catalan data
   a. *sek* and *seɣə* are "related" in a grammar in the same way that *go* and *went* are related in the grammar of an English speaker. They share some part of their meaning, but each is memorized as an idiosyncratic entity. The same holds for *sɛk* and *sɛkə*.
   b. The members of each pair of words are related morphologically by the presence vs. absence of a suffix, and the alternants of the root (and the distribution of those alternants) are memorized—the root

for 'blind' is *sek* in the masc. and *seɣ* in the fem.; the root for 'dry' is *sɛk* in both the masc. and the fem.

c. The invariant [k] of *sɛk* 'dry' in various environments conforms to a recurring pattern in the language, as does the alternating [k]/[ɣ] of *sek / seɣə* 'blind'. However, both alternants of the *sek* and *seɣə* pattern are stored in memory, and declarative rules determine which is used in particular environments.

d. A single form /sek/ is stored for the 'blind' word, and a single form /sɛk/ is stored for the 'dry' word, but the former also is stored with a stipulation that the /k/ changes to [ɣ] under certain circumstances (say, between vowels).

e. A single form /seɣ/ is stored for 'blind' and general phonological rules convert this, and all cases of /ɣ/ to [k] when it is at the end of a syllable. For this morpheme, the rules yield [sek]. A single form /sɛk/ is stored for 'dry'.

f. A single form /seg/ is stored for "blind" and general phonological rules convert this, and all cases of /g/ to [k] when it is at the end of a syllable. Other general rules convert the /g/ to [ɣ] between vowels.[4] For this morpheme, the rules yield [sek]. As above, a single form /sɛk/ is stored for 'dry'.

g. A single form /seG/ is stored for 'blind', where G denotes an abstract velar obstruent with no specification for voicing or continuancy, and general phonological rules convert this, and all cases of /G/ to [k] when it is at the end of a syllable. Other general rules convert the /G/ to [ɣ] between vowels. As above, a single form /sɛk/ is stored for 'dry'.

Solutions (5a) and (5b), and perhaps (5c), entail a view of grammar that denies the relevance of generativity. Rejection of these solutions can be supported by establishing the existence of productivity—not productivity of behavior, but grammatical productivity. In the next section we examine some old and new arguments for productivity in phonology. These considerations will allow us to reject solutions (5a–c) immediately.

For us, the most interesting issues arise in comparing the merits of solutions (5d–g)—the solutions that have been taken most seriously in the generative phonology tradition. In the course of the book we will continually make reference to these solutions, as we draw on various considerations and additional data to assist us in choosing among them.

---

[4] Or rather between continuants, as we will see.

1.5 Traditional arguments for generativity in phonology

There are at least four arguments in the classical generative literature for rejecting the null hypothesis for phonology—the idea that the pronunciation of words is memorized. The recursiveness of syntax rules out the possibility of memorizing sentences, but it has been claimed that phonology does not have any clear cases of recursion. Thus other arguments for generativity have been adduced, including the following:

- Distributional regularities
- Alternations
- The *wug* test
- Borrowings

The standard argument based on distributional regularities runs as follows. In the absence of a rule system that derives non-contrastive, "allophonic" variation from underlying abstract segments, observed regularities—such as the fact that the distribution of unaspirated and aspirated stops in English is completely predictable from phonological context—would be a curious coincidence. Since science must explain regularities in observed phenomena as deriving from general principles, phonological science must posit phonological rules to model allophony.

Alternations—variations in the surface form of a morpheme depending on phonological context—are a particular kind of distributional regularity. In addition to the non-contrastive phonetic distinctions mentioned above, such alternations may also show neutralizations of segments that are distinct in some environments. For example, after non-stridents, the English plural marker for nouns has the form [s] after voiceless sounds and [z] after voiced sounds. Again, the regularity of patterning cries out for a principled explanation, and typically linguists posit that the pronunciation as a correspondent of the segment /s/ is derived by rule from an underlying morpheme consisting of just the phoneme /z/. The distinction between /s/ and /z/ is neutralized in favor of [s] after voiceless non-strident sounds.[5]

The *wug* test (Berko 1958) refers to well-known experimental work with children and adults which seems to confirm the notion that alternations are the product of rule application. When presented with nouns in the singular invented by the experimenter and prompted for a plural form, both adults and young children tended to adhere to the pattern described above—[s] after

---

[5] For those not familiar with the argument, /z/ is chosen as basic, since [s] can occur after voiced sounds, as in *fal*[s]*e* in contrast with *fall*[z].

voiceless non-strident sounds, [z] after voiced ones. Since they could not have memorized the plurals of novel words, which were, after all, just created by the experimenter, they must have applied a rule to generate them.

Foreign accents and pronunciation of foreign words are also invoked to support the idea that pronunciation is best modeled by appeal to a grammar, rather than listed pronunciations, since speakers tend to assimilate words from other languages to the phonology of their own language, despite apparent evidence to the contrary from the foreign speakers' pronunciations. For example, English speakers tend to aspirate voiceless stops in syllable onset position when learning Spanish or French.

We believe strongly in the existence of a productive phonological component, and we probably would accept some version of each of these arguments as valid. However, we acknowledge that some of our own arguments later in the book may appear to be at odds with aspects of these classical positions. For example, we will adopt the position that certain phenomena widely considered to be phonological merely reflect generalizations about the lexicon. Thus at times the existence of sets of seemingly related forms in a lexicon may be due solely to the regularity of language change, rather than to computational or representational properties of the phonological system. By providing a "diachronic" account for these regularities, we are accepting the responsibility that science should account for the observed data, but shifting that responsibility outside of phonological theory, narrowly construed.

We will not dwell here on the potential weaknesses of the traditional arguments discussed above, because we believe we can fortify the argument for generativity and abstract representation with other considerations.

Memory.   First, the null hypothesis, presented in the form "Words are stored in memory as pronounced", cannot be literally true. We know that even a single word from a single speaker varies in its acoustics on different occasions of utterance. Furthermore, we know that we do not pronounce words with the same acoustic properties (reflecting voice quality, affect, loudness, environmental noise) that were present when we learned the word—a child does not pronounce words learned from deep-voiced women differently from words learned from squeaky-voiced men, for example. So while there is memory involved in pronunciation, it is a very special kind of memory—it is a representation consisting of abstract symbolic primitives, transduced from speech signals by the human speech-processing system. These primitives are known as phonological features. The features are the equivalence classes of phonology.

Speech rate. Another argument against pronunciation as pure imitation from memory comes from the obvious fact that we do not always speak at the same rate. So, the abstract representation of a vowel, say, has to be fed into an output system that can vary its actual duration as a physical event. In fact, a long vowel spoken at a fast speech rate may have the same duration as a short vowel spoken slowly. Again, we do not pronounce all words which were learned from speakers in a hurry at a fast rate, and all words learned from a more leisurely speaker at a slower one. Speech rate variation appears to fall along a continuum, and thus actual pronunciations of speech sounds cannot be stored as discrete tokens. There must, therefore, be rules that map abstract representations to actual utterances.

Intonation. Intonation—the mapping of pitch and stress contours onto syntactic phrases—constitutes another argument for generativity, and may in fact parallel the arguments for generativity in syntax. Since sentences are of unbounded length, and since the pronunciation of every sentence must have an associated intonation pattern, there must be a generative mechanism for assigning intonation to the unbounded set of strings of words generable by the syntax.

1.6 Does it matter which rules and representations we posit?

It would appear that any number of the explanations provided in (5a–g) above could adequately account for the phenomenon observed in Catalan. Does it matter, then, which of these extensionally equivalent solutions we opt for? We present here arguments that it does, indeed, matter.

1.6.1 *I-phonology, E-phonology, and B-phonology*

Suppose that a child, call him Baby Z, is acquiring an "English-type" grammar, the output of which includes forms like [kʰæt]. It seems clear that cognitive scientists, phonologists in particular, should set as an ultimate goal finding a solution to the first of the following questions (which is the harder and more interesting one), and they should not be satisfied with merely answering the second.

- What knowledge state underlies Baby Z's output such that he says [kʰæt]?
- What is the set of possible knowledge states that could lead to Baby Z saying [kʰæt]?

The answer to the first question correctly entails a concern with I-language, language conceived of as knowledge, a matter of "individual psychology" (Chomsky 1986). In other words, phonology is computation over symbolic representations by the phonological component of the mind/brain. Let's refer to this approach as the I-phonology approach. The second is merely concerned with defining extensionally equivalent E-languages, i.e. language conceived of as sets (or potential sets) of utterances, tokens of behavior. This "E-phonology" approach may involve some interesting theorizing on the formal properties of grammars, both humanly attainable ones and others; however, it cannot be adopted as a well-grounded conception of phonology as cognitive science.

We will argue that much of the phonological literature, both before and since the advent of Optimality Theory (Prince and Smolensky 1993), has given up on answering questions of the first type. In fact, phonologists have turned away from this goal in at least two ways. First, those we will call "E-phonologists" concern themselves with the formal issues entailed by the second type of question. It is important to note, however, that like "I-phonologists" they are concerned with mappings between input and output *representations*, although it is not always clear what the status of these representations is for E-phonologists (e.g. whether or not they are mental representations).

Others have turned further from the goal of I-phonology in their sometimes tacit rejection of the generative assumption that grammar, including, of course, phonology, is only about knowledge and representations. Instead this work is concerned with more superficial,[6] data-fitting theories of speech output as *behavior*. We can thus refer to this as the "B-phonology" school.

We can characterize the concerns of the three-way distinction we now have with these questions:

- I-phonology: "Which humanly attainable knowledge state underlies Baby Z's computation over phonological representations?"
- E-phonology: "What is the set of formal systems that would output the same representations as Baby Z's phonology outputs?"[7]
- B-phonology: "What can we say about the *sounds* Baby Z makes?"

---

[6] This word is meant in the sense of "observable", not in a necessarily pejorative sense, although we do believe the approach is misguided.

[7] There is yet another possible sub-distinction: some E-phonologists might concern themselves with only humanly attainable formal systems. We will argue that it is useful to assume the position that, given the hypothesized invariance of the language faculty, only one grammar is attainable on exposure to a given set of input data.

The "evaluation procedures" discussed in *The Sound Pattern of English* (Chomsky and Halle 1968) and subsequent work were meant to answer questions of the first type, but Anderson's (1985: 327) remarks on the topic are telling: "Early concern for evaluation procedures...turned out to be something of a dead end...the appeal of feature counting went away...not with a bang, but with a whimper." In this book we discuss some simple examples which suggest that prospects for answering the first type of question are not as bleak as they have seemed in the past, and that I-phonology is thus a viable enterprise.

Once we recognize that the I-language approach forces us to accept the existence of a correct answer to the question of the nature of Baby Z's phonology, the next step is to ask how we might go about finding the correct answer. In other words, how do we choose among extensionally equivalent grammars? We identify two techniques which are often used in the generative literature, but not always explicitly identified. Both techniques will be exploited in subsequent chapters.

One method for choosing from a set of extensionally equivalent grammars is to develop a model of language acquisition which has as its endpoint one of the competing models of the acquired grammar. If one theory is compatible with an elegant and insightful acquisition model, and the others are not, then the first is to be preferred.

The second technique is to use cross-linguistic argumentation. Already in *Syntactic Structures*, Chomsky's (1957) stated goal was a general theory of language, one in which notions like "phoneme" and "noun" are not defined on a language-particular basis. Thus, if only one of several extensionally equivalent grammars of a language L is compatible in its inventory of primitive elements with the grammars of other languages, then it is tentatively preferable over its rivals as the "correct" grammar of L.

In the remainder of this chapter we focus on the first of these techniques and attempt to revive these issues by redefining the relationship between the study of phonological computation *per se* and phonological acquisition and learnability. In addition to making positive proposals, we will point out where other models of phonology have strayed from the pursuit of I-phonology. For example, with respect to Optimality Theory, we will argue here that the notion of Richness of the Base has no place in a theory of I-phonology.

1.6.2 *Two reasons to look at acquisition*

Given Kiparsky's (1973: 17) observation that "Children learning their native language do not have the interests of linguists at heart", it is necessary that we view phonology from the learner's perspective. Our reward for such attention to the acquisition process will be twofold. First of all, paying attention to acquisition can tell us what we need *not* worry about. For example, the OT literature is rife with claims of OT's superiority at accounting for conspiracies: "One of the principal reasons that rule-based theory has come under attack is that it offers no satisfactory explanation for conspiracies" (Kager 1997: 463). Kiparsky (1973) has argued convincingly, however, that generative phonology does not need the notion of conspiracy. Here is our interpretation of Kiparsky's argument.

(6)   The epiphenomenality of conspiracies (based on Kiparsky 1973: 75ff.)

   a.   A conspiracy is a set of rules that are "functionally related", i.e. they lead to the same kinds of output configuration such as "all syllables are open".
   b.   If a language has such a set of rules, then these rules will tend to be surface true, that is, transparent. Otherwise they would not contribute to the "conspiracy".
   c.   Non-transparent (opaque) rules are not surface true.
   d.   Rules that are not surface true are hard for a learner to learn.
   e.   Things that are hard to learn are more likely *not* to be learned than things which are easy to learn (by definition).
   f.   Failure to learn aspects of the ambient language constitutes a diachronic change.
   g.   Therefore, (E-)languages are more likely to lose a given instance of opacity than gain such an instance of opacity.
   h.   Therefore, grammars are likely to look as though they have conspiracies.

In other words, the existence of conspiracies is an epiphenomenon to be attributed to the fact that languages tend to have transparent rules. This in turn is an epiphenomenon derived from the undeniable fact that individual languages must be learned.

Kiparsky's explanation of conspiracies depends on the fact that acquisition can be *unsuccessful*, resulting in so-called "language change" (Hale 2007). In other words, tendencies such as "conspiracies" are to be explained by reference to diachronic linguistics, where the goal is to define possible changes and to explain why certain changes are more or less likely to occur. We now turn to the question of what *successful* acquisition can potentially tell us.

The second benefit of paying attention to acquisition is that it allows us to take seriously the idea expressed in Chomsky (1986:3) and elsewhere that Universal Grammar (UG) *is* the Language Acquisition Device (LAD). In other words, the LAD constrains the set of possible languages by determining how the learner assigns analyses to data provided in the environment, the Primary Linguistic Data (PLD). There are several advantages to such an approach. First, we need no "principles" of UG which are not derivable from, or reducible to, the nature of the LAD. Since we obviously need a learning algorithm (the LAD), a theory with just an LAD is *ceteris paribus* better than a theory with an LAD *and* stipulated principles of UG. This approach also obviates the need for an evaluation metric. Learners never compare extensionally equivalent grammars for simplicity or economy; they just construct the one grammar that is determined by the LAD. This means that there is no reason to introduce the terms "simplicity" and "economy" into the theory, since they are contentless labels for aspects of the LAD that are not derivable; that is, they are arbitrary.

Note that even if the attempt to collapse UG and the LAD is ultimately misguided, this is not a bad kind of mistake to make. Attempting to collapse the two can lead to the discovery that *some* aspects of our current theory of UG are derivable from the nature of the LAD. Using such findings, we can formulate a more streamlined version of UG (*qua* set of stipulated properties of the language faculty not derivable from the LAD), even if we cannot reduce its contents completely.

1.6.3 *Phonological systems are partially learned*

One aspect of the discussion in section 1.6.1 above is a criticism of the use of the facts of phonetic substance in developing models of UG. We come back to this issue in Chapter 7, where we develop arguments for a purely formal approach to phonology. In this section we argue, in apparent contradiction to this point, that in some ways phonologists have been *too* formal in their methods. The contradiction is merely apparent, however; the problem is mostly one of focus. Since, as Chomsky (1986) puts it, generative linguistics is concerned with matters of "individual psychology", the regularities in the output of linguistic systems need to be seen as the result of innate and learned factors. Focusing on purely formal statements concerning potential in situ grammars which are extensionally equivalent misses something critical in that it does not force us to discover *the correct grammar* that constitutes knowledge of some language. Some examples will prove helpful.

Kenstowicz and Kisseberth (1979: 215) provide a useful formulation of Kiparsky's Alternation Condition (AC):

Each language has an inventory of segments appearing in underlying representations. Call these segments phonemes. The UR of a morpheme may not contain a phoneme /x/ that is always realized phonetically as identical to the realization of some other phoneme /y/.

We need not worry about which, if any, version of the Alternation Condition is best, or even if the condition is valid in any form—our point here is one of perspective. If we want to equate UG with the LAD, then, instead of proposing the Alternation Condition as a principle of UG, we should ask: "How does the child set up underlying representations? What is the learning algorithm that is used to capture the apparently real patterns manifested by alternations and the distribution of speech sounds?" Kiparsky (1973: 65) pretty much says this in referring to one version of the Alternation Condition: "a situation which I termed *absolute neutralization* is either impossible or hard to learn, and should therefore in an explanatory theory of phonology be excluded or specified as not highly valued." The explanatory theory Kiparsky refers to is phonological UG. Once we equate UG and the LAD, Kiparsky's stipulated Alternation Condition becomes unnecessary. If this suggestion is valid, then it is perhaps unfortunate that some later work fails to adopt this position, and the Alternation Condition is treated as a formal *principle* that constrains grammars (including the lexicon), rather than expressing a generalization about how they are constructed.

   It is ironic to note that while a fair amount was written on the Alternation Condition in the pre-OT era, studies of phonological acquisition posited rules of supposed child phonological systems that violated the Alternation Condition. For example, children who do not distinguish [ʃ] from [s] because of a purported rule /ʃ/ > [s] that neutralizes the two are in blatant violation of the Alternation Condition, which is, recall, a limitation imposed on human grammars by the genetic code. If the Alternation Condition is conceived as a principle of UG, it is not possible for it to be violated by any human grammars, even those of children. A coherent theory that takes acquisition into account will provide a learning algorithm that tells us how underlying representations are inferred from the PLD (in part by denying the existence of "child phonology rules" as we shall see). Therefore such a theory does not need the Alternation Condition, as others have concluded before us (e.g. Kenstowicz 1994). This book is our attempt to ground such a theory.

1.6.4 *Richness of the Base*

Can we relate any of this to the currently dominant theory of phonology, Optimality Theory? One oft-touted property of OT is the notion of Richness

of the Base. Assuming Richness of the Base and given an appropriate constraint ranking, a speaker of English could have any one of a number of forms
stored for the lexical item that surfaces as [kʰæt]. For example, they could
have /kʰæt/, /kæt/ or /k!æt/. If, say, constraints against clicks and constraints
demanding that voiceless stops be aspirated word-initially are ranked high,
then all these inputs would surface as [kʰæt]. In other words the surface
inventory is not so much a function of the inputs, but more a result of the
ranking.

As Kager (1999) puts it, Richness of the Base is a "principle" that means that
"no specific property can be stated at the level of underlying representations".
That is, there are no morpheme structure constraints (MSCs) of any kind,
including restrictions against certain sequences of segments or against certain
feature combinations. Kager (1999: 31–2) shows that a single OT ranking
for English could generate the correct output forms [sæd] 'sad' and [sæ̃nd]
'sand' using any combination of nasal and non-nasal vowels in underlying
forms. That is, the ranking produces the right output for any of the lexicons
in (7):

(7)   Ranking: $^{*}V_{ORAL}N >> ^{*}V_{NASAL} >> $ Ident-IO(nasal)

Input		Output
/sæ̃d/ & /sæ̃nd/	>	[sæd] & [sæ̃nd]
/sæd/ & /sæ̃nd/	>	[sæd] & [sæ̃nd]
/sæ̃d/ & /sænd/	>	[sæd] & [sæ̃nd]
/sæd/ & /sænd/	>	[sæd] & [sæ̃nd]

The highest-ranked constraint is violated when an oral vowel occurs directly
before a nasal consonant. The next constraint is violated by the appearance
of nasal vowels in output forms. The lowest constraint demands input–
output identity for the feature [nasal]. This ranking of a context-sensitive
markedness constraint above a potentially conflicting context-free markedness constraint, and both above a faithfulness constraint, is an example of
the standard OT account of allophonic variation. The proposed ranking
generates the right results without being tied to a unique view of what the
lexical items are. This is a useful demonstration of an interesting mathematical property of OT grammars, but we argue that it is psychologically
uninteresting.

Ridding phonological theory of MSCs is clearly a laudable goal, since
such constraints serve merely to state descriptive generalizations about the
memorized content of the lexicon of a particular language. Even if we, as
linguists, find some generalizations in our description of the lexicon, there is
no reason to posit these generalizations as part of the speaker's knowledge of

their language, since they are computationally inert and thus irrelevant to the input–output mappings that the grammar is responsible for. Now, one might argue that this is what all phonological statements achieve: a generalization over a body of individual tokens. For example, the aspiration rule of English just restates a generalization about aspiration in surface forms of English. However, the difference between MSCs and phonological rules should be clear: the former generalize over stored, i.e. memorized, information, whereas the latter are meant to capture productive patterns of generated information. That is, phonological rules are intensional statements, consistent with the I-language perspective. They cannot be extensional statements, since speakers are assumed not to store surface forms. The MSCs just redundantly capture facts about the lexicon, which by definition must be extensionally represented as a list. If Richness of the Base were meant merely as a descriptive statement about OT grammars in comparison to other models, it would impossible to find fault with it: other models incorporate MSCs and explicit characterizations of underlying inventories, whereas OT grammars do not. It is odd, however to call Richness of the Base a "principle", since in effect it just names entitities that are *not* part of the theory. It is also the case that OT grammars do not contain electrons or beliefs; but a statement to this effect is not part of the theory, nor should it be. So, even the benign use of Richness of the Base is tainted by the practice of taking it to be a principle of grammar: there are an infinite number of such "principles" of exclusion (see Chapter 8).

It is instructive to consider just how the "principle" of Richness of the Base is used in actual OT practice. McCarthy (2003a: 29) invokes Richness of the Base to avoid selecting a single underlying representation for a given morpheme: "with faithfulness bottom-ranked, the choice of input [among three alternatives] doesn't matter, since all map to [the same surface form]. So there is no need to restrict the inputs." McCarthy's constraint ranking generates the same (correct) output representation for all three of the input forms he considers, so he has solved in some sense an analytical problem which confronts any scientist: how can I construct a formal system which could account for the data in question (in this case, by generating it)? However, we feel that it is critical to distinguish between three very different problems which confront the linguist in approaching a body of data. We will refer to them as the Artificial Intelligence (AI) Problem, the Linguist's Problem, and the Human's Problem. They are described in (8).

(8)   Three problems
   • *The AI Problem*: AI research is concerned with simulation of human intelligence or behavior without regard to whether the model proposed

matches the computational methods used by humans. In the cognitive science literature, this is described as the requirement that the computer model be weakly equivalent to the human—it must generate the same outputs. While this is a non-trivial task, it is less demanding than a requirement of strong equivalence in which the model makes use of the same representations and computations as the human. (See Pylyshyn 1984: ch. 4.)

- *The Linguist's Problem*: In modeling a mental grammar, a specific, physically instantiated knowledge state, a linguist may be faced with choices which cannot be determined from the available data. Since scientific models are always somewhat incomplete, this should be seen as a normal state of affairs. However, it should not be assumed that the indeterminacy can never be overcome: more data may be forthcoming or indirect forms of reasoning may be applied. An example of the latter is discussed by Chomsky (1986: 38): "Because evidence from Japanese can evidently bear on the correctness of a theory of S_0 [the initial state of the grammar-mrh & cr], it can have indirect—but very powerful—bearing on the choice of the grammar that attempts to characterize the I-language attained by a speaker of English." In other words, evidence from one language should bear on the best analysis of other languages. If two hypotheses, A and B, concerning UG (or the Language Acquisition Device, the LAD) are empirically adequate to explain the acquisition of English, and two hypotheses, A and C, are adequate to explain the acquisition of Japanese, then we should select A as the best available hypothesis about the nature of UG.

- *The Human's Problem*: Since the learner acquires *some* particular grammar, he or she must have an algorithm for selecting specific representations and rules among a range of extensionally equivalent ones. We assume a deterministic learning algorithm, so that the learner is not faced with a choice, in any meaningful sense—the choice is part of the Linguist's Problem.

McCarthy has solved the AI Problem to which the data he is considering give rise. However, linguistics is not AI. Instead of recognizing that he is faced with the Linguist's Problem (which is to figure out how learners solve the Human's Problem), McCarthy abdicates the job of phonologist *qua* cognitive scientist by claiming that the choice between competing input forms "doesn't matter".

Finding the solution to the Human's Problem may be difficult because of the Linguist's Problem, but the solution surely does matter. McCarthy is confusing various issues in advocating no restrictions on inputs. There is no question of "restricting" the inputs in the sense of positing MSCs as part of the grammar, but rather a question of figuring out which inputs the learner constructs given the observed data. It is something of a perversion of terms to label a hypothesis about what the LAD does "a restriction on underlying representation", when in fact what is involved is merely a function of what happens when the acquirer arrives at a solution, given data and a learning algorithm.

Consider an additional discussion of Richness of the Base in the OT literature:

> The set of possible inputs to the grammars of all languages is the same. The grammatical inventories of languages are defined as the forms appearing in the structural descriptions that emerge from the grammar when it is fed the universal set of all possible inputs. Thus, systematic differences in inventories arise from different constraint rankings, not different inputs. The lexicon of a language is a sample from the inventory of possible inputs; all properties of the lexicon arise indirectly from the grammar, which delimits the inventory from which the lexicon is drawn. There are no morpheme structure constraints on phonological inputs, no lexical parameter that determines whether a language has *pro*. (Tesar and Smolensky 1998: 252)

However, if the inventory is due to the constraint ranking, then what determines the ranking? The answer is obviously that richness of the base expresses exactly the wrong generalization. The inventory present in the ambient language, or rather, the inventory detected by the learner from the Primary Linguistic Data, together with the Language Acquisition Device, determines the ranking.

Now it is not a problem that OT with Richness of the Base would allow apparent violations of the Alternation Condition (by merging all underlying clicks with plain velars, for example), since the Alternation Condition is not part of the theory. However, who, if not phonologists, will be responsible for deciding whether the child has underlying /kʰæt/, /kæt/ or /k!æt/? Since we are interested in I-language, we can (and must) ask which is the correct grammar, not just what is the class of extensionally equivalent, descriptively adequate grammars.

The two approaches under consideration correspond to the questions we began with in section 1.6.1, which we repeat here for convenience:

- I-phonology: "Which humanly attainable knowledge state underlies Baby Z's computation over phonological representations?"
- E-phonology: "What is the set of formal systems that would output the same representations as Baby Z's phonology outputs?"
- B-phonology: "What can we say about the *sounds* Baby Z makes?"

If we believe that our job ends when we can answer the second question, and that the first is not important or perhaps not even coherent, then we will have sided with the anti-mentalism of Quine (who maintained that it is incoherent to ask which of two extensionally equivalent grammars represents the best scientific hypothesis) on the I-/E-language debate.[8]

We see then that Richness of the Base is actually a *symptom* of not having an explicit learning algorithm. It represents an abdication of the responsibility to attempt to determine just what the speaker has stored. Of course, one can attempt to provide OT with an explicit learning algorithm, but then Richness of the Base becomes irrelevant to the development of a scientific account of linguistic knowledge. This characterization of the anti-mentalism implicit in many OT analyses is explicit in the quotation of McCarthy (2003a: 29) given above, which says that the decision about the stored form of lexical items "doesn't matter". McCarthy is confusing the issue of the linguist designing a grammar, *qua* computational system, with the problem of discovering which *mental* grammar it is that the learner has acquired.

We think that there is a deep confusion of epistemology and ontology in the literature surrounding this issue—an impression reinforced by McCarthy's (2003b: 1) comments elsewhere on the matter:

One reason for this neglect of ROTB is probably the perception that it is just an inconvenient obstacle for the analyst or an abstruse theoretical concept without relevance to daily life in phonology. Indeed, it has even been suggested that "the notion of richness of the base [is] a computational curiosity of OT grammars that may be quite irrelevant to human language". (Hale and Reiss 1998: 600)

In referring to "daily life in phonology", McCarthy is using the term to refer to the academic study of the phonological component of the human language faculty. However, the issue is not whether Richness of the Base is a useful heuristic for phonologists in the daily life of doing phonology (although we can't conceive of how this could be the case), but whether it is a property of the *object of study* of phonologists. The term "phonology" is used with the same systematic ambiguity as "physics" to refer both to the object of study and to the study itself. But nobody believes that the nature of the physical world is determined by what physicists do in their daily life at the blackboard or in the lab to make discoveries. Are we being unfair? Consider the next sentence in McCarthy's paper (2003b):

---

[8] See Chomsky (1986) for discussion of Quine's views.

In this paper I will argue, on the contrary, that ROTB can be a positive aid to the analyst, helping to solve a perennial puzzle in generative phonology, indeterminate underlying representations

Once again, Richness of the Base is described as part of *doing* phonology, not as part of the object of study. Only confusion can arise from such careless flip-flopping between these two domains.

1.7 Outline of the book

The preceding discussion has introduced some of our working assumptions concerning the goals of phonology (and linguistic theory more generally), some data that is widely assumed to fall within the purview of the field, and some justification for a non-superficial, generative model of phonology. All of these issues will be revisited throughout the book, which is divided into four Parts. Part I deals with a central issue which confronts anyone trying to construct a UG-based theory of phonological knowledge and computation: acquisition. Chapter 2 presents our account of the notion of the "Subset Principle" in phonological acquisition, presenting a very different take on the matter from the one generally advocated. In Chapter 3 we deal in considerable detail with the complex matters arising from the need to respect the well-known competence/performance distinction in the study of human linguistic systems, including, of course, those of children.

Part II of the book focuses on a problem which we have dubbed "substance abuse" in phonological theory. The gist of this portion of the book is that if we take seriously (and *we* do) the generative notion that grammar, including its phonological component, is a property of individual minds, and the modern cognitive science conception of the mind as a set of computational devices (or "modules"), then phonology will involve computation over abstract mental entities. Since these entities will not have the properties of tongues, lips, and vocal folds, phonology will not be grounded in the facts of articulatory practice; and since the entities over which phonological computation takes place are not acoustic waves, nor the body's physiological response to such waves, phonology will not be grounded in facts of human perception (Chapter 6). And, finally, since the computational system owes neither its aetiology nor its constitution to the statistical properties of the set of attested human languages, phonology will not be typologically grounded (Chapter 7).[9]

---

[9] We do not obviously intend to exclude the possibility that an understanding of the computational entities and processes made available by UG for phonological computation will provide an account for some aspects of language typology or phonetics—but note the *directionality* of the implication. Some typological or phonetic facts may find a natural explanation once we have come to understand the

In Part III we discuss aspects of some of the proposed models of phonology which have come to be called "Optimality Theory". In Chapter 8 we discuss some conceptual difficulties which in our view confront any constraint-based approach to phonological computation. In Chapter 9 we discuss two somewhat different aspects of the concept of "Output–Output" Correspondence, which plays a significant role in some OT research.

Part IV presents the major conclusions of the book. In Chapter 10 we sketch out some ideas, building upon our arguments in the earlier parts of the book, for the future of phonological research, presenting as well our final solution to the Catalan problem outlined earlier in this chapter. It is thus no exaggeration to say that the whole book serves as justification for solutions to the two simple problems we have presented in this introduction, the Georgian allophone problem and the Catalan neutralization problem. The book concludes with some final remarks.

We cannot end this introduction without one further note, inspired in large part by the helpful comments of those who have read through this book in manuscript form.[10] The arguments in this book are stated with an enthusiasm and forcefulness that some take as overly strong. We have gone to some trouble to point out, in the beginning of this introduction, the extreme ignorance which the phonological community, including ourselves, is presently in. There is nothing shameful or surprising in this: the scientific study of phonological matters is a domain of human activity very much in its infancy. There are many different approaches to the issues which we concern ourselves with in this book; and, although we are critical of many, though by no means all, of them (for what we feel are good reasons), we believe diversity of opinion and approach is a healthy sign. There are those who do not believe in segments, those who do not believe that an "internalist" perspective on the nature of "language" is appropriate or even possible, those who reject innateness, or anything but the storing of whole word-forms in the lexicon: this book is largely not directed towards these scholars (though they might find some profit in reading it). There is a community of scholars who, in contrast to the above, share a common set of assumptions about the nature of the phonological enterprise: segments exist and are themselves made up of more primitive features; long-term lexical storage is of morphemes; the grammar is a property of individual minds/brains and is computational in nature; one must distinguish between competence (the underlying system) and performance (its

computational structure of phonological UG, but phonological UG will not have the properties it has *because* of the typological or phonetic facts.

[10] This includes several anonymous reviewers, whom we would like to take this opportunity to thank.

use), etc. Our primary target audience for this book is those who accept these, and related, "generative" assumptions, for we argue in considerable detail in this book that such scholars often offer explanations and propose models and analyses which are largely *inconsistent* with these assumptions—assumptions which they nevertheless continue to avow a belief in. A logically consistent approach to phonology, whatever one's grounding assumptions, is what we are arguing for. Those who make different grounding assumptions should argue, in our view, forcefully and coherently for the utility of their approach. This is what we have attempted to do here for our own, we think relatively mundane, set of grounding assumptions.

Part I
Phonological UG and acquisition

2

The Subset Principle in phonology

2.1 Introduction

This chapter is an extended explication with relevance to phonological theory of the following quotation: "In any computational theory, 'learning' can consist only of creating novel combinations of primitives alrady innately available" (Jackendoff 1990: 40). We refer to this position as the Innateness of Primitives Principle (IofPP). This position has been formulated and defended most eloquently by Jerry Fodor (e.g. 1975); however, an earlier formulation is in Pylyshyn (1973). Karl Popper (1962) has made essentially the same point, for all knowledge, including conscious scientific reasoning. In more or less explicit forms, the argument appears to be an ancient one that has never been completely refuted by connectionists or any other anti-nativist school. We will demonstrate the logical necessity of IofPP with a set of model languages, then show how a great deal of work on the acquisition of phonological inventories is inconsistent with IofPP. We then propose an alternate theory which *is* consistent with IofPP, which, we assume, lies at the core of the Innateness Hypothesis.

The chain of reasoning we pursue in explicating the IofPP can be summarized as follows. Intelligence (by which we intend merely cognition) consists of the construction and manipulation of symbolic representations. Interacting intelligently with the world requires the ability to *parse* input (assign it a representation). Learning is a form of intelligent interaction with the world; thus learning requires parsing inputs into representations. Without an innate set of representational primitives, learning cannot begin.

We demonstrate further that our theory, unlike traditional views concerning the acquisition of phonological inventories, is consistent with the Subset Principle (SP), properly defined. We argue that the Subset Principle is also a logical necessity for linguistic theory, although we propose that it must be reconceptualized somewhat, for both phonology and syntax. In brief, the SP is to be defined over stored representations, including the representations that constitute the structural description of rules, and not over grammars or sets of sentences. The essence of the SP, as we restate it, is that representations at an earlier stage of acquisition must be *more highly specified* than those at a later stage. Because of the inverse relationship between the number of features used to define a set of representations and the number of members in the set, our view of the SP will sometimes be in direct conflict with pretheoretical intuitions, as well as with the suggestions of other scholars. After introducing the Subset Principle, we illustrate the basics of our approach using toy grammars in potentially excruciating detail. The reader's indulgence in that section will we hope, be repaid when we turn to real linguistic examples.

2.2 The Subset Principle in learnability theory

The Subset Principle is a result in learnability theory that is assumed to be built into the Human Language Acquisition Device so as to constrain the hypotheses that a learner makes (Hamburger and Wexler 1975). We will first sketch the SP as it is traditionally presented and then present a critique of the traditional formulation that will help us achieve a better understanding of the SP when we turn to phonology.

Imagine a species C that is innately endowed so as to be able to acquire only languages that contain sentences consisting of strings of tokens of a single symbol a. Here are some of the languages that a member of C can learn:

(9) Languages available to species C:
- $\mathcal{L}_1 = a$
- $\mathcal{L}_2 = a, aa$
- $\mathcal{L}_3 = a, aa, aaa$
- ...
- $\mathcal{L}_n = a, aa \ldots a^n$

Since the specific language acquired can vary for a member of C, we need a theory of how a baby C learns the language of its environment. The question that concerns us is thus: "How does the learner converge on the correct $\mathcal{L}_i$?" It seems clear that one of the simplest ways for the the learner to end up with the correct grammar would be if a grown-up C could just tell a baby C "Around here we speak $\mathcal{L}_{64}$" or whatever the appropriate grammar is.

This scenario is implausible for a model of human language acquisition for a variety of reasons. First of all, it requires innate knowledge of *another* language, the one in which adults would issue such instructions to the acquirers. Second, it requires that adults have conscious knowledge of the grammar of their language and that they be able to convey that information to acquirers.

A second method of ensuring successful acquisition would be to allow babies to freely generate sentences, i.e. strings of *a*s, but have adults convey to them, by some kind of negative reinforcement, the information that certain of the strings the babies produce are ungrammatical. For example, if a baby C utters *aaaaaaa* and receives the appropriate negative feedback, the baby will know that this string is ill-formed and thus the target language must be $\mathcal{L}_i$ for $i \in \{1 \ldots 6\}$. This kind of negative evidence immediately rules out the infinite set of possible languages for $i \geq 7$. If the learner at some point received negative feedback for uttering *aaaaa*, then it would know that the target language is $\mathcal{L}_i$ for $i \in \{1 \ldots 4\}$. If we assume that there is a finite period for acquisition, say until puberty, then at puberty the learner will fix $\mathcal{L}_i$ with $i = n - 1$ where n is the smallest number such that the child was told that a^n is ungrammatical.

This scenario again appears to be implausible as a model of human language acquisition (even if we grant that human languages could be ordered like the languages available to C). First, the model requires innate capacity to recognize that some kind of sporadically supplied negative reinforcement, say a bite on the nose, signals ungrammaticality, as opposed to some other undesirable behavior on the child's part. Second, it requires that babies can identify the locus of ungrammaticality—imagine getting a bite on the nose for saying *Me don't likes dat* when trying to learn Standard English. What should the baby conclude? Is it being bitten for using the wrong pronoun form? For the inflection on *likes*? For the stop in *dat*? Third, empirical studies of humans suggest that children do not get much correction for their speech—and if it is sporadic, how are they to recognize it as being relevant to speech, since they also get sporadic correction for sticking things into electrical outlets? Fourth, the correction they do get from parents tends to be related to content, not form: a child who says something fresh is likely to be chided no matter how well-formed the utterance, and a child who says something sweet will be praised even if the utterance contains errors. See Marcus (1993) for references, as well as other arguments supporting the assumption of an acquisition model that does not rely on negative evidence.

So, children are not told what the correct grammar is and they do not learn it by being corrected. Instead, it appears that they have to learn the correct grammar by inducing it from what they hear. There are tremendous complexities involved in this scenario as well, since we know that kids learn despite the fact that people around them talk simultaneously, get cut off, lose their train of thought and make errors in grammatical form due to attentional failure, and we also know that kids learn language even in a multilingual context where utterances are not presented with labels like "I am a Spanish utterance" and "I am a French utterance". Still, we are going to assume that language learning on the basis of positive evidence alone is possible and is what humans children do.

Before we return to language acquisition among the C, let's be clear that negative evidence would be additional evidence. Linguists attempt to model the path of acquisition under the assumption that the learner does not get negative evidence. In other words, we are potentially making our job harder than it need be if it turns out that there is some kind of negative evidence in fact available to learners. However, if we can successfully model language acquisition assuming "no negative evidence", then it is a logical necessity that our model will work with negative evidence in addition to positive evidence.

So, how must a Language Acquisition Device be designed if it is going to work on the basis of positive evidence alone? What if a baby C were to suppose that the best strategy is to make the assumption that anything goes, and that the target language is $\mathcal{L}_\infty$—that arbitrarily long strings of *as* are grammatical? Every piece of input the baby hears would be consistent with this hypothesis. If the target language were in fact $\mathcal{L}_{17}$ the learner would have a grammar that could generate everything in the environment, which would include a, aa, aaa, ... a^{17}. The problem is that the learner would *overgenerate*, producing a^{18}, a^{137} and so on. No positive evidence would tell the learner that the posited grammar is wrong, and by hypothesis, the learner cannot use negative evidence.

The solution to this dilemma is that the learner should assume as an initial hypothesis that the target language is $\mathcal{L}_1$. If the learner hears *aaaa* it will revise its hypothesis to $\mathcal{L}_4$; if a^{63} is encountered, it will revise to $\mathcal{L}_{63}$. At the end of the grammar acquisition process,[1] the learner will finalize the grammar to $\mathcal{L}_n$ where a^n is the longest sentence it has heard. This strategy ensures that the learner will not ever make a hypothesis that requires negative evidence to correct.

This is the standard view of the Subset Principle: the learner's initial hypothesis must be the language that is a subset of possible later hypotheses. Since the set of grammatical sentences in $\mathcal{L}_1$ is a subset of the set of sentences in every other $\mathcal{L}_i$, this language must correspond to the initial hypothesis. This hypothesis is revised when the learner encounters positive evidence.

While the argument presented appears to be logically valid, there is an obvious problem with the approach. We are assuming the I-language approach

---

[1] For justification of the hypothesis that the acquisition process has a termination point, see Hale (2007: 13ff.).

of Chomsky (1986), which considers a grammar to be internal, individual and *intensional*. The grammar *is* the language under this view, and thus the language is a computational system, *not* a set of sentences. The discussion above, and thus the standard conception of the Subset Principle, is cast in an extensionalist view of languages as sets of sentences. This distinction will prove crucial when we turn to the understanding of the SP in phonology below.

Another problem with the traditional view is that it does not explain how the learner can parse input forms that are not compatible with the current state of the grammar. If the learner's initial grammar $\mathcal{L}_1$ does not generate, say a^{22}, then how can the learner assign a representation to such a form when it is encountered? Given their current knowledge state, they should be forced to parse a^{22} as 22 distinct sentences! Our approach to the Subset Principle, and to learning in general, which allows rich initial representations, avoids this problem.

In the next section we illustrate the Innateness of Primitive Principle, and then go on to show its relevance to our reconceptualization of the Subset Principle.

2.3 Card grammars

In this section we illustrate the logic behind Jackendoff's statement quoted at the beginning of this chapter by using model languages consisting of sets of playing cards from a normal deck. In this analogy, cards correspond to sentences of natural languages. From our point of view as observers, a card c will be grammatical, ungrammatical or neither to a "speaker" of G.[2] We further assume that learners of these "card languages" are endowed with an innate card language faculty. We will explore the effect of tinkering with "Card UG" below.

In general, Card UG will be a computational system, consisting of a set of entities and a set of logical operators defined over these entities. Our general assumptions in building our "grammars" are sketched in (10).

(10)   General principles
   • Each card is grammatical, ungrammatical or neither.
   • A grammar is a set of conditions on cards.
   • UG is a set of primitives, including:
       • entities (features);
       • logical operators defined over these entities.

---

[2] The reason for the third possibility will become clear below.

- A card c is "grammatical" with respect to a grammar G iff c satisfies the conditions imposed by G. In such a case we will say, informally, that c is "in G".

We will now explore how the nature of Card UG limits the set of possible languages available to a learner.

2.3.1 *UG1*

Assume first that UG makes available to the learner the (privative) feature NUMBERCARD which characterizes cards that bear the numbers two through ten. Further assume that UG makes available the four suits: clubs, diamonds, hearts, spades (♣, ♢, ♡, ♠). These also function as privative features.[3] Finally, assume that UG makes available the logical operator AND, which allows for the conjunction of features in structural descriptions. We call this version of universal grammar UG1.

(11)   UG1
   - Features:

     NUMBERCARD

     ♣, ♢, ♡, ♠
   - Operators: AND

2.3.1.1 *Possible grammars given UG1*   Now consider some possible grammars, given the definition of UG1. Our first grammar is G_1, which is characterized as follows: $G_1 = $ [NUMBERCARD]. This is to be read as "A sentence/card is in G_1 if and only if it is a numbercard." So, the king of diamonds is ungrammatical in G_1. This is because a king is not a numbercard. On the other hand the six of diamonds and the three of clubs are both grammatical in G_1.

Consider a second possible grammar G_2, characterized as follows: $G_2 = $ [NUMBERCARD AND ♢]. This is to be read as "A sentence/card is in G_2 if and only if it is a diamond numbercard." In this grammar the king of diamonds is still ungrammatical, but so is the three of clubs. The six of diamonds is obviously grammatical.

Now consider G_3, defined as follows: $G_3 = $ [♠]. That is, "A sentence/card is in G_3 if and only if it is a spade." We hope it's obvious to the reader just what the grammatical sentences of this grammar are, but we would now like to focus on a different question: what, for one who has G_3 as their

---

[3] Note that only one of these suit features can characterize any given card. Such restrictions will not concern us further.

system for generating analyses of card sentences, is the representation of 5♠? K♠? 5♣? The answers are [NUMBERCARD AND ♠], [♠] and *[NUMBERCARD AND ♣],[4] respectively. Only the third is ungrammatical, since it is not a spade.

Finally, consider G_4, which is characterized by no features at all. In other words, it places no restrictions on which cards are grammatical: $G_4 = [\ ]$. That is to say, "Every sentence/card is in G_4." But now, is this completely true? The answer is that it is true of all the cards characterizable by UG1, say the fifty-two cards that can be assigned a representation given UG1. However, a tarot card or even a Joker would not be grammatical in G_4, given UG1. (Thinking ahead a bit, what would their representation be?)

2.3.1.2 *Impossible grammars given UG1*   Since any given UG delimits the set of possible grammars, it is also instructive to consider a few impossible grammars, under the assumption of UG1. Consider first (non-)grammar F_1 described as follows: F_1 = [PICTURECARD]. In other words, "A sentence/card is in F_1 if and only if it is a picturecard." Clearly this is an impossible grammar, since UG1 does not provide for a class of all and only picture cards. (Recall that NUMBERCARD is privative by hypothesis.) Similarly, consider F_2 = [NUMBERCARD OR ◇]: "A sentence/card is in F_2 if and only if it is a numbercard or a diamond (or both)." This is an impossible grammar, since UG1 does not provide the logical operator OR. Next consider a potential grammar with severely limited expressive capacity: F_3 = [6 AND ♠], i.e. "A sentence/card is in F_3 if and only if it is the six of spades." This grammar is impossible given UG1, since UG1 does not provide the means to parse a card with the property "six" as being different from any other numbercard.

2.3.2 *UG2*

Now imagine another species endowed with a different universal grammar called UG2, characterized by the following features: [±PICTURE], which is equivalent to having the mutually exclusive privative features [NUMBERCARD, PICTURECARD], and [±RED], which is equivalent to having the mutually

---

[4] We are assuming that the learner retains access to the UG-given features, even if these features are not used in the acquired language. Rejecting this assumption would not substantively affect the argument, but would unncessarily complicate the exposition. As one can see in the present instance, since the representation of the five of clubs would otherwise be [NUMBERCARD], its grammaticality is unaffected by this simplification. We are indebted to Afton Lewis for discussions on this point.

exclusive features [RED, BLACK]. UG2, like UG1, provides the operator AND.

(12)   UG2
- Features:
  [±PICTURE]
  [±red]
- Operators: AND

2.3.2.1 *Some possible grammars given UG2*   A possible grammar given UG2 is G_5 = [+RED AND −PICTURE]: "A sentence/card is in G_5 if and only if it is a red numbercard." What is the representation of 7◇ in this grammar? What about 7♡? And 7♠? The answers are [+RED AND −PICTURE], [+RED AND −PICTURE] and *[−RED AND −PICTURE], respectively. Since the suits are not distinguishable given UG2, the learner parses the two red cards as [+RED]. Since the numbers are indistinguishable given UG2 (as was the case with UG1), the fact that the three cards in question are all sevens is lost to the learner. They are all just [−PICTURE]. Now consider G_6 = [+RED]: "A sentence/card is in G_6 if and only if it is a red card." This grammar will include all the red cards, hearts and diamonds, number and picturecards, though of course these distinctions are not made by creatures endowed with UG2—they are only made by beings whose genetic endowment equips them to represent such contrasts.

2.3.2.2 *Some impossible grammars given UG2*   It should be easy now to see that the following two potential grammars are impossible given UG2.

- F_4 = [♠]
  "A sentence/card is in F_4 if and only if it is a spade."
- F_5 = [+PICTURE OR −RED]
  "A sentence/card is in F_5 if and only if it is a picture card or a black card (or both)."

The first is impossible since UG2 does not distinguish the suits. The second, because UG2 does not provide OR. Note, however, that although F_4 is impossible assuming UG2, its specification is identical to the grammar G_3 which is allowed by UG1. So, again, the nature of UG determines the set of possible grammars. It is worth pointing out that because of this, positing a specific UG allows us to pick between some extensionally equivalent grammars (thus transcending the limitations of the "AI Problem" discussed in Chapter 1).

2.3.3 *UG3*

We leave it to the reader to confirm that the following characterization of a third UG, UG3, allows for G_7, G_8 and G_9, but excludes F_6, F_7 and F_8.

(13)   Description of UG3
- Features:
  [PICTURECARD]
  [2,3,4,5,6,7,8,9,10]
  [±RED]
- Operators: AND, OR

(14)   Some possible grammars given UG3
- $G_7 = [+\text{RED AND } 9]$
  "A sentence/card is in G_7 if and only if it is a red nine."
- $G_8 = [-\text{RED AND PICTURECARD}]$
  "A sentence/card is in G_8 if and only if it is a black picture card."
- $G_9 = [\text{PICTURECARD OR} +\text{RED}]$.
  "A sentence/card is in G_9 if and only if it is a red card or a picture card (or both)."

(15)   Some impossible grammars given UG3
- $F_6 = [\spadesuit]$
  "A sentence/card is in F_6 if and only if it is a spade."
- $F_7 = [\text{NUMBER}]$
  "A sentence/card is in F_7 if and only if it is a numbercard."
- $F_8 = [-\text{RED AND Q}]$
  "A sentence/card is in F_8 if and only if it is a black queen."

It is worth pointing out that, given UG3, it is possible to acquire a grammar which is *extensionally* equivalent to F_7: "A sentence/card is grammatical if it is [2 OR 3 OR 4 OR 5 OR 6 OR 7 OR 8 OR 9 OR 10]." As we have argued in the previous chapter, the goal of linguistic theory is to discover the "correct" model of a speaker's grammar, one that is, for example, compatible with a theory of UG that underlies all human languages. In defining I-language, a matter of "individual psychology", as the domain of inquiry for linguistics, Chomsky (1986) has argued convincingly that the fact that knowledge of language is instantiated in individual minds/brains means that there is necessarily a "correct" characterization of a speaker's grammar (or grammars).

It is also worth stressing that we have demonstrated how the nature of UG limits the set of possible grammars—the set of achievable final states of the language faculty is partially determined by what is present at the initial state.

2.3.4 *An impoverished UG4*

Now imagine that UG4 provides only a single privative feature: [$\diamond$]. What happens if we expose a learner to 5$\diamond$? The learner parses (constructs a representation for) [$\diamond$]. The "5" is unparsable. It is not *linguistic* information (obviously, we are using "linguistic" in a special card grammar sense, here). Now, expose the learner to "6$\heartsuit$". The learner parses nothing! There is *no* linguistic information in the input. (A linguistic parallel would be the parse of a belch by a human phonological system.) In fact only two grammars can be defined given UG4. $G_{10} = [\diamond]$ allows all and only diamond cards as grammatical utterances. $G_{11} = [\ ]$, which imposes no limitations of what is grammatical, defines, actually, a grammar which is extensionally equivalent to G_{10}—i.e. the two contain the same sentences, but these sentences are generated by different grammars. The reason is that, given G_{11}, cards can either be assigned the representation $\diamond$, or they are not parsed at all. So the only cards that will count as linguistic entities are the diamonds. (What happens if we instead make a binary feature [$\pm\diamond$]?)

2.3.5 *A really impoverished UG5*

What if UG provides nothing at all—no features and no operators? Then, no matter what we expose the learner to, nothing will be parsed. It follows that the starting point for the grammar we ultimately construct cannot be an empty slate, since, to quote Jackendoff again, "[w]ithout Mental Grammar, there's no language perception—just noise" (Jackendoff 1994: 164). To reiterate: The set of primitives supplied by UG determines the set of possible grammars that can be described. Without any primitives, no grammar can be described. The card language faculty of a creature endowed with UG5 will parse any given card in the same way as it will parse a tarot card, the *Mona Lisa*, or the smell of pepperoni. Any innate system which parses such entities distinctly must be endowed with a mechanism for distinguishing between them. This mechanism, obviously, must ultimately be innate.[5]

Before we move on, consider the contrast between a really large 2$\spadesuit$ (like a prop for a magician) and a really small one (like a card from a travel deck), as depicted in Figure 2.1. Obviously these two cards differ physically—one is

---

[5] By "ultimately" we do not mean to exclude the possibility that the entities exploited by the computational system might be constructed out of more primitive features. But at some point the primitives involved must be innate. We return to this point a little later in the main text.

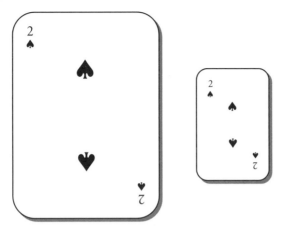

FIGURE 2.1 A non-"linguistic" card contrast

big and one is small. They may even have different patterns on their backs and differ in many other ways. But the two cards are *linguistically identical*. They differ in the same way that whispering and shouting a given word differ, i.e. they differ only paralinguistically.

Crucially, our claim is not that the contrast in card size will be *imperceptible* to an acquirer—merely that no size information will be used in the construction of the representations relevant to the "linguistic" module; other modules of mind may well exploit (and of course parse) size information. That is, given a particular card UG, the relevance of specific contrasts that fall within the perceptual capabilities of the learner for card grammar learning must be made explicit. The set of possible card grammars consists precisely of those which are UG-consistent. The fact that a learner can perceive the difference between large cards and small ones, or between a card on the ceiling and a card on the floor, will not be relevant to the *grammatical* learning task, for which the two cards are members of an equivalence class (i.e. representationally non-distinct). For a learner for whom these contrasts are perceptible, any theory which fails to recognize innate primitives within the card grammar domain will fail to properly constrain the set of possible grammars—i.e. the primitives of grammar construction *cannot* arise from the primitives of perception.

We have been forced to the logical conclusion that there must be something at the initial state of the grammar in order to allow learning to occur. However, one might object: "Maybe there are more basic primitives at the initial state. For example, if we are sensitive to the difference between straight and curved lines we could discover the distinction between ◇ and ♡." This is perfectly reasonable. It just means that, say, "straight" vs. "curved" are the innate primitives. But—ya gotta start with something! That something is Universal Grammar.

It should now be obvious that we are heading toward the conclusion that children must "know" (i.e. have innate access to) the set of phonological features used in all of the languages of the world. This is how the IofPP will be extended in this chapter; but it is equally clear that the same conclusion holds for primitive operators like the AND and OR of card languages, or whatever are the operators of real grammars (in both phonology and syntax).

Obviously, we are not claiming that the set of primitives of phonology corresponds exactly to the set of distinctive features referred to in the literature. There is no question that some of the features have yet to be identified or properly distinguished from others (for some recent speculation on this matter, see Hale et al. 2007). In some cases a currently assumed feature may represent a conglomeration of the actual primitives of phonological representation. However, *by definition*, UG, the innate component of the language faculty, consists of the elements of linguistic representation which cannot be derived from anything else.

Consider a proposal that Q is necessary for the acquisition of human language and that Q is innate. Critics of the proposed innateness of Q must formulate their criticism in one of two ways. Either they must provide a learning path which is not dependent on Q—i.e. they must challenge the claim that Q is *necessary* for the acquisition of human language—or they must derive Q from some other more basic entities and processes (such as R), themselves available to the acquirer innately. In the absence of such alternatives, the criticism is invalid. The second alternative is the favorite of so-called constructivist theories of cognitive development. However, note that the appeal to "general learning mechanisms", without specifying in detail what the set of actual primitives involved in any such mechanisms are, is not a responsible critique of the nativist stance.

We sympathize with one reader of this discussion who noted that the "card" grammar discussion appears to go into relatively painful detail about matters which should be a priori fairly clear; and we beg the reader's forgiveness. However, we have found that for both readers of this chapter and for the field in general, coming to grips with the basic insight that in order to learn over a given set of a data, the learner must possess the relevant representational primitives *within the learning domain*, has proven immensely difficult. Far from being our own idiosyncratic conclusion, we find that this view of specialized "organs" for learning has gained widespread acceptance in a variety of domains of cognitive science, as a development of Chomsky's work on language.

Another reviewer of this book is puzzled (or rather, shocked) by our complete dismissal of exemplar theory and the idea of statistical learning to *construct* categories. Ultimately the debate boils down to the larger issue of empiricist vs. rationalist theories of learning. We think that our card languages demonstrate the reasoning behind the rationalist view, and we place ourselves in the tradition of other cognitive scientists like Gallistel (1996). As far as we can tell, the issue was settled long ago, and even recognized by some enlightened phoneticians, such as Hammarberg (1976), who points out that phonetic analysis (by scientists and babies) cannot even begin without the a priori categories of phonology. The categories of phonology cannot be inherent in the signal, or else any creature with good enough *hearing* should be able to acquire them. See Hammarberg (1976: 334–5) for discussion.

2.4 Acquisition of phonological inventories: the standard view

In this section we summarize and critique a theory that we see as characterizing the mainstream view on the acquisition of phonological inventories. We choose Rice and Avery (1995) because these authors are particulary lucid in their claims, and thus serve well as a basis for comparison with our proposal. The central claims of these authors are as follows:

- Minimality: Initially the child's representational apparatus consists of a minimal set of primitives, say, C and V.
- Monotonicity: Representational capacity is expanded as further primitives become available.

What these claims mean is that a child's phonological representation apparatus is initially highly impoverished and is enriched over the course of acquisition. So, for example, a word like [ma] must be represented as just /CV/ at the initial stages of acquisition; later it may be represented as /[C, +son][V,−hi]/; yet later as /[C, +son, +labial][V,−hi,+bk]/; and ultimately as fully specified as the target language requires.[6]

Rice and Avery do not explicitly invoke the Subset Principle (SP), but their account of the learning path looks superficially as though it conforms to the SP. For example, the child moves from having a small phonological inventory to having a larger one which contains all the feature contrasts, and thus all

---

[6] Our example uses an ad hoc feature system, but the point should be clear.

the underlying segments, present at the earlier stages. This traditional view, which we will reject, continues the same basic attitude towards children's phonological development and its reflection in their speech output as that expressed by Jakobson (1941/1968). A standard version of this view is sketched in (16): the early states of the grammar contain a limited number of vowels, e.g. a single vowel or the three "basic" vowels represented here; acquisition of a larger inventory leads to a superset of this early inventory.

(16)   The Subset Principle in the traditional model (to be rejected)

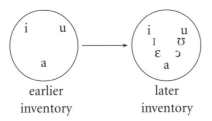

earlier   later
inventory   inventory

Now, we must ask ourselves if it is indeed possible to get from the earlier stage to the later stage sketched above. We believe that such a learning path is not possible given standard assumptions about the language faculty. First, assume the child is at a three-vowel stage, as above. Then any vowel that the child is presented with must be parsed as one of the three, or else it will not be parsed at all. This claim follows from the definition of parsing: to parse a string is to assign it a linguistic representation. A representation can only be assigned using the available representational apparatus. In the case of vowels under discussion, this gives rise to two distinct logical possibilities. A child at the three-vowel stage, presented with an [ɪ], could, under certain assumptions, parse it as an instance of the (ATR underspecified)[7] high front vowel [i]. Alternatively, the learner could fail to parse the segment as a vowel at all. No other possibilities exist under the traditional view, and neither of these possibilities will lead to an expansion of the vowel inventory. Clearly, if the learner could parse the [ɪ] as a vowel, distinct from [i], this would entail the learner having access to the feature contrast which is, by hypothesis, not available.

It is sometimes suggested (e.g. Ingram 1995: 77) that the child's grammar makes use of two kinds of representation: a phonological representation, which starts out with access to a minimal set of features, and a phonetic or acoustic representation, which makes use of fully specified phonetic feature matrices. One might imagine that the child stores contrasts

---

[7] We return to this matter in section 2.5 below.

in the phonetic representations until the phonology is "ready" for them, at which time previously identical phonological representations can be distinguished by accessing their corresponding (stored) phonetic representation. This view suffers from at least three difficulties. First, the desired "simplicity" or "poverty" of the child's grammar is not attained, but rather just holds at one level of the grammar—"phonetic" representations are neither "simple" nor "impoverished". Second, as assumed by Pinker (1984) and many others, the child's grammar should be considered to differ from the adults quantitatively, not qualitatively (since, after all, children are small humans). Having this extra lexicon would surely constitute a qualitative difference between child and adult grammars. In fact, it would appear to endow them with a *more*, not *less*, complex grammar than adults. Third, in generative grammar, surface representations are not stored. They are *generated*. In fact, explaining the capacity to create and process an unbounded number of utterances from finite means is perhaps the *raison d'être* of the generative program. Indeed, the storage of surface forms would vitiate the need for phonology at all—the child, and the adult as well, could simply pronounce the stored surface forms.

A variant of the two-lexicon hypothesis is that the special, additional lexicon that children have is not feature-based, but is instead based on "raw acoustic images" (i.e. non-linguistic representations). This version of the proposal shares the three aforementioned problems, but is further burdened by the evidence that speech is recognized and processed differently from other sounds immediately from birth. Thus there is no reason to believe that children would store speech input as raw acoustic signals to a greater extent than adults do (as in the occasional case where we remember the manner in which a particular word was spoken). Note that storing raw acoustic images exclusively is not only irrelevant to language acquisition, but is in fact an impediment to the process of extracting a discrete, constant representation from vastly variant tokens.

Theories like those of Calabrese (1988; 2005) posit a universal set of markedness statements that are "deactivated" upon exposure to positive evidence that a given featural distinction is exploited in the target language. In Chapter 7 of this book we argue that markedness is not a coherent notion, and that informal statistical arguments for the marked status of given feature configurations are flawed. In addition to such problems, a theory like that of Calabrese faces other difficulties. First, the types of implicational universal concerning phonological inventories which such theories build upon are devoid of empirical content, since the theory does allow for "accidental" gaps to occur. For example, most markedness theories posit that [t] is less marked than [k].

However, there is at least one language, Hawaiian, which has [k], but not [t], due to a fairly recent sound change. In order to have any explanatory value, such a theory must predict that Hawaiian speakers would accept [t] as a possible Hawaiian sound, but be unable to provide any examples of its occurrence. Although we have not done the empirical work, we find such a scenario implausible. Now, a theory that allows arbitrarily structured inventories will obviously allow allegedly motivated ones. Therefore, a theory that proposes that phonological inventories are not constrained by markedness considerations allows for those that follow from markedness arguments, as well as those which do not. Removing markedness from phonological theory thus leads to no loss in empirical coverage.

To summarize, Rice and Avery's theory, and those like it, must be rejected as unparsimonious, incompatible with the generative program, and incapable of modeling a successful learning path. In the following section we discuss the Subset Principle (SP) of acquisition in general terms. We then apply the SP to the problem of the acquisition of phonological inventories.

2.5 The Subset Principle and features

It is worthwhile to remember that the skepticism with which the claim of "no negative evidence" is sometimes treated is misguided. The availability of negative evidence greatly *simplifies* a learner's task. Thus, as we pointed out above, any scholar who assumes "no negative evidence" is undertaking a harder job than one who assumes that the child does get negative evidence. If we can find a successful learning algorithm that does not rely on negative evidence, it will by necessity be successful even if negative evidence is provided. However, a learning algorithm that makes use of negative evidence may not succeed using only positive evidence. There are no explicit proposals concerning the kind of negative evidence that children get for phonology, and there are explicit arguments (Marcus 1993) that negative evidence is not used in syntactic acquisition. We therefore take upon ourselves the more difficult task of accounting for phonological acquisition without appeal to negative evidence.

We consider the relevance of the SP to acquisition to be beyond question, once the assumption is made that children are not sensitive to negative evidence in the course of acquisition. In other words, the SP can be viewed as a corollary to the acquisition principle of "no negative evidence". The effect of the SP is to prevent the learner from making overly broad generalizations which cannot be corrected on the basis of positive evidence alone. We take the essence of the SP to be, therefore, a kind of restrictiveness. In other words, the initial state of the grammar, S_0, is maximally restrictive, and learning consists of relaxing restrictions. Our task, then, is to figure out how these restrictions are formulated (in terms of features, parameters, etc.).

Despite the fact that the SP was first formulated for phonology (Dell 1981) it has been more widely discussed in the syntactic acquisition literature, for example by Berwick (1986) and Wexler and Manzini (1987). Therefore, it may be useful to first review how the SP has been applied to a syntactic problem, as a lead-up to our reinterpretation. Given our concerns here, the discussion of syntactic phenomena will be informal.

In a comparative study of acquisition of anaphora, Hyams and Sigurjóns-dóttir (1990) compare the binding conditions on Icelandic *sig* and English *himself/herself*. In simple terms, we can characterize the anaphors in the two languages as follows: Icelandic anaphors need to be bound; English anaphors need to be bound in the minimal S. So, English is more restrictive; it imposes more conditions on anaphors than Icelandic does. The difference is represented by the schematic sentences in (17). In English, the anaphor can only be coreferential with the NP in the same clause, whereas in Icelandic, the anaphor can be coreferential with an antecedent in a higher clause.

(17) Anaphors in English and Icelandic
- English: John$_i$ asked Bill$_j$ to shave self$_{*i/j}$
- Icelandic: John$_i$ asked Bill$_j$ to shave self$_{i/j}$

We can represent the greater restrictiveness of English as in (18), and conclude that English corresponds to the initial state (in this respect).

(18) Relative restrictiveness on anaphors

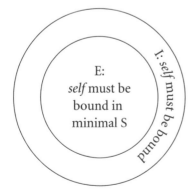

We can also represent the relationship of the two languages as an implicational relationship, as in (19).

(19)   The SP as an implicational hierarchy

    a.   Anaphor must be bound in the minimal S $\Rightarrow$ Anaphor must be bound.

    b.   Anaphor must be bound $\nRightarrow$ Anaphor must be bound in minimal S.

One of the reasons that the SP has fallen out of favor in discussions of syntactic acquisition is that a number of prominent contemporary syntactic theories (e.g. Minimalism) assume an invariant syntactic component cross-linguistically. It becomes unclear how to state subset relations among languages if they all have the same syntax. In fact, the solution to this problem is quite simple in our view, and is completely compatible with a theory like Minimalism. The SP in syntax should be defined with reference to the representation of lexical entries (functional and lexical categories).[8]

If we represent the distinction between English and Icelandic in terms of lexical features of the anaphors, instead of in terms of parameter settings, as has been done traditionally, we might propose the model in (20), where English anaphors are marked as [+bound, +local] whereas Icelandic anaphors are marked only as [+bound].

(20)   Features for anaphors

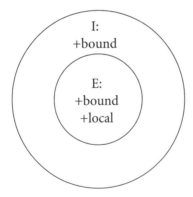

This brings us to a point which, though obvious, is crucial to our argument. Despite the simplicity of the argument, it it precisely the failure to grasp this

---

[8] Despite the fact that the parameterization of Principle A that motivated work on the acquisition of long-distance anaphora is somewhat obsolete, we can retain it as an example. It is clearly beyond the scope of this book to account for binding theory and all issues in syntactic acquisition. Our revision of the SP from parametric terms to featural terms may very well revive some old discussions in syntactic acquisition.

point which has led to the misinterpretations of the SP in phonology. The point can be formulaically stated as: fewer features equals more entities. That is, assuming that feature combination is restricted to conjunction (as required by the notion "natural class"), the size of a class varies inversely with the number of features used to define the class. This is stated more formally in (21).

(21)   Fewer features = more entities
       Let F and G be sets of features such that R(F) is the set of entities defined by F and R(G) is the set of entities defined by G. If G is a subset of F, then R(F) is a subset of R(G). That is F $\supset$ G $\leftrightarrow$ R(G) $\supset$ R(F).

At the risk of appearing pedantic, we now present a non-linguistic example of this principle. The properties of being "odd" and being "less than 10" can be used to characterize, positively or negatively, subsets of the set of positive whole numbers. Let's assume that, like linguistic features in lexical representations, these features can only be combined conjunctively. As shown on the left-hand side of (22), the set of properties, or features, containing both "odd" and "< 10" contains the two sets which contain only one of these features. On the right-hand side, however, we see that the containment relation goes in the other direction: the set of numbers which are both odd and less than 10 is contained within the set of odd numbers and within the set of numbers less than 10.

(22)   A non-linguistic example

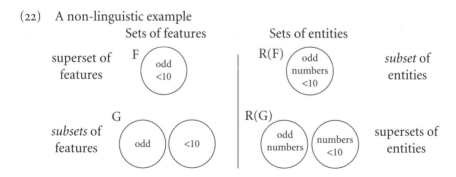

We can now return to our linguistic example and see that the same inverse relation holds. On the left-hand side of (23) we see a superset of features containing a subset of features, but on the right-hand side we see that the interpretations associated with anaphors are in the inverse relationship, i.e. the class of all anaphors contains the class of locally bound anaphors.

(23)   A linguistic example

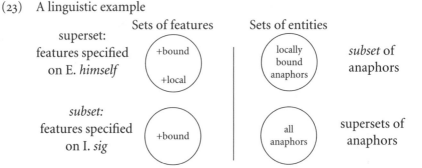

So, English represents the subset or initial state for the acquisition of anaphors by virtue of the fact that it uses a *superset* of features to restrict its characterization of pronouns. Of course, if we adopt a more modern view of syntax, the subset–superset relation is between the features that specify the English lexical item vs. the Icelandic one.

Before we come back to phonology, we will return briefly to the card languages. In order to be consistent with the SP, what strategy should a learner endowed with UG1 employ? Recall that UG1 provides the four suits, the category NUMBERCARD, and the operator AND. Compare a learner L_1 who must learn $G_1 = $ [NUMBERCARD] to one L_2 who must learn $G_2 = $ [NUMBERCARD AND $\Diamond$]. Since we assume that the learners belong to the same species and thus are endowed not only with identical UGs (UG1), but also with identical language acquisition devices, we must assume that they go about learning in the same way. Confronted with, say, [5$\Diamond$], our theory—which gives the learners full access to the primitives provided by UG1—requires both learners to construct a maximally specific parse, namely [NUMBERCARD AND $\Diamond$].[9] Both learners will first assume that all grammatical cards must be diamond numbercards. L_2 will never get conflicting data and thus the learning path is complete for this learner. L_1 *will* get conflicting information, i.e. positive evidence, consisting of numbercards which are *not* diamonds. Thus, L_1 will have to relax restrictions on the definition of a grammatical card to arrive at G_1. In both cases the learning strategy will be successful. And note that more features are needed to state the constraints which characterize the more restrictive G_2.

The traditional view of inventory acquisition can also be modeled using card languages. Imagine two learners, Z_1 and Z_2, with target grammars G_1 and G_2 respectively, again both genetically endowed with UG1. By hypothesis,

---

[9] Of course, this is maximal given UG1. With another UG it may be possible to be more specific and parse the "5" as a "5".

these learners under the traditional view do not have access at the initial state to the full set of UG1 primitives. Their representational capacities allow them only to construct representations using a single primitive from UG1, say, [NUMBERCARD] at the initial stage. Presented with [5♢], both Z_1 and Z_2 will hypothesize that their target grammar is characterized by [NUMBERCARD], i.e. that every grammatical sentences be a numbercard. Z_1 will be fine, since that is indeed the target grammar, but Z_2 will be in trouble. All future data will be consistent with this first hypothesis, since that data will consist completely of numbercards that just happen to be diamonds. Note that even when additional primitives (e.g. AND, ♢, ♠, ♣, ♡) become available, the existence of a stored lexical representation consisting solely of [NUMBERCARD] and assumed by the learner to be grammatical precludes construction of the more restrictive target grammar.

2.6 SP and segment "inventories"

2.6.1 *Further problems with the traditional view*

Recall that the traditional view of inventory acquisition appears to conform to the SP: earlier states have fewer segments than later states. There are two reasons to be skeptical of this superficial impression. First, there is no reason to expect "segments" to play a role in the learning path, since features are the primitives of phonological theory. Second, the inverse relationship of features and natural classes discussed above leads to an alternative interpretation, as (24) shows.

(24) The class of back vowels contains the class of back, rounded vowels.

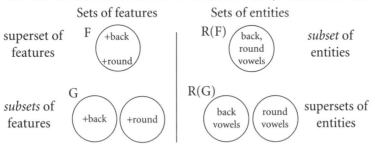

The third and final issue concerns phonetic space. Consider two languages, one with a rich vowel inventory and one with a restricted inventory, shown in (25). The direction of the subset–superset relationship is not so clear when faced with two ways of looking at the problem: (i) numbers of "segments" and (ii) phonological space.

(25)   Phonological space assigned to high front vowels in two vowel systems: which is the subset?

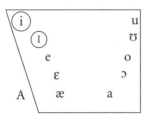 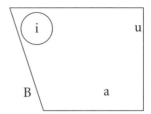

The traditional view of inventory acquisition in (16) fails to take account of the fact that the *space* occupied by a high, front, non-round vowel underspecified for ATR may be identical to that occupied by the two fully specified vowels [i] and [ɪ]. The traditional view of acquisition sees the acquirer as moving from state B to state A; however, it is clear that the subdivision of the underspecified high front unround vowel space into two more restrictive target spaces does not involve going from a subset to a superset—unless one defines the relevant sets over IPA symbols, rather than over phonetic space or phonological features.

The arguments we have offered to this point favor choosing the language with more restrictive, i.e. richer, representations and narrower phonological space associated with individual vowels as the initial state. In other words, the representational primitives of phonology must all be innately available to the learner.

Note that our claim is couched in intensional terms. We are *not* claiming that children are born with all vowels or with lexical items containing all vowels. They *are* born with the representational apparatus to parse all possible vowel distinctions. In Gallistel's (1996) terms, they are born with a specific "learning organ".

2.6.2 *The learning path*

In order to provide learnability arguments to support this proposal and further justify rejecting the traditional theory, we must answer the two questions in (26). Below we provide arguments using hypothetical languages to justify the answers we provide.

(26)   The questions
   a.   Can the traditional view lead to a growing inventory? No, so it must be rejected.
   b.   Can the proposed view lead to a shrinking inventory? YES.

To explain the answer to (26a), consider the acquisition of /dip/ vs. /dɪp/ in a hypothetical language which maintains the [i] / [ɪ] contrast on the surface. In the traditional view of the growth of vowel inventories, the contrast is unlearnable initially, and the two words will be acquired as homophones. Without access to a difference in representation, the phonetic difference between the two vowels cannot be evaluated. The so-called "positive evidence" often invoked to allow inventory expansion is not sufficient if that evidence cannot be assigned a representation. That is, the contrast cannot be parsed linguistically if the child does not have the appropriate representational apparatus. This is a fundamental assumption of linguistic theory. It is equivalent to saying that a language that uses a feature which is not available to humans is unlearnable, which is tautologically true given the standard definition of UG. If a child did not have access to a feature provided by UG, then the child could not store this distinction for future use; each lexical entry would have to be relearned at each stage, since each lexical entry could potentially contain the newly "acquired" feature. Since no lexical item would, under such a scenario, be *finally* acquired until all features came "on line" and since, at that point, the learning model is equivalent to our own, it is hard to see what the complicating assumption of a monotonically expanding feature set buys us. It is, in any event, contra-indicated by the acquisition evidence. On the other hand, if the distinction is available at S_0, then acquisition of contrastive lexical items is trivial.

We now turn to (26b), loss of a "wrong" potential contrast—i.e. /dip/ and /dɪp/ collapse to /dip/ in some language with a three-vowel system. The challenge to the theory proposed in this chapter can be stated thus: How does a grammar which has more potential vowels than the target grammar end up *not* making use of irrelevant contrasts? Two cases must be distinguished.

(27)　Two distinct cases for the "collapse" of contrast
　　a.　Unobserved contrasts: If the target language does not present forms such as [dɪp], then there may never be any reason to remove [+ATR] from the representation of /dip/. Access to the universal feature set allows the *potential* for any contrast, not its realization. This is clearly relevant to underspecification theory in that we assume e.g. that /i/ will never lose its [+ATR] specification without grammar internal motivation (see below).
　　b.　Phonetic underspecification: Imagine the child hears [dip] and stores it as such, specified [+ATR]. Since this child has access to all the features and since its learning conforms to the SP, it assumes that representations must be maximally restrictive (specified). This

word cannot be stored with just a [−back, +hi] vowel; it must be stored as a [−back, +hi, +ATR, −round] vowel. Given the variability of articulation in some three-vowel systems, this child may also hear something more akin to phonetic [dɪp] for what the speaker intends to be the same lexical item as the acquirer's existing [dip] representation. The child, under our proposal, will then mistakenly (from the point of view of the target grammar) posit a new lexical item, ending up with a pair of synonyms, /dip/ and /dɪp/. A process of lexicon optimization, responsible for collapsing synonyms, will determine that eliminating the [ATR] feature from these segments will collapse these synonyms as a single lexeme (and general elimination of the feature would lead to no collapse of non-synonyms). [ATR] will thus be seen as no longer relevant to the phonology of the language and thus will be excluded from representations. This proposal is very similar to the uniqueness principle of morphology (Wexler and Culicover 1980).[10]

Note at this point that the confusion is largely notational. In losing the /i/–/ɪ/ contrast the grammar moves from containing two vowels [−back, +hi, +ATR, −round] and [−back, +hi, −ATR, −round], which we happen to denote as /i/ and /ɪ/, to one [−back, +hi, −round] which we somewhat arbitrarily denote as /i/.

(28)   Lexicon optimization

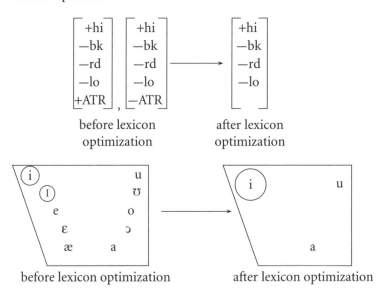

$$\begin{bmatrix} +hi \\ -bk \\ -rd \\ -lo \\ +ATR \end{bmatrix}, \begin{bmatrix} +hi \\ -bk \\ -rd \\ -lo \\ -ATR \end{bmatrix} \longrightarrow \begin{bmatrix} +hi \\ -bk \\ -rd \\ -lo \end{bmatrix}$$

before lexicon optimization   after lexicon optimization

before lexicon optimization   after lexicon optimization

---

[10] Note that this algorithm does not affect all redundant features, merely those which behave as though they are *phonetically* underspecified.

Clearly, this account needs to be further developed by an explicit model of lexicon optimization. See Hale and Reiss (1997) for some suggestions.

It is worth examining in some detail just how the "traditional" analysis—which assumes that not all of the features are available to the acquirer at the initial state—fares in this "shrinking inventory" task. The ultimate target in the hypothetical case sketched above is the representation of a high, front, non-round vowel underspecified along the ATR dimension. Assume that the "marked" feature ATR is not available at some early stage in the acquisition task. Given the broad phonetic target space of our hypothetical three-vowel system, the acquirer will hear both [dip] and [dɪp]; however, given the child's limited representational apparatus, s/he will posit representations which are underspecified along the ATR dimension. These are in fact the correct representations, and one might therefore assume that the child's learning task with respect to these vowels would be complete—and that the swift and direct nature of the acquisition in this case would lend support to the traditional model.

But how could the child *know* s/he was done? An acquirer would also assume, at this stage, underspecified representations in the case of a different ambient language which *did* make use of ATR features. That is, the fact that all high, front, non-round vowels are underspecified in our hypothetical case is a language-specific property which must be learned by explicit evidence. In fact, when the ATR feature becomes available for the construction of representations, the learner will begin to (wrongly, vis-à-vis the target language) construct fully specified representations (just as s/he must do so correctly when exposed to a language such as English, in which ATR is contrastive). This is because, in the hypothetical case under discussion, the broad target space for the ATR-underspecified vowel allows for hits in both the [dip] and [dɪp] space. The adults providing the evidence for the target language will therefore produce hits throughout the broad target space. Of course, the child cannot know in advance if s/he is learning a language that uses ATR contrastively.

At this point, the child will face the same learning task as the learner initially faced under our assumptions regarding the learning path (as outlined above): s/he will need access to some type of "lexicon optimization" in order to learn that the [i]/[ɪ] difference now posited for certain lexemes is in fact non-contrastive. In other words, the learning path for such a language under the traditional scenario consists of the learning path under our proposed scenario preceded by an additional stage that is of no use to the learner. The initial lack of availability of ATR as a feature to be used in the construction of lexical representations thus works to the acquirer's advantage *neither* in the "growing inventory" *nor* in the "shrinking shrinking" scenarios.

2.6.3 *Empirical evidence*

In addition to being logically consistent with standard assumptions of learnability theory and linguistic theory, our proposal of innate access to full representational apparatus is also plausible in light of well-established empirical studies. For example, psycholinguistic experiments show that even newborns can distinguish sounds that constitute possible phonetic contrasts in the languages of the world, and that by 10 months of age they have lost some of their power of discrimination. So language acquisition is, in a very real sense, a process of loss—we are "deafened" by our experience.[11] Given that very young infants appear to be sensitive to contrasts that are used in the languages of the world, a theory of phonological acquisition that reflects their innate phonetic capacities seems preferable to one that must grant these well-supported results (e.g. Streeter 1976; Goodman and Nussbaum 1994) but then claim that children's phonological capacities are severely impoverished.[12] Our proposal represents the null hypothesis.

Innate access to categorical, rather than gradient, phonological features is also consistent with the well-established studies of categorical perception of speech in infants (e.g. Miller and Eimas 1983). Indeed, it is possible to define the phonetics/phonology boundary as consisting of a distinction between categorical and gradient phenomena. A reviewer of this book objected to the idea that categorical perception could have any bearing on the innateness of phonological categories: "The notion that categorical perception is somehow revealing of innate access to categorical phonological features is ridiculous. After all, the exact same kind of categorical perception of speech stimuli (of the same kind) has been demonstrated in macaques and Japanese quail...and surely they are not privileged with such innate access." This comment reflects a common error of reasoning—the claim that something is innate to humans does not preclude it being innate to another species as well—think of innate aspects of our visual processing which are found in many other species. Perhaps the categories that we map to phonological discrete categories are not used in anything like a phonological system by other species, but this has no bearing on their innateness in humans. Innateness is

---

[11] These are the so-called phoneme discrimination tests. The trouble with the term "phoneme discrimination" is that phonemes can only be defined on the basis of lexical contrasts (such as minimal pairs). Since a one-month-old infant is not distinguishing sounds on the basis of a phonemic contrast in his or her own lexicon, a better term would be "discrimination of potential phonemes": "In general, it should be observed that 'minimal pair' is not an elementary notion. It cannot be defined in phonetic terms, but only in terms of a completed phonemic analysis" (Chomsky 1964: 97).

[12] For an extensive criticism of the widely misunderstood results of Maye and Gerken (2002) in this regard, see Kissock (2002), with which we are in full agreement.

not to be confused with uniqueness. Surely macaques and quail *are* innately endowed with categorical perception, but they can't map their categories to a linguistic system. It is important to realize that *to the macaque or quail* the experiments do not utilize *speech*—there is no such thing for them. Speech is only speech to a human with a speech-processing system (including a grammar).

Finally, we know that children's representational ability is always far ahead of what we perceive to be their speech output:

...they appear, in many respects, to have adult-like representations, which are reflected, among other things, in their vociferous rejections of adult imitations...(Faber and Best 1994: 266–7)

For further discussion of the competence/performance gap in child language, see the next chapter.

The model we have constructed is strikingly parallel (though not of course identical) to Patricia Kuhl's work on the perceptual magnet effect (e.g. Kuhl and Iverson 1995; see Hawkins 1999 for a useful overview). According to this theory, the auditory space of infants is divided by a set of natural (innate) boundaries that provide an upper limit on the number of possible vowel contrasts in human language. Early exposure to speech provides the child with information about which of the categories defined by these boundaries are exploited in the ambient language. Some of the innately available categories which are not used are still discriminated in experimental situations. During development, the vowel space is reorganized in that certain of the innate boundaries come to be ignored in linguistic processing. The regions of the vowel space on either side of these boundaries are merged into a single category from the linguistic perspective.

The parallel between the innately provided maximum number of, say, vowel distinctions and an innate set of phonological features that can define vowels is obvious. It is also obvious that the auditory system imposes upper limits on the number of contrasts made by speech perception modules, which in turn imposes limits on the number of constrasts made by the grammar. As Pylyshyn (1984: 151) points out, the "*computationally relevant* states are a tiny subset of [a system's] physically discriminable states", and the "former are typically a complex function of the latter". So, it is not necessary to come to a decision about which layer of Kuhl's model best corresponds to the level of featural (linguistic) representations. We can just note that the model of the learning path proposed here converges nicely with Kuhl's model, despite the fact that the latter is often seen as supporting exemplar-based statistical learning models which we reject.

2.6.4 *Summary*

We can summarize the argument of this chapter up to this point in the following way:

(29)   Summary of arguments
      A. Subset Principle Argument
          a. The Subset Principle reflects restrictiveness in the initial state.
          b. Greater restrictiveness is encoded through fuller specification.
          ∴. All features must be available for representations at S_0.
      B. Learnability Argument
          a. Linguistic representations contain features.
          b. If a feature F is unavailable at stage L_j, then positive evidence of F cannot be evaluated by the learner since the learner cannot evaluate representations with respect to F.
          ∴. All features must be available for representations at S_0.
      C. Empirical Argument
          a. Infants appear to be innately sensitive to any possible phonological contrast.
          b. Phonological contrasts are parsed and represented in terms of features.
          ∴. All features must be available for representations at S_0.

Since acquisition involves real-world performance in both production and comprehension, our arguments represent a useful idealization. Children will fail to acquire adult representations in some cases; the explanation for this is not to be sought in an impoverished grammar, but rather in performance factors (for further discussion, see Chapter 3).

2.7 Innateness and maturation

It has been suggested that the claims of innateness argued for in this chapter can be replaced by appeal to maturation. We reintroduce here here some general concerns voiced above about such an approach to phonological phenomena. First of all, as we pointed out in considerable detail above, if a given featural distinction is not available at a certain stage of acquisition, then by definition the child cannot differentiate representations that are distinguished in the adult grammar by means of this feature. So, such representations could only be acquired as identical ("homophonous"). Once the relevant feature is made available by maturation, it cannot just be "plugged" into the learner's lexicon in the appropriate places with respect to the adult lexicon. Instead, the child must *relearn* the relevant forms (by exposure to them). Of course, since the acquirer won't know *which* forms are the "relevant" ones, s/he will simply have to relearn the entire lexicon. In other words, the maturation view just consists of a sequences of learning and unlearning, and the last of these learning stages, i.e. at the end of the relevant maturation sequence, corresponds to the stage of full access to the universal feature set. This is our initial stage and the state required to lead to full acquisition.

Second, appeal to maturation in representational capacity is based on superficial impressions of children's *speech*, and not a principled analysis of their linguistic abilities. Such an analysis should make reference to careful acoustic and articulatory examination of their speech, as well as to their comprehension abilities. We go through the relevant facts and arguments in some detail in Chapter 3 of this book, so we provide only a brief overview here. Studies of the acoustics of child speech has shown that sounds that are perceived as identical (merged) by adult transcribers are, in fact, distinct (Kornfeld and Goehl 1974; Gibbon 1990). For example, a child who sounds to adults as if s/he is merging initial [r] and [w] is not in fact doing so. Therefore, there is no reason to believe that the child lacks the representational apparatus necessary to encode such distinctions.[13] Instead, the child merely lacks the ability to articulate the relevant distinction with sufficient clarity for adult transcribers. This inability can be due to physiological immaturity, overloaded resources in motor planning, attentional deficits, lexical access delays, etc. The fact that children's pronunciation typically improves when they focus on the task of articulation supports the "performance" view we espouse.

If children's speech output were a reliable indicator of the state of the grammar, we would expect that they would be able to parse their own speech. However, Dodd (1975) showed that, at a point when they successfully parse recorded speech of unfamiliar adults, children systematically fail to parse aspects of their own recorded speech when it deviates from adult output.

A third argument against the appeal to maturation is one of parsimony. The infant speech perception studies cited above suggest that children innately possess an ability which is relevant to the categorization of speech sounds. The maturation hypothesis entails poor representational capacity at the stage when discrimination abilities are most sharp and increased representational capacity just as discrimination abilities are being attenuated.

The final justification for our approach, as opposed to a maturational view, is adopted basically from Pinker (1984). When we find that children's speech

---

[13] This is especially true given their ability to distinguish them in comprehension.

output differs from that of adults, we can assume that the difference is due to a discrepancy in performance systems, or to a hypothesized discrepancy in a representational capacity, or to both. We know that children's (cognitive and physiological) performance systems are extremely underdeveloped. Therefore, even in the absence of logical arguments against such a discrepancy in representational capacity, we would be forced by Occam's Razor to assume as the null hypothesis that the discrepancy in output is due *only* to the immaturity of the performance systems. Of course, this hypothesis is subject to revision, but it represents the most constrained model available. Now, the only reason we have seen invoked to posit stages of maturation in a representational capacity is to account for observed differences in speech output over time. However, since we know that the performance systems are becoming more and more adult-like over time, we can, and must, attempt to derive developmental stages from this (non-grammatical) maturation which is independently necessary for a full account of development.

2.8 Conclusions

In addition to providing a basis for a coherent analysis of phonological acquisition, we believe that our model also provides some insight into the history of phonological theorizing. In the context of the Jakobsonian model of initially impoverished representations, it made sense to assume that languages ended up with high degrees of underspecification. Adding fewer contrasts represented a shorter learning path, and thus a more elegant acquisition model. We are not aware of this rationale being made explicit anywhere, but it seems relevant. However, in the context of a model that strips away representational matter when forced to by the nature of the evidence, excessive underspecification represents an unmotivated extension of the learning path. Thus our model actually favors a phonology with minimal underspecification.

We hope to have explicated Jackendoff's statement and thus shown that the Innateness Hypothesis is perhaps a misnomer for a logical necessity, the Innateness of Primitives Principle. Given its generality, we look forward to extending the reasoning used here to other areas of linguistic theory, such as the acquisition of the syntactic features that distinguish lexical items. In addition to the logical arguments we provide, we have shown that our view converges strongly with empirical work concerning children's speech comprehension capabilities. We also find that our model more accurately mirrors the child's learning path, since children do not appear to need to relearn each lexical item when they begin to show a new contrast in pronunciation—which is what would be predicted by a view that denies early access to all features.

We took pains to illustrate the logic of the Innateness of Primitives Principle. While several readers of this discussion objected to its length, we have chosen to maintain it in its current form because of the oddness of the conclusion it leads us to. The notion that infants must have access to all the representational apparatus of UG *is* odd, but as Pylyshyn (1984: xxii) has pointed out:

[I]f you believe P, and you believe that P entails Q, then even if Q seems more than a little odd, you have some intellectual obligation to take seriously the possibility that Q may be true, nonetheless.

We see this chapter as a step towards fulfilling this intellectual obligation.

3

Competence and performance in phonological acquisition

3.1 What is "child phonology"?

This chapter draws on the generative literature in phonological acquisition, as well as on the work of phoneticians and psycholinguists, in an attempt to propose a unified view of the acquisition of phonological competence. In an oft-quoted passage Chomsky (1965) characterizes the goals of linguistic theory as follows:

Linguistic theory is concerned primarily with an ideal speaker listener, in a completely homogeneous speech community, who knows its language perfectly and is unaffected by such grammatically irrelevant conditions as *memory limitations, distractions, shifts of attention and interest, and errors (random or characteristic)* in applying his knowledge of the language in actual performance. This seems to me to have been the position of the founders of modern general linguistics, and no cogent reason for modifying it has been offered. To study actual linguistic performance, we must consider the interaction of a variety of factors, of which the underlying competence of the speaker-hearer is only one. In this respect, study of language is no different from empirical investigation of other complex phenomena. (Emphasis added.)

The emphasized part of this quotation describes psychological properties which hold of no one more fully than of children, yet the phonological acquisition literature seems virtually unanimous in attributing the disparity between comprehension and production found in children to the grammar.[1] Why should this be so? The answer to this question seems to lie in the *nature* of children's errors. It is not simply the fact that children "misarticulate", since adults frequently do the same, but rather that they produce *systematic* misarticulations. Since one of the most salient attributes of grammars (and the property which ultimately justifies positing generative analyses) is precisely their systematicity, it is perhaps not surprising that researchers have analyzed child speech output using phonological theories. However, we believe such an

---

[1] Notable exceptions include Chomsky (1964), and Faber and Best (1994).

approach is mistaken. We hope to show in what follows that the empirical evidence gathered thus far on most "systematic errors" in child speech does not justify appealing for explanation to natural language grammatical systems, nor, indeed, to the acquisition of those systems. We will argue instead that they are best accounted for in terms of a variety of extragrammatical factors (cognitive and physiological), which can be broadly categorized as "performance".

3.1.1 *Arguments against "child phonology"*

It seems preferable, a priori, to assume that child and adult grammars are organized by the same computational principles and contain the same sorts of process. If this is an accurate assumption, then it is problematic that certain frequent aspects of "child phonology" have long been known to have no parallels in adult phonological systems. One of the most widely discussed phenomena found in "child phonology" is that of "consonant harmony", responsible, for example, for the realization of "duck" as [gək].[2] Another, less widely discussed phenomenon is children's tendency to voice onset consonants. However, the total absence of across-the-board initial stop-voicing and place harmony in adult phonological systems indicates that such processes may not be possible in human phonological systems. Obviously, attributing them to children's grammars would be seriously misguided, if this is so.

On the other hand, it has been pointed out that children often devoice codas and that similar processes occur in languages such as German and Russian. Examples such as this seem to support a supposed parallelism between acquisition and cross-linguistic tendencies, and constitute the basis of much of the literature on markedness theory, from Jakobson to Stampe, as well as to the positing of well-formedness constraints in current Optimality Theory. However, this appears to be a rather opportunistic appeal to "markedness". If "markedness" is responsible for apparent parallels between child and adult phonological output (and is due to a fundamental mechanism of the grammar), then we do not expect to find "more marked" output in children,[3] let alone output which results from processes unattested in adult language.

Pseudophonological (i.e. performance-related) effects (like coda devoicing) have been documented among populations other than children. Johnson et al. (1990) report on the intoxicated speech of the captain of the *Exxon Valdez*

---

[2] This example, as well as several additional ones, has been discussed in this respect by Drachman (1978). Note that while we use square brackets, we do not in fact believe that such forms are phonetic *representations*. Such forms represent, in the way IPA strings in brackets often do, impressionistic renderings of the waveform of the strings.

[3] See below for examples of children's "highly marked" output.

around the time of the accident at Prince William Sound, Alaska. They note, as do other studies of intoxicated speech, that the realization of segments may be affected by blood alcohol level. They include the following among their list of observed effects:

(30)   Some features of intoxicated speech
   • misarticulation of /r/ and /l/
   • final devoicing
   • deaffrication

The accurate articulation of /r/, /l/, and affricates, as well as the existence of a voicing contrast in final position, all represent "marked" features of English whose presence in the grammatical output is attributed, within OT theory, to relatively high-ranked faithfulness constraints regarding the features of the segments in question (and by the absence of neutralizing rules in other theories). To account for Captain Hazelwood's output we have two options: (1) these instances of the "emergence of the unmarked" are to be attributed to the impairment of his *performance system* by alcohol; or (2) the consumption of alcohol in sufficient quantities leads to constraint reranking or rule addition in adult grammars. Under any kind of even vaguely modern conception of the nature of the "grammar," (1) must be thought the more likely hypothesis. The Hazelwood evidence demonstrates that the presence of "emergence of the unmarked" effects in children's bodily output—even systematic effects— does not license unreflective attribution of these patterns to the effects of the grammar, rather than to the "impairment" of the child's performance capacity by the immature state of his or her physiological and cognitive systems.

   Of course, this does not prove that none of the cited cases of "child phonology" is due to the grammar, but it does demonstrate that other explanations are potentially available. Whether the output which forms the basis for the grammatical analyses proposed in work on child language represents output of the grammar or output of the "performance system" is an empirical question, presumably to be resolved by a sophisticated consideration of the relevant learning-theoretic and competence investigation process, just as it is in the case of adult output.

   A serious look at the data on child phonology reveals an additional problem: knowing what exactly constitutes evidence. Consider, for example, the following attempts at producing adult [pʰɛ̃n] *pen* collected from a 15-month-old child in a 30-minute period: [mã˞], [ṽ], [dɛ^dn], [hɪn], [ᵐbõ], [pʰɪn], [tʰn̩tʰn̩tʰn̩] [baʰ], [dhauɴ], [buã] (Ferguson 1986, cited in Faber and Best 1994). As troubling as this data may seem for the presumed "systematicity" of "child phonology", the empirical situation is actually quite a bit worse than these transcriptions suggest. Child speech output used in acquisition study has almost invariably been subjected to what Lust (2006: 132) calls "Rich Interpretation"[4] by the investigators involved, and thus the transcriptions have been "patched" by being filtered through the grammar of the adult listener who is also a speaker of English. Earlier studies such as Kornfeld and Goehl (1974) indicate that transcriptions of child speech are rife with inaccuracy, in that acoustic analysis reveals subtle distinctions, for example, between supposedly merged adult /r/ and /w/, which transcribers tend not to observe.[5] In any event, the existence of the type of data presented by Ferguson (1986) means that *any* use of production evidence will have to selectively cull the data (i.e. recognize the important role of "performance" factors in children's output).

Recent research by Stoel-Gammon and colleagues (e.g. Stoel-Gammon 2004; Sosa and Stoel-Gammon 2006) supports the general impression that children's speech production displays a high degree of variability. For example, Sosa and Stoel-Gammon (2006) discuss what they call "intra-word variability" in acquirers in their second year of life. They define (2006: 32) "intra-word variability" as what takes place when "multiple tokens of the same word are produced differently at the same point in time (same chronological age, recording session, etc.)". They conclude their investigations of the data they collected as follows (2006: 48):

Longitudinal variability rates observed for four children between the ages of 1;0 and 2;0 confirm that intra-word variability is prevalent during the earliest stages of lexical acquisition. Furthermore, these results reveal that high rates of variability continue well beyond the first 50–100 word stage. In fact, intra-word variability in these children peaked at the acquisition of about 150–200 words and this peak coincided with the onset of combined speech.

Two matters regarding this study are worth emphasizing, both pointed out by the authors themselves. The first is that the procedures used in their study for determining whether there was variability in production of a given lexical item "likely underestimate actual levels of intra-word variability" (2006: 35), not least because

---

[4] Lust's own examples in this area involve syntactic acquisition, but of course the same reasoning holds in the phonological domain.

[5] As Faber and Best (1994: 264) state, "[The] child may, despite the apparent lack of contrast, have acoustic differences between *red* and *wed* such that the initial consonants are perceived by adults as representing the same phonemic category."

[v]ariations in vowel quality did not contribute to variability for the purposes of this study. For example, productions of the word *duck* as [dʌt] and [dʌʔ] were considered different, whereas production of *duck* and [dʌ] and [dɛ] were considered the same.

Thus the conclusion of these researchers that variability is prevalent in the children in their study is based on a metric which misses a great deal of the actual variability of children's productions.

Secondly, the author's extend their claims of variability into the third year of life, noting that (2006: 43):

... there is a considerable amount of intra-word variability in the speech of typically developing children even at two years of age ... A recent study by Stoel-Gammon (2004), using a similar data set and a similar variability measure, suggests that this variability continues even into the third year of life.

In approaching an explanation for this high degree of variability, the authors are of course aware of the possible role of some performance factors:

Another factor that certainly influences variability is the development of neuromotor control for speech that occurs during this period of early language acquisition. Young children have been found to demonstrate high levels of variability in many different aspects of motor control. In general, motor development might be summarized as a process of increasing accuracy and decreasing variability (Kent 1992; Smith and Goffman 1998). With regards to the specific musculature used to produce speech, the same types of observations have been made; the speech and non-speech orofacial movements of children tend to be less accurate and more variable than those of adults (Smith and Goffman 1998; Clark, Robin, McCullagh and Schmidt 2001). Thus, some of the observed variability in production of individual words by young children may be attributable to general inability of the speech control system.

Unfortunately, as the authors note, "[t]hese factors ... will not be considered in detail in this study", which focuses instead on what we would consider a highly speculative account which invokes some poorly defined representational incapacity on the child's part.

It seems clear that factors known to play a role in the performance of complex, orchestrated physical activities by any human, including attention to the specific task at hand (as opposed to the countless other impinging demands for attention), fatigue, anxiety, etc., vary from moment to moment, doubtless more so in children than in adults. It would be astonishing if the productions of children were *not* variable given the role of such factors in their behavior, and it would be a tremendous mistake to draw conclusions about the child's underlying competence from the existence of this variability without sophisticated, non-superficial consideration of the matter.

The conclusion we would hope to derive from the arguments given above is that it is not at all obvious that a competence-only based account for children's speech output is a desirable goal. Children's output is actually not very parallel to so-called "unmarked" aspects of adult languages when considered *in toto*. Furthermore, children's output can be demonstrated to parallel systematic, yet unambiguously non-grammatical, performance effects, as seen in intoxicated speech.

It is also well known that children's non-grammatical abilities, such as physiological aptitude at performance and short-term memory capacity are limited. Even when their performance appears to parallel that of adults, we know, for instance, that their control of respiration and voicing differs qualitatively from that of adults (Faber and Best 1994: 269). Occam's Razor demands attributing aspects of their speech output to these factors as the null hypothesis.

3.1.2 *Some non-arguments against a performance system account*

3.1.2.1 *Chainshifts*   In his justly famous study of the acquisition of English phonology by his son Amahl, N. Smith (1973) presents three reasons why the "mappings" he posits from adult surface forms to child output forms are "part of the child's competence rather than of his performance" (1973: 148), including:

- puzzles;
- metathesis;
- recidivism.

All of these phenomena display a superficial similarity to what are sometimes called "chainshifts". They are all, but especially the "puzzles" problem, still regularly and widely cited in the acquisition literature as compelling arguments against performance-based accounts of so-called "child phonology" (see e.g. the positive comments in Lust 2006: 163, and the use of structurally identical data by Smolensky 1996, to be discussed in greater detail below). We find this use of these arguments, by Smith and by most researchers on child phonology since the appearance of his work, somewhat baffling, since the phenomena in question seem to us to offer no real challenge to performance-based accounts. In fact, we believe they support such accounts in a relatively straightforward manner. For this reason, we will go through the three phenomena, using some of Smith's original data, in some detail. Since they relate to what in the end we will argue is a single unifying dynamic, we will reserve our critical assessment of these phenomena until after we have presented a simple illustrative case of each.

The first and most famous phenomenon identified by Smith concerns the pronunciation by Amahl at a certain stage in his development of the words *puzzle* and *puddle*. At this stage, he pronounced adult non-final *z* as *d*, thus producing [pʌdəl] for adult *puzzle*. At this same stage, Amahl velarized coronals before "dark" *l*, and for this reason he produced [pʌgəl] for adult *puddle*. The question which Smith raises regarding these forms (and similarly patterning data) is this: since Amahl actually says [pʌdəl] (when trying to pronounce *puzzle*), one can hardly claim that he is incapable of producing such a string. But why, then, doesn't he say [pʌdəl] for *puddle*? It would seem that physiology cannot be the problem. The label "chainshift" is appropriate for such a case, because in one and the same context *z* → *d* AND *d* → *g*.

The metathesis data concerns Amahl's pronunciation of the word *icicle* at a certain stage of his development. He says this word [aɪkitəl], a form which clearly displays a metathesis (since the *t* should be a reflex of adult *s*). When he said this form, Amahl was at the stage at which he velarized dentals before "dark" *l*, so when Smith gave him the (nonsense) word [aɪkitəl] to say, Amahl said [aɪkikəl], as expected. But the pronunciation of *icicle* shows that he does produce dentals before "dark" *l*, so why does he fail to do so in the made-up target [aɪkitəl], or, indeed, in other *-tle* cases in English? The argument again is that, since Amahl produces the sequences, physiological incapacity cannot possibly provide an explanation. This is a "chainshift"-like effect, since *t* → *k* before "dark" *l*, but in some sense a *k* in this environment (if also preceded by a *t*) becomes a *t*.

Finally, one of the cases of "recidivism" cited by Smith runs as follows. At an early stage of his speech production, both adult *l* and adult *s* show up as *ḍ* in Amahl's speech; thus both *light* and *side* are pronounced [ḍaɪt] at this stage. At a later stage, *l* came to be realized in many environments, including the one of interest to us here, as *l* in Amahl's productions. At this point, *light* was pronounced [laɪt] while *side* was still being pronounced [ḍaɪt]. At the next stage, initial *s* in some environments (including those of interest to us here) also came to be pronounced *l* by Amahl, leading to a renewed collapse of the apparently acquired (at the second stage) contrast between *light* and *side* (hence the term "recidivism"). The question which seems to bother Smith in this case is why, having acquired a mechanism for differentially articulating *s* and *l*, Amahl seemed to lose that ability. The implication is that such a loss of ability is inconsistent with a model of steadily increasing performance capacity. Again, this case is structurally very similar to the chainshift cases discussed above.

We fully agree with Smith's assertion (1973: 150), regarding the *puddle/puzzle* case, that it might appear at first sight "as if the child is incapable of producing a particular sequence...But this clearly is false: the child can produce the sequence correctly, but only as the reflex of the wrong input..."[6] We seriously doubt that anyone has ever contended that children's organs of articulation cannot be placed in a configuration such that a *d* or an *l*, or indeed any other possible human speech sound, might emerge from their vocal tract. Of course, we believe that it has also long been recognized that the bodily production of a sound which is similar to a speech sound, e.g. of a long *s*-like noise to represent a leaking tire, is not "pronunciation of an *s*". The production of a given phonological segment is a relationship between two entities: the phonetic output representation of the segment in question in the mind of the speaker and an articulatory or acoustic event in the world. Can Amahl pronounce, i.e. bring to realization in the world, his mental representation [d] in the word *puddle*? If Smith's data is reliable (and we see no reason to challenge it on this score), the answer is no, he cannot. Can he reliably pronounce his mental representation [z] in *puzzle* as a bodily output of a *z*-type? No, he cannot. Neither of these incapacities on Amahl's part represents an ability to *pronounce* a [d] in this position—a capacity which Amahl simply does not possess at this stage of development of his performance system. That his performance system causes his mis-articulated [z] to sound—to his father's ears in any event (and here real caution must be observed)—like the sound made when an adult accurately pronounces a [d] is simply of no significance for our understanding of Amahl's competence.

Similarly, Amahl can produce reliably neither the target sequence [sikəl] (as in *icicle*) nor the sequence [kitəl] (as in Smith's made-up word [aɪkitəl]), producing the former as [kitəl] and the latter as [kikəl]. Again, we have two *articulatory incapacities* of the developing child. Neither of these incapacities provides the slightest bit of evidence that Amahl has some particular *ability* to pronounce (i.e. bring to realization in the world) either of the relevant target strings.

Finally, in the alleged case of recidivism we have evidence which looks for all the world like stepwise maturational development of Amahl's cognitive and physiological performance system. We agree with Smith (and argue for this position at length in this chapter) that Amahl's representations of *side* and *light* are adult-like throughout the period under study. His performance system has a variety of incapacities regarding the articulation of a target [l], and another partly distinct set of incapacities regarding the articulation of a target [s]. At no point did he *learn* to distinguish [l] from [s]: these mental

[6] The sentence actually continues "and can easily identify such pairs as *riddle* and *wriggle* correctly". The importance of this comprehension capacity is vastly under-appreciated, as we argue in detail in this chapter.

target articulations are distinguished by him *throughout* the learning period. There was thus no learned capacity for him to show recidivism with respect to. What we see instead is the steady development of skill in the realization of a target [l] (in the relevant position), which progresses (in this environment) more rapidly than that for Amahl's realization of a target [s]. As his performance systems go through their normal maturational development, [s] shows various realizations (in various environments); sometimes these realizations are identical to the realizations of other segments at the same stage, sometimes they are not. But the fact that Amahl has acquired the capacity to accurately hit his target [l]s in this context simply has no implications, or (to word it more cautiously) no implications that we understand at present, for his capacity to hit his target [s]s. What Smith has shown is that at some stages Amahl's incapacity regarding target [s] leads his realizations of that segment to sound to his father just like an (accurately or inaccurately) articulated target [l] and at other stages in his development it does not. Far from providing an argument *against* a strong role for performance-based accounts of alleged "child phonology", the "recidivism" argument, like the others offered up by Smith, seem to us to offer very strong support for such accounts.

In his own criticism of performance-based accounts for some attributes of children's speech, Smolensky (1996) asserts that "invoking severe performance difficulties to account for the impoverishment of production relative to comprehension has several problems." He goes on to point out that "[g]ross formulations of this hypothesis, essentially claiming that children don't produce, say, a particular segment because their motor control hasn't yet mastered it" run into problems due to the chainshift data and the fact that children may imitate the relevant sounds. He cites as an example of chainshifts the following: children who produce *thick* as [fɪk] cannot be said to be unable to produce [θ], since they produce this sound when saying *sick* as [θɪk]. In discarding the "gross formulations" of a performance-based account, Smolensky fails to consider a more coherent alternative such as the one we have just outlined. The merger *in performance* of target [θ] and target [f] could be attributed to any intervening cognitive or motor process. A performance-based account simply holds that, when the performance system is given (by the grammar) the command to make a [θ], the vocal tract generates a sound *like* [f]. Given the commands to make an [s], the vocal tract may produce something *like* a [θ], resulting in an apparent chainshift.[7]

---

[7] Note that, when we write [s], we are writing a phonetic symbol—i.e. a linguistic entity which is generated by the grammar. This is not to be confused with a physiological act which happens to

We note in passing that Smolensky never actually demonstrates how the Optimality Theoretic grammar he advocates can allow a child to produce a [θ] for an underlying /s/, but [f] for underlying /θ/. The treatment of chainshifts and other opacity effects has been one of the most difficult issues for OT. Reiss (1995; 1996), and others have demonstrated why a well-constrained OT grammar has difficulty with chainshifts. Simply put the problem is this: if the optimal output for underlying /θ/ is [f], why isn't [f] also a better output for underlying /s/ than [θ] is? Or similarly, [θ] is as well-formed (with respect to Well-Formedness constraints) whether it corresponds to underlying /θ/ or /s/, and it is more faithful to /θ/; therefore, it should be the optimal candidate for the realization of /θ/.[8] At any rate, none of the existing proposals for dealing with opacity in Optimality Theory holds that chainshifts represent an *unmarked*, initial state of UG-phonology. The phenomenon of chainshifts appears, rather, to be highly marked and thus, given the assumptions made within OT concerning markedness and acquisition, must be the result of learning. Smolensky offers no plausible learning path which would lead the acquirer from the initial state to the highly marked constraint-ranking which would trigger chainshifts, and indeed it seems extremely unlikely that any such path could be coherently posited. There is *no* evidence in the PLD presented to a child acquiring English, for example, which would lead them to posit a constraint ranking which generated the [θ] > [f] but [s] > [θ] chainshift. Moreover, becoming a competent adult speaker would then require readjusting the grammar (by resetting constraint parameters or by reranking complex constraints so low as to be inactive) so as to attain the adult grammar which has no chainshifts, just as the initial state of the grammar had none. Such "Duke of York" models of the learning path are intuitively unappealing.

Moreover, this is not the only way in which Smolensky's invocation of the chainshift data runs foul of standard OT assumptions regarding markedness. The initial ranking is intended, within OT, to represent a grammar which generates only maximally unmarked output. However, the segment [s] is less marked than [θ] according to any of the standard criteria used in markedness theories—[s] is more common cross-linguistically, any language with a [θ] also has an [s], French speakers (e.g.) say [s] for English [θ], etc.

---

look and sound like an [s], but is not an [s] *qua* linguistic representation. Sapir's famous comparison between a voiceless [ʍ] and the sound of a person blowing out a candle comes to mind.

[8] Given a theory of phonology which contains rules which apply in an ordered derivation, chainshifts are predicted to occur. In that sense, opacity has no status in a rule-based grammar. Opacity is just a point of logic, a possible result of applying rules in some order. As pointed out earlier, this was recognized by Kiparsky and Menn (1977: 73): "Opacity is a property of the relation between the grammar and the data. An opaque rule is not more complex, merely harder to discover."

In short, the existence of chainshifts and related phenomena is not evidence against a performance-based account of the "systematic errors" of child speech. Indeed, under standard OT assumptions about segmental markedness and the cross-linguistic markedness of opacity, it would appear to offer strong support in favor of the type of performance-based account we are advocating here.

3.1.2.2 *Imitation*   Smolensky (1996) argues that the higher level of performance during direct imitation (citing Menn and Mathei 1992) provides further evidence for a competence-based model. Unfortunately, this appears to contradict his own approach to the study of child speech output. There are two distinct accounts for what has been labeled "imitation": (1) increased performance skill under concentration and (2) parroting. Under our account it is precisely during intense concentration on the act of performance that the child will perform better in carrying out the instructions provided by the grammar. Parroting clearly has no grammatical basis: a speaker of English can parrot a Cree sentence fairly well without acquiring a Cree grammar.

Under Smolensky's competence-only approach, neither of these types of "imitation" can be accounted for. In the first type, since Smolensky assumes the *grammar* is responsible for e.g. realization of [θ] as [f], increased attention to performance should lead only to a clearer hit of the target [f]. In the second type, to account for an English speaker's ability to imitate Cree, Smolensky would have to assume instantaneous acquisition of Cree constraint rankings. Clearly, accounts for "imitation" phenomena which invoke the performance system are to be preferred.

3.2 Optimality Theory and the competence/performance "dilemma"

We are discussing Smolensky (1996) rather extensively in this chapter because his work represents one of the most explicit attempts to address competence vs. performance concerns regarding "child phonology" in the vast literature on phonological acquisition. He proposes in that work an Optimality Theoretic (OT) resolution of the well-known comprehension/production dilemma in child language, which arises from the observation that children appear to be capable of parsing (i.e. comprehending) more elaborate structures than those which appear in their own output. We argue that Smolensky's model encounters two serious difficulties — the first concerning his proposed parsing algorithm, and the second concerning the issue of the learnability of underlying forms. We offer alternative parsing algorithms, and examine their implications for learnability and the initial ranking of OT constraints. Finally, we re-emphasize, based on evidence from a variety of sources, that the resolution of the comprehension/production dilemma lies not in phonological domain (linguistic competence), but rather in the domain of implementation of linguistic knowledge (performance). With a revision of certain aspects of the OT model for children's phonologies and of learnability theory in phonology, we attempt here to contribute both to research on OT and to the study of phonological acquisition generally. It is not our aim in this chapter to argue for or against OT approaches to phonology. We will not hesitate, however, to point out flaws in the *application* of OT in the current literature. We hope that the improvements in the application of OT which we propose, as well as mention of points in which the theory seems to fare worse than alternative approaches, will lead to the kind of progress in the fields of phonology and acquisition that transcends the parochialism of particular frameworks.

3.2.1 *The phonological enterprise*

We adopt the standard generative view that the study of phonology involves a characterization of mental representations and computations involving these representations. This view can be contrasted with with conceptions of phonology centered around the characterization of "tendencies" and "trends" sometimes subsumed under the ill-defined notion of "markedness". For example, McCarthy (1988) has asserted that "[t]he goal of phonology is the construction of a theory in which *cross-linguistically common* [*but not necessarily universal—* MH&CR] and well-established processes emerge from very simple combinations of the descriptive parameters of the model" (emphasis added). As we argued in Chapter 1, we take the goal to be the development of a theory of *possible* human languages (i.e. the restrictions imposed upon the human language faculty by UG), not "common" (statistically preponderant) human languages.[9] "Common" features are artifacts of the sampling process, phonetic factors grammaticalized through historical change/acquisition (cf. Hale 2007), etc., some of which are interesting and important domains of inquiry, but, all of which are, strictly speaking, extragrammatical.

The study of acquisition includes a characterization of the initial state of the grammar, S_0, and a theory of a learning path from S_0 to a subsequent state S_n. Our point of view is a strongly innatist approach to child grammar, but proposes a performance-based account of many of the peculiarities of children's speech production. There exist various hypotheses in the acquisition

---

[9] Briefly, the question of what gets counted in determining "commonness" leads to insurmountable difficulties, given the standard assumption among generative linguists that the object of study is computational systems, not speech communities.

literature which are directly relevant to these assumptions. Some of these are outlined, contrastively, in (31) and (32) below.

(31) The nature of child phonology
   a.   The Strong Identity Hypothesis, which holds that child phonology is governed by the same principles as adult phonology.
   b.   The view that child phonology is fundamentally distinct from adult phonology—licensing processes unattested in adult language, dependent on a series of developmental stages, etc.
(32) The nature of the evidence
   a.   Deviations from target forms—in children's as well as adults' grammars—are to be attributed to performance effects, including non-linguistic cognitive and motor processing.
   b.   Many deviations from target forms are the result of "child phonology" (i.e. the child's phonological competence)—grammatical effects for which the target language provides no evidence.

We believe that both empirical evidence and learnability considerations favor the (a) hypotheses—that is, we support the Strong Identity Hypothesis and the hypothesis that deviations from targets are largely due to performance effects.

   By contrast, Smolensky (1996) uncritically follows most of the phonological acquisition literature in attempting to account for the peculiarities of children's speech output and the well-known discrepancy between their inaccurate production of adult words and their extremely accurate parsing of adult speech by appealing to the state of their grammars. In particular, he rejects the notion that there is a "dramatically greater performance/competence gap for children" (1996: 1). He proposes that a single OT grammar can generate both adult-like comprehension and child-like production. In order to model the observed discrepancy between the two domains, he assumes that at the initial state of the grammar, S_0, OT Well-formedness (W) constraints are ranked above Faithfulness (F) constraints.[10] Smolenksy's proposal is represented in (33):

(33) Smolensky's proposed initial state
      Well-formedness constraints $\gg$ Faithfulness constraints

---

[10] F-constraints value correspondence between input forms (underlying representations) and output forms (surface phonetic representations). W-constraints value "unmarked" output.

3.2.2 *Smolensky's parsing algorithm*

Smolensky ingeniously proposes a distinction between the nature of production and comprehension in an OT model. The distinction is sketched in (34) and (35):

(34)   Production: OT grammar selects the most "harmonic" *output/surface form* (from the set of candidates which GEN provides) for a given *input/UR*

(35)   Comprehension: (the same) OT grammar selects the most harmonic *input/UR* for a given observed *output/surface form*

Smolenksy's model is intuitively satisfying. As he states, "What differs between 'production' and 'comprehension' is only *which structures compete*: structures that share the same underlying form in the former case, structures that share the same surface form in the latter case" (1996: 3). Note that this parsing model is meant to be valid for all grammars—those of adults as well as those of children.

   The result of making such a distinction is that the two operations will not always lead to the same input–output mapping, for example, at S_0. In (36) we have adapted Smolensky's constraint tableaux to show how the distinction works. Compare a child's pronunciation of a stored lexeme /kæt/ to the comprehension of this same lexeme as pronounced by an adult.[11] Since the W-constraints are all ranked high, every possible candidate form except for the most unmarked will violate some W-constraints. Like Smolensky, we have not distinguished among candidates on the basis of which specific W-constraints they violate, since this does not affect the argument. Again following Smolensky, we assume that the universally least marked output representation is [ta]. Since this candidate violates no W-constraints, it is selected by the grammar at this stage as the optimal surface form. Note that the same candidate will surface no matter what input form is used at this stage of the grammar.

   In the bottom half of the tableau we illustrate how, in Smolensky's system, the child, who systematically pronounces /kæt/ as [ta], is nevertheless able to parse adult [kæt] accurately as /kæt/, using the same grammar that is responsible for the output [ta]. Since the W-constraints represent surface well-formedness conditions, and the output, [kæt], is a given, the mapping from any possible underlying representation to this surface form will violate the same W-constraints. The surface form is known a priori to violate constraints

---

[11]   Following Smolensky, we ignore details of the pronunciation such as the aspiration on the initial voiceless stop.

against the presence of a coda, of an [æ] and of a dorsal consonant. Therefore, it is left to the F-constraints to select the most harmonic, the optimal, input-output mapping.

(36)   Comprehension and production (following Smolensky 1996)[12]
- Production: /kæt/ pronounced [ta] ("emergence of the unmarked").
- Comprehension: [kæt] parsed as /kæt/, not /skæti/, since mapping of /kæt/ to [kæt] is more harmonic than /skæti/ to [kæt] (only F-constraints matter).

	Candidates	W-constraints (*æ, *Dorsal, *Coda...)	F-constraints (Parse, Fill,...)
PRODUCTION			
UR /kæt/			
☞	[ta]		*
	[kæt]	*!	
	[skæti]	*!	*
	[dajpəræʃ]	*!	*
	etc.	*!	*
COMPREHENSION			
Surface [kæt]			
	/ta/	*	*!
→	/kæt/	*	
	/skæti/	*	*!
	/dajpəræʃ/	*	*!
	etc.	*	*!

The winner in comprehension is marked with an arrow, →.

Observe that Smolensky departs from most work on phonological acquisition in implicitly assuming (correctly, we believe) that children have access to the full set of universal features in constructing URs and that they store URs fully and accurately specified, according to what they hear in the target language.[13] Therefore, under Smolensky's own analysis the notion of Richness

---

[12] Smolensky (1996: 7) says: "What is given is the surface form, so the competing structures now [*i.e. in comprehension*—MH&CR] are all those which are pronounced [kæt]." This is uninterpretable for child language as stated since, by Smolensky's hypothesis, the grammar is responsible initially for maximally "unmarked" pronunciation. There is no UR at this stage which is *pronounced* [kæt], even though adult [kæt] can be parsed as such. It seems clear from the discussion that Smolensky is trying to say that the mappings from every possible UR to surface candidate [kæt] are compared. The UR corresponding to the most harmonic mapping is the winner.

[13] We would qualify this by allowing for errors in parsing, which lead to incorrect representations. This is to be distinguished from merely incomplete representations assumed by researchers who posit that the child does not have access to all the features of the universal feature inventory. See the previous chapter for arguments against the latter position. Since Smolensky denies the relevance of performance in the characterization of language acquisition, he cannot appeal to such parsing errors.

of the Base (e.g. Prince and Smolensky 1993: 191) is irrelevant (at least in the case of non-alternating forms) to the acquisition process. Richness of the Base, you will recall from the discussion above, is a claim about the nature of OT grammars which states that there can be great latitude in the form of URs. For example, someone with a grammar of English could have all voiceless surface velar stops stored as clicks. Given the appropriate constraint ranking, viz., with constraints against clicks ranked high, the surface forms could still be pronounced with normal velar stops. But given Smolensky's own assumptions about how parsing and the acquisition of URs proceeds, /kæt/, for example, could never be stored with a click. As a result, Smolensky appears to agree with our position: the notion of Richness of the Base is a computational curiosity of OT grammars which is irrelevant to human language.

Note, in anticipation of the discussion to follow, that (a) given the arbitrariness of the sign, the child must first hear adult [kæt], store /kæt/, and associate this UR with the appropriate meaning before being able to generate the production mapping of /kæt/ to [ta] that Smolensky assumes; and (b) that as soon as the child does generate this form, the discrepancy between the child form and the adult form leads to a massive reranking of the constraints. In particular, it will trigger the demotion of most relevant W-constraints below the F-constraints that (even in the adult grammar) assure that the UR and surface forms of this word are in most respects identical. Smolensky's presumed initial high ranking of W-constraints thus leads to immediate promotion of those F-constraints which are relevant to each lexical item acquired.

3.2.3 *Flaws in the parsing algorithm*

The parsing algorithm that Smolensky proposes is meant to characterize comprehension by both children and adults. Unfortunately, this algorithm suffers from a serious flaw. We believe that this flaw precludes using such a model for the purposes of either child or adult language. The flaw lies in the fact that since the algorithm generates the *most* harmonic mapping from a UR to a surface form, it will never be able to account for the well-attested and widespread phenomenon of surface ambiguity (neutralization) in natural language. A simple and well-known example will reveal this, though it is worth pointing out that any example which shows the effects of a phonological merger would do as well.[14]

This idealization does not, however, affect the structure of his argument, which up to this point we accept.

[14] In earlier work we used an example from Fijian.

Our example comes from German, which has two surface forms [rat], one derived from the UR /rat/ and the other from /rad/. We can capture the phenomenon of coda devoicing in German by assuming that a constraint against voiced codas is ranked above constraints demanding faithfulness to underlying voicing values. The relevant aspects of German grammar are sketched in (37).

(37)   German surface ambiguity
   • /rat/ > [rat] 'advice' & /rad/ > [rat] 'wheel'
   • *VOICEDCODA ≫ FAITH[VOICE]

Consider what happens when a surface form [rat] is parsed by a speaker of German, using Smolensky's algorithm. Since the surface form is a given in parsing and since the choice of UR is left to the F-constraints, the most harmonic mapping from a UR to [rat] will be from the UR /rat/. The mapping from UR /rad/ to surface [rat] violates the same W-constraints as the mapping from /rat/ to [rat], but the former violates more F-constraints than the latter.

Indeed, in any case of surface merger, only the most "unmarked" underlying lexeme will be chosen by the parse, since this lexeme provides the most faithful mapping. Note that this flaw in Smolensky's comprehension model is independent of the issue of the initial ranking of F-constraints—i.e the model produces the wrong result both for children (who, according to Smolensky—though we do not share this assumption—have low-ranked F-constraints) and adults (who have elevated selected Faithfulness constraints).

Smolensky's proposed resolution of the comprehension/production dilemma thus gives rise to an unresolvable empirical problem: in any case of surface phonological merger, only the more "unmarked" underlying lexeme can be comprehended by the parser. This is contra-indicated by a wealth of evidence from virtually every human language. Note that the same difficulty arises in the case of syntactic comprehension: Smolensky's algorithm generates only the *most* harmonic parse for a given, potentially ambiguous, overt string.

Any appeal to top-down processing to resolve this dilemma is inconsistent with well-established priming effects: "The general picture of lexical access during speech perception, then, is that it initially can discriminate only on phonological grounds. Only somewhat later in processing, after the syntactic and conceptual processors have gotten access to the list of possible candidates, can the ultimate choice of word be determined" (Jackendoff 1987: 103; cf. references therein). In other words, the phonology makes multiple candidates available to further processing. Smolensky's discussion thus makes the basic error of treating the mapping of UR to SR as an invertible function, which it clearly cannot be, given the existence of neutralization.

3.2.4 *Smolensky's learnability argument*

Smolensky provides a brief discussion of the mechanism of constraint-demotion in an OT model of the acquisition process (1996: 12). The learning algorithm is given as follows. At the initial stage, the child uses his/her grammar to parse (and produce) overt phonetic forms. This grammar diverges from the target, since all W-constraints outrank all F-constraints. Subsequently,

> The full structural descriptions assigned to the overt data are then used in the Error-Driven version...of the Constraint Demotion ranking algorithm (Tesar and Smolensky 1993): *whenever* the structural description which has just been assigned to the overt data (comprehension) is less harmonic than the current grammar's output (production), relevant constraints are demoted to make the comprehension parse the more harmonic. This yields a new grammar...(Smolensky 1996: 12; emphasis added.)

In the case discussed by Smolensky in which a child produces [ta] for the underlying representation /kæt/, but correctly parses [kæt] as /kæt/, the structural description of the production mapping is more harmonic than that of the comprehension mapping. This is because the production process does not contain violations of highly ranked W-constraints such as *CODA, *DORSAL, etc., whereas the comprehension process violates these constraints. When the child compares the structural description assigned to the overt data with that of the grammar's output and finds that the former is less harmonic, the necessary W-constraints are reranked such that they are lower than the relevant F-constraints.

3.2.5 *Flaws in the learnability argument*

The state of knowledge ("grammar") required for Smolensky's resolution of the comprehension/production dilemma in child language *cannot exist* given his learning algorithm. The virtual simultaneity of events which share a cause–effect relationship resulting from the application of this algorithm *precludes* a difference in comprehension and production via the mechanism asserted by Smolensky. We can illustrate this with the example just cited. The child must first correctly parse [kæt] as corresponding to underlying /kæt/. This is a necessary prerequisite to the acquisition of that lexeme (and the assumption is that the child must be able to do this in spite of having e.g. *DORSAL ranked high). As soon as the child has done this, he/she will make the relevant comparison between the harmony of the comprehension form and that of his/her production form. The child will ascertain that the comprehension form is less harmonic than the production form, and the relevant W-constraints will be demoted below the relevant F-constraints. As a result, there can be no stable stage during which the child produces [ta] for /kæt/, i.e. no stable state in which production is consistently different (for a given stage in acquisition) than comprehension. Thus the grammar posited by Smolensky, which produces [ta] for /kæt/ but correctly parses [kæt] as /kæt/, could never exist. A stage which cannot exist cannot provide an account of stable features of child speech output of this type.

3.2.6 *An alternative parsing model*

If we are to account for surface ambiguity, Smolensky's parsing algorithm must be replaced with one which generates a set of parses, not a single parse. We propose two such algorithms. In this book we offer many arguments against OT as currently practiced; however, our main goal in this chapter is to focus on issues surrounding the competence/performance gap in child speech. Therefore, we attempt to couch our discussion in terms of an OT-type model. In (38) we sketch an algorithm which is in the non-procedural spirit of classical OT. Under the assumption that massive computational complexity will ultimately be amenable to effective modeling, the algorithm culls the set of all possible URs to select those which can serve as a parse for a given surface form.

(38)   "Shrinking" algorithm in the "spirit of classical OT"
       To select a set of possible parses for a surface form Φ (a) GEN generates all possible URs; $\Psi_i, i = 1,\ldots$ (b) for each UR Ψ_i GEN generates all possible surface candidates; (c) for each UR Ψ_i whose optimal output is Φ, Ψ_i is a parse for Φ.

In (39) we sketch a more procedural algorithm which starts with a set of parses containing only the one form which is identical to the surface form. The algorithm expands the hypothesis space of the parse by "undoing" the effects of W-constraints.[15]

(39)   "Expanding" algorithm
       • Let the set Ψ of possible parses for Φ be equal to Φ; $\Psi = \{\Phi\}$. (This means that the first member of the set of candidate parses is identical to the surface form.)
       • Start at the highest-ranked constraint and proceed through the ranked constraint hierarchy.

---

[15] This bears some similarity to recent proposals concerning Harmonic Serialism by McCarthy (e.g. McCarthy 2006).

- When an F-constraint which refers to a feature G is encountered, "fix" the candidate set with respect to G. That is, all subsequent candidates must be identical to some Ψ_i with respect to the feature G.
- When a W-constraint is encountered, expand candidate set Ψ along precisely the dimension specified by the W-constraint. That is, add candidates Ψ_i to the hypothesis space Ψ which differ from some pre-existing candidate only in violating the current W-constraint.
- The algorithm ends when there is no remaining W-constraint which dominates an F-constraint. The parse candidate set thus produced $\Psi = \{\Psi_i, i = 1, \ldots, k\}$ represents the set of URs which will be neutralized to Φ by the grammar.

We can illustrate the operation of the algorithm in (39) by contrasting the parsing of English [rat] vs. [rad] with that of the ambiguous German [rat], assuming the URs in (40). (We have chosen the algorithm in (39) for purely expository purposes. The same result will be obtained using the algorithm in (38).)

(40)   Contrastive parsing[16]
- English: /rat/ 'rot' and /rad/ 'rod'
- German: /rat/ 'advice' and /rad/ 'wheel'

Since English does not have coda devoicing, we can assume that the ranking of *VOICEDCODA relative to FAITH[VOICE] in English is the opposite of that assumed for German, above. The operation of the parsing algorithm is sketched in (41), where a single UR is associated with surface [rat].

(41)   English parse of [rat]: FAITH[VOICE] $\gg$ *VOICEDCODA
- The candidate set consists of /rat/.
- The voicing specification of all segments in /rat/ is fixed by FAITH[VOICE].
- The candidate set is not increased by *VOICEDCODA, since [voice] has been "fixed" in previous step.
- The overt form is associated to a *single* UR, /rat/.

In German, on the other hand, the algorithm leads to an ambiguous parse, as desired, shown in (42).

(42)   German parse of [rat]: *VOICEDCODA $\gg$ FAITH[VOICE]
- The candidate set consists of /rat/.
- The candidate set is expanded to /rat/ AND /rad/ by "undoing" the W-constraint *VOICEDCODA.

---

[16] The "English" in question is that of the (Midwestern) first author.

- The voicing specification of all segments in both /rat/ AND /rad/ is fixed by FAITH[VOICE].
- The overt form is ambiguous—derivable from both /rat/ and /rad/.

Whichever algorithm turns out to be more useful, both of our proposed parsing algorithms are superior to Smolensky's, since they generate a *set* of candidate URs for a given surface form. Note that the argument developed here for phonology applies to the parsing of syntax as well, whereas Smolensky's model will not generate differing underlying structures for sentences which are ambiguous on the surface. Theories of phonological and syntactic comprehension must account for such ambiguity. Any model which targets the most harmonic parse (i.e. a *single* candidate) instead of a set of acceptable parses fails to capture a critical aspect of natural language.

3.2.7 *An alternative learning path*

We now turn to a consideration of the implications of these parsing algorithms for the study of the learnability of OT grammars. There is, first of all, an intuitive argument to be made against the position held by Smolensky and virtually every other scholar writing about the learning of OT grammars. Since surface forms and underlying forms tend to be "fairly close" in adult grammars, it is clear that most F-constraints must ultimately be ranked higher than W-constraints. A theory which assumes that the F-constraints start out ranked high seems preferable a priori to one which posits massive reranking. Obviously, our intuitions in this regard are not universally shared, as illustrated by Prince and Tesar (1999: n. 2): "Swimming against the tide, Hale & Reiss 1997 insist on F≫M as the default."[17] We hope to justify our intuitions in the following paragraphs.

This intuitive argument can be supported by a demonstration that a parsing algorithm that actually works *requires* that F-constraints be initially ranked high in UG so that learners can converge on a lexicon. In contrast to

---

[17] Ironically, their footnote continues as follows: "For them, then, word learning yields no learning of phonology. To replace M≫F learning, they offer an 'algorithm' that regrettably sets out to generate and then sort the entirety of an infinite set in its preliminary stages." They reference here an unpublished paper of ours; however, the argument is laid out already in our 1998 *Linguistic Inquiry* paper. Prince and Tesar appear to be taking us to task for adopting, as we do for the sake of argument, the idea that a learner has an OT grammar that evaluates (intensionally) an infinite candidate set, and that this grammar is used in acquisition. We are mystified by their apparent disdain for these assumptions, which are widely shared in OT research on phonology, not least in their own contributions to that field.

Smolensky, then, we propose that the initial state of the grammar must be that shown in (43).

(43) At S_0: Faithfulness constraints $\gg$ Well-formedness constraints

With the initial ranking proposed in (43) there is a single outcome to each parse at S_0. With the opposite initial ranking proposed by Smolensky in (31), a parsing algorithm like (38), which eliminates candidates from an initially infinite set, will generate the empty set; and an algorithm like (39), which adds candidates to an initially unary set, will explode the candidate set to include all possible URs. A lexicon is *unacquirable* under either scenario.

The table in (44) below illustrates the acquisition of English /rat/ and /rad/ (forms AB) as opposed to German /rat/ and /rad/ (forms C–F), based on exposure to relevant surface forms. The German forms ending in [-əs] are genitive singular forms of the relevant nouns; because the stem-final stops occur between vowels, i.e. in onset position, in these forms, coda devoicing is not relevant. In the top half of the table we sketch the learning path under our assumption that all F-constraints are ranked high. Using either parsing algorithm, (38) or (39), the learner will be able to converge on a single UR for each surface form. Using (38), the high ranking of all F-constraints ensures that the optimal candidate is identical to the input form. Using (39), the high ranking of all F-constraints "fixes" the value of all features of the surface form before the W-constraints can expand the set of candidate parses, again producing a single, fully faithful parse at the initial state.

The parse chosen is the correct one with respect to the relevant adult grammar in each case except for form E. Ultimately, when the grammar generates the alternations due to coda devoicing, forms E and F will have to be collapsed. This process is obviously intimately related to the process of constraint reranking, whereby *VOICEDCODA is raised above FAITH [VOICE] to obtain the grammar of German.

(44) Comparing HIFAITH and LOFAITH at S_0 using a parser that works

WITH F CONSTRAINTS RANKED HIGH		
Surface Form	Initial Hypothesis for UR	Path to adult UR
A. rat	rat	Unique, correct UR is selected initially.
B. rad	rad	Unique, correct UR is selected initially.
C. rat	rat	Unique, correct UR is selected initially.
D. ratəs	rat	Unique, correct UR is selected initially.
E. rat	rat	E & F stored differently, later collapsed by
F. radəs	rad	storing /rad/ and raising *VOICEDCODA.

With F constraints ranked LOW		
Surface Form	Initial Hypothesis for UR	Path to adult UR
A. rat	Ø *or* rat, ratOʂ, bəbə...	There can be no learning path: each
B. rad	Ø *or* rat, ratOʂ, bəbə...	production yields the maximally
C. rat	Ø *or* rat, ratOʂ, bəbə...	unmarked utterance, say *ta*, as S
D. ratəs	Ø *or* rat, ratOʂ, bəbə...	desired, but each parse yields Ø by (38)
E. rat	Ø *or* rat, ratOʂ, bəbə...	or else everything generated by the
F. radəs	Ø *or* rat, ratOʂ, bəbə...	UG-given W-constraints by (39).

The bottom half of the table illustrates the problem with assuming that F-constraints are initially ranked low. As shown by Smolensky, the production mapping will generate the maximally unmarked [ta] at the initial state. However, (38) will generate no parses—there is no UR which will surface as [rat] at this stage, since every UR will surface as [ta]. Algorithm (39) will generate an infinite set of candidate parses, since no features of the surface form Φ will be "fixed" before the W-constraints expand the parse set to include forms with every possible W-constraint violation.

To appreciate that constraint reranking and choice of UR are part of the same task, it may be helpful to think about the most basic lesson in rule-based phonology: the interdependence of the choice of UR and the establishment of phonological rules. Unfortunately, the obvious fact that the reranking of constraints and the collapsing of predictable allomorphs to a single form are two aspects of a single process has not been consistently recognized in the literature:

(45) Tesar and Smolensky (1993: 1)

Under the assumption of innate knowledge of the universal constraints, the primary task of the learner is the DETERMINATION OF THE DOMINANCE RANKING of these constraints which is particular to the target language. We will present a simple and efficient algorithm for solving this problem, ASSUMING A GIVEN SET OF HYPOTHESIZED UNDERLYING FORMS. (Concerning the problem of acquiring underlying forms, see the discussion of "optimality in the lexicon" in P & S 1993, Par. 9). (Emphasis added.)

Turning to Prince and Smolensky (1993: par. 9) we find:

(46) Prince and Smolensky (1993: 192)

Lexicon Optimization. Suppose that several different inputs $I_1, I_2, \ldots I_n$, when parsed by A GRAMMAR G [i.e. *ranked constraint hierarchy*—MRH&CR] lead to corresponding outputs $O_1, O_2, \ldots, O_n$, all of which are realized as the same phonetic form Φ—these inputs are all *phonetically* identical with respect to G.

Now one of these outputs must be the most harmonic, by virtue of incurring the least significant violation marks: suppose this optimal one is labelled O_k. Then the learner should CHOOSE FOR THE UNDERLYING FORM for Φ the input I_k.

We might refer to this approach as the *Teufelkreis* or "vicious circle" theory of language acquisition: the child needs a ranking to get URs and needs URs to get a ranking.[18] In more recent work Tesar and Smolensky have acknowledged the flaw in their approach, but consign a solution to the status of "one of the next steps in [their] research program" (1998: sec. 9).[19] They also propose that the child must make an "initial guess" as to the correct UR for each surface form. In our view, the only coherent interpretation of "guess" is the initial hypothesis provided by the learning algorithm—this is what "guess" means in a formal learning theory. Tesar (1997) states explicitly that he will "avoid the challenging problem of identifying and learning underlying forms, and assume that for a given overt form, the underlying form is apparent" (sec. 2). The only coherent interpretation of this is that URs are initially identical to observed (and produced—see below) surface forms. This follows from our initial assumptions, since it is equivalent to assuming that Faithfulness constraints are initially ranked higher than all Well-formedness constraints. Prince and Smolensky's (1993) process of Lexicon Optimization has a second drawback in addition to the *Teufelkreis* issue: as pointed out by Inkelas (1994), it only works for non-alternating morphemes, those that have a single surface realization.

So, constraint reranking and choice of a lexicon are part of the same task. Using the algorithm we have proposed, the learner can converge on a lexicon *only* if F-constraints are initially ranked *above* W-constraints. Again, referring to rule-based phonology, this is the equivalent of saying that the child has no rules at S_0, i.e. that adult phonetic forms are stored as perceived by learners. As we indicated above, this assumption actually leads to the simplest view of the learning path—one that does not require massive reranking with each newly acquired lexeme.

---

[18] Smolensky's model discussed above attempts to address this problem, but fails for reasons we have discussed.

[19] Unfortunately, their initial suggestions for a solution do not appear promising, since they rely crucially on Output–output Faithfulness constraints and context-sensitive Faithfulness constraints. Both these powerful devices have been criticized by us on empirical and theoretical grounds; we summarize and expand our earlier criticisms in Ch. 9 of this book. Recent work in OT continues to attempt to address this persistent problem.

3.2.8 *Summary*

We now summarize the major points in our argument thus far. First, Smolensky's parsing algorithm selects only the most "harmonic" UR, so it fails to account for surface ambiguity due to neutralization in any human language. Second, an algorithm which associates a perceived form with a set of possible URs is needed, since surface ambiguity does exist. Finally, using such an algorithm in acquisition, the learner can converge on a lexicon only if F-constraints are initially ranked above W-constraints.

For the moment, note that the "emergence of the unmarked" has been touted as a property of children's speech derived from the initial ranking assumed by Smolensky and others. Given our learnability arguments thus far, we are forced to conclude that emergence of the unmarked is irrelevant to the description of children's grammars. In the rest of this chapter we return to our argument that, although superficially implausible, it is in fact the case that children's grammars are faithful to observed (adult) target forms.

3.3 The nature of phonological acquisition

In addition to the empirical and "learning-theoretic" difficulties with Smolensky's approach to acquisition, we believe that the motivation for Smolensky's position is flawed. As we have seen, child speech output does not parallel unmarked adult speech, in general. In addition, there is clear evidence that "there is a dramatically greater competence/performance gap for children" (Smolensky 1996: 1)—a hypothesis Smolensky rejects despite a rich body of empirical evidence to the contrary. Note that this holds in speech as in virtually every other domain of physical activity. We will now sketch an alternative theory which, we believe, avoids the shortcomings of Smolensky's proposal. In particular, we build upon our earlier demonstration that if one adopts an OT framework at all, the initial state of the grammar must have all F-constraints ranked above all W-constraints in order to allow for the acquisition of a lexicon. We also assume, as demonstrated in Chapter 2, that children must have access to, and make use of, the full universal phonological feature set.

An evaluation of our hypothesis involves confronting the difficult problem of distinguishing, in children as we do in adults (in keeping with the Strong Identity Hypothesis), between an output of the phonology (a mental representation) and a real-time output of the body under some particular circumstances (those in effect at the time of utterance). The standard approach to the study of the speech of adults can be sketched as in (47) below.

(47)   Adult speech[20]
          underlying representation: X
                                         | Phonology
                                         ↓

              output of grammar: Y
                                         | Cognitive and physiological
                                         ↓   performance systems
                    output of body: Z

The phonology represents a mapping relationship between the underlying representation, X, and the output of the phonology for the string in question, Y.[21] The performance system of the speaker, responsible for directing the body to "hit" the output target in question, leverages the current state of its memory access and retrieval systems, as well as its articulatory planning system, to convert the mental representation Y to a set of articulatory commands which, filtered by contingent environmental factors (including accidental features of the body in question—its size, shape of its resonating cavities, etc.—as well as contingent features of the context in which the body finds itself at the moment of utterance—air pressure, humidity, wind speed and direction, etc.), generate an acoustic output, Z. Each of the arrows in (47) represents a mapping relationship: the grammar is responsible for the mapping of lexical entries onto output representations, the production system (and environmental factors) for mapping the output representation onto an acoustic realization. It is to be expected that these relationships, therefore, will be relatively systematic and regular; indeed, such systematicity is implicit in the notion of "mapping relationship".[22] As is well known from the study of adult phonetics, Z is highly variable (e.g. multiple articulations of /æ/ from the same speaker in the same session in the same phonological environment will still differ from one another acoustically). Given the complex set of factors determining its form (cognitive and physical attributes—stable and accidental—of the speaker as well as numerous environmental effects), this is to be expected. Note that Z cannot, under any circumstances, be the same as Y: Y is a mental representation and Z is an acoustic (or articulatory) event.

[20] A more sophisticated representation of the relevant process is presented in Ch. 5.

[21] It may be for some phonologies (e.g. if they are maximally faithful with respect to the relevant features, in OT terms, or have no rules which affect the relevant segments, in a rule-based system) that X = Y.

[22] We are unlikely to be in a position to ascertain the systematicity of the effects of contingent environmental factors in most cases. The relevant information is not typically provided in studies of phonetic output.

It is widely acknowledged that while the speech perception skills of even very young infants are highly developed (Goodman and Nussbaum 1994), the articulatory skills of these same infants are much less sophisticated. Indeed, the general conception is that the sensitivity of the speech perception system is generally reduced over time to attend only (or primarily) to those distinctions critical for parsing the target language, while the production system moves from a state of virtually complete inarticulateness to a comprehensive ability to articulate the target language. We would not be surprised, then, if the effects of an immature and generally incompetent production system on the Y of (47) were more dramatic than the effects of the adult production system. That is, we would predict from general considerations such as these that Z should be more distant from Y (and more variable in its realization of a given Y) in children than it is in adults—this, indeed, is the definition of immature control of the production system.

The importance of distinguishing between the output of the body and the output of the grammar is not lessened by the difficulty of the task. The significance of the undertaking is often noted; in her survey of phonological acquisition, for example, Macken (1995: 672) notes that "we must attempt the difficult, perhaps impossible, task of separating the grammar from the processor". If we fail to rise to this challenge, we have abandoned the core concern of linguistics: to understand the nature of human linguistic competence.

The goal of distinguishing between these various effects can be stated as a simple question: how can we determine Y given the variability of Z? Even in the case of adults, where the relationship between Y and Z is assumed to be relatively close and stable over time, this question has proven to be a considerable challenge. We have shown that the parsing system involves essentially the same mechanisms as the generating system, applied in "reverse", as it were. That is, given some other person's output Z, the listener strips Z of contingent effects of the body and environment (such as the cues as to speaker identity), thereby generating a hypothesized Y. The listener then "undoes" the effects of the phonological computational system, thereby recovering an underlying representation, X, (or, in the case of ambiguous strings, a set of underlying representations) which would be expected, given the listener's grammar, to generate Y. The lexical item(s) corresponding to this X is (are) then accessed and passed to the other computational components of the grammar.

Factoring out the effects of the body and environment, i.e. converting a given Z to its corresponding Y, involves sophisticated implicit knowledge on the part of the listener regarding the effects of different physiological properties (male vs. female, large resonating cavities vs. small, etc.) and external conditions (passing train, high wind, etc.) on the acoustic information contained in any given Z. The ability of listeners to successfully perform this conversion is key to their ability to parse a given real-time acoustic realization of /kæt/ as being a reflex of 'cat' regardless of what speaker produced it under what conditions. It is important to note that, in this model of parsing, the listener's own bodily output, the listener's Z for a given Y, is completely irrelevant. The listener, who may be a 40-year-old male, does not compare the output of a 12-year-old female to his own bodily output. His bodily output reflects the grammar output "augmented" by the effects of his own body and its context of utterance. Instead, he compares his hypothesis regarding the output of her grammar to the output of his own grammar, his Y (which does not have speaker-specific characteristics, except of course for possible idiolectal features).[23]

The Strong Identity Hypothesis would lead us to believe, in agreement with Smolensky, that it would be most sound, methodologically, to assume that precisely the same components and processes are to be posited for child speaker-listeners as we have sketched above for adults. If this is correct, it seems clear that the study of children's phonological parsing provides us with a critical tool to access information regarding Y without confronting directly the problems raised by the child's immature control of his or her output performance system. Parsing bypasses the listener's bodily output (Z), accessing instead the listener's grammar output (Y) and phonological system to arrive at an X (or several Xs). Therefore, the study of children's parsing skills makes manifest aspects of the relationship between Y and Z which a study of children's bodily output alone may be unable to reveal.[24]

An example may help make this clear. It is well known that at a certain stage in their development, children learning English may fail to distinguish, in their bodily output, between /s/ and /ʃ/, producing both *Sue* and *shoe* as [su]. There are three likely scenarios which could account for this phenomenon, sketched in (48A–C).

---

[23] Again, a more comprehensive and sophisticated account of the processes discussed in this paragraph will be found in Ch. 5.

[24] We assume that performance factors—e.g. distraction, shifts of attention—play a role in comprehension as well, but that they are much less dramatic than those affecting production, and thus we ignore them here. As Madelyn Kissock (p.c.) points out, it is standard in syntactic investigation to use grammaticality judgements, rather than output sampling, to determine a speaker's syntactic competence. Comprehension testing in children, we would argue, provides the closest possible parallel to grammaticality judgements.

(48)   Three views of the s/š merger in child speech

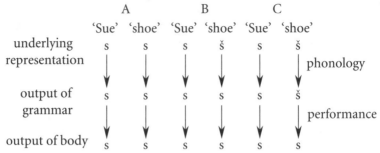

	A		B		C	
	'Sue'	'shoe'	'Sue'	'shoe'	'Sue'	'shoe'
underlying representation	s	s	s	š	s	š
output of grammar	s	s	s	s	s	š
output of body	s	s	s	s	s	s

(phonology applies from underlying representation to output of grammar; performance applies from output of grammar to output of body)

Under the scenario in (48A), the child has constructed identical underlying representations for both *Sue* and *shoe*, each /s/-initial. Nothing affects these URs in the computational component of the phonology,[25] and the performance system implements the segments (more or less) accurately. Thus the body produces something [s]-like (abstracting away from the speaker-specific and environmentally induced effects). This hypothesis can be excluded on several grounds. First, it implies that the child's innate perceptual sensitivity to phonologically relevant contrasts in acoustic signals is of no use in the acquisition of the grammar, for it is not exploited in the construction of underlying representations. Second, it is difficult to imagine how a child who had posited the system in (A) could ever acquire English: the child accepts both adult [š] and adult [s] as realizations of his/her /s/, i.e. s/he has constructed the acoustic target space for /s/ as covering both the [s] and the [š] space of universal phonetics. The child will thus posit for the lexemes *ship*, *sip*, *shame*, *same* the underlying representations /sɪp/, /sɪp/, /sem/, and /sem/. Since the child accepts both adult [s] and [š] as "hits" for his/her own target [s], no positive evidence will ever reveal that the phonological system posited by the child fails to match that of the adult.[26] While the lexicon will contain more homophony than the adult lexicon, homophony must be permitted (given *night* and *knight*), so homophony alone will not rule out the child's constructed grammar. Indeed, the fact that homophony can come into being through diachronic change indicates that this type of event does indeed take place on occasion. However, it cannot hold in our case, which assumes that the child eventually converges upon the adult output. Since scenario A essentially precludes acquisition of the s/š contrast, it must be rejected.

[25] Note that even this scenario would require that Faithfulness to /s/ be ranked higher in the phonology than any W-constraint that would favor changing /s/, say, to [t].

[26] As we have shown in Ch. 2, this is due to the Subset Principle, properly construed.

Scenario B holds that the child, by virtue of his/her inborn sensitivity to phonetic contrasts of potential phonological relevance, has constructed accurate underlying representations for *Sue* and *shoe*, encoding the s/š contrast correctly. However, the child has ranked the constraints in the phonology in such a manner that Faithfulness to /š/ is ranked *lower* than a well-formedness constraint such as *š (i.e. "do not have a [š] in the output representation"). As can be seen from the tableau in (48), the correct output (for the hypothetical child speaker) will be generated by such a scenario.[27]

(49)   Hypothesis (B): the s/š-merger

	*š	FAITH
☞ šu > su		*
šu > šu	*!	
☞ su > su		
su > šu	*!	*

It should be noted that the scenario hypothesized under (B) is a standard example—indeed, it is the definition—of *structural ambiguity*: distinct underlying structures have the same representation in the output of the grammar.[28]

Under scenario (C) in (48) the child's underlying representations are, as in the (B) scenario, set up correctly. However, under this scenario, the output of the grammar maintains the s/š contrast. The failure on the part of the child to distinguish between the two segments in his/her speech output is attributed to a shortcoming of the performance system, which responds to the instruction to produce a [š] by emitting something like a [s] instead.[29] Such mismatches

---

[27] We have simplified the set of F-constraints—which should be separated into one constraint for each feature—into a single super-constraint FAITH, following the practice of Gnanadesikan (1995). This is of course just an abbreviation of the real tableau; however, this "abbreviatory" convention may have serious empirical consequences.

[28] Structural ambiguity (48B) is distinct from lexical ambiguity (48A), where identity in input structures is responsible for the ambiguity of the output, as well as from production ambiguity (48C), where forms which are distinct at the level of the output of the grammar are produced the same due to the operations of the performance system. Cases of so-called "phonetic underspecification", which we will discuss in some detail in Ch. 6, are interesting to consider in this regard, as would be widely cited instances of syntactic ambiguity. Unfortunately, it would take us too far afield if we were to pursue this matter in the present context.

[29] Note, crucially, the wording of the text. We have not asserted that the speaker cannot say an [š]. The instruction to produce an [š] results in an [s]-like realization, but the instruction to produce some other segment (e.g. [tš]), run through the same performance-impaired system, may well give rise to an [š]-like articulatory event.

A reviewer suggests that "markedness" considerations must be relevant in accounting for why the two underlying fricatives merge as [s], or an [s]-like sound, rather than a [š]-like sound. If there are real tendencies in the direction of performance mergers, then such data must play a role in developing a

are, as pointed out above, to be expected if one assumes, as everyone does, that the child is not a fully competent articulator or processor.

The question of whether or not we can distinguish between the output of the grammar and the output of the body amounts to this: is there any empirical evidence that bears on the question of whether the child has [s] or [š] as the output of the *grammar* in the word for "shoe" at the stage of acquisition under discussion? Given (48), there is of course a simple test which will resolve the question. Since the child, like any adult, is assumed to use the output of his or her own grammar to parse input from other speakers, rather than the output of his or her own body, it can be seen that if the child treats other speakers' [šu] as *shoe* and other speakers' [su] as *Sue*, then the contrast between [s] and [š] persists to the level of the output of the grammar. It is well known that children are indeed capable of identifying accurately whether an adult has said *Sue* or *shoe* in spite of their own production merger at this stage. Indeed, they reject adult renderings of *shoe* as [su]—in spite of the fact that the adult output then matches their own—strongly supporting the hypothesis that their parser is not making reference to their own bodily output form.[30]

Additional support for this conception of the child's parsing mechanism can be seen in the results of Dodd (1975), as mentioned above. Recall that Dodd showed that children failed to parse taped versions of *their own output* when it differed significantly from the output of an adult. Only by recognizing the irrelevance of the child's Z-form, the output of their body, to the parsing procedure can this result be accounted for.

Note that, under hypothesis (48B), the consistent and accurate parsing of the adult [s]:[š] contrast by children is completely unexpected (except under Smolensky's account, which we have shown to be untenable). Some earlier approaches to the study of children's phonology, which adopted Hypothesis B, needed to invoke special "perception" grammars, distinct from "production"

theory of children's *performance*. Ida Toivonen (p.c.) has provided us with tapes of a Swedish-speaking child who consistently pronounces Swedish /s/ as something that sounds like a voiceless lateral fricative. Not only is this sound absent from the ambient language, but it is surely more "marked" than [s] according to any of the usual (often non-formal) metrics of markedness. The apparently widespread phenomenon of gestural overlap in children's speech production (see Masilon and Ross 1996) gives rise to articulatory events which, if analyzed as grammatical output, would necessarily lead to the conclusion that childrens" grammars contain *more highly marked* representations than those of the target language in a great many instances, as we have argued above.

[30] See e.g. Faber and Best (1994: 266–7): "these studies show that by the time infants are starting productive use of language they can already discriminate almost all of the phonological contrasts of their native language. While they cannot yet produce adult-like forms, they appear, in many respects, to have adult-like representations, which are reflected, among other things, in their vociferous rejections of adult imitations of their phonologically impoverished productions."

grammars (Ingram 1976; 1989*a*; 1989*b*). These perception grammars allowed the child direct access to underlying forms (rather than having the parser operate on the output of the child "production" grammar). As Hale and Reiss (1998) and Smolensky himself note, such a theory is far too powerful, severing the connection between the child's linguistic competence and that of adults.

3.4 Faith at S$_0$

It does not matter how small you are, if you have faith and a plan of action. (Fidel Castro, *New York Times*, 22 April 1959)

We continue in this section our argument that a compelling case can be made for the assumption we made in (43) that all F-constraints are ranked, at S$_0$, above all W-constraints.[31]

The key to understanding acquisition under OT assumptions (or, indeed, under rule-based assumptions) is centered around the answer to the question of why there are well-formedness constraints (or, in rule-based systems, rules) at all. Since we assume, with most other researchers on child language, that children's perception of adult output forms is quite accurate, what prevents the simple storage of strings to which the child is exposed (reduced to linguistically relevant featural representations) both as input form and output form? This, of course, gets at the question of why we assume that phonology exists at all. We will not go through again the well-established experimental results which show that allophonic relations exist, nor the *wug* test and related empirical evidence for the existence of phonological processes. It is clear, however, that two phenomena, both involving "optimizing" lexical storage, are of potential relevance to this issue: (1) the elimination of redundancy due to "allophonic" variation; and (2) the reduction of the size of the lexicon by linking morphologically related forms via phonological processes (forms which may have been representationally distinct before the linking).[32] The relevance of these issues for the development of a solution to the problem posed by the alternations present in the Catalan problem from Chapter 1 should be clear. The only "work" the computational component of the phonological system

---

[31] This still describes a rather large class of possible UGs: there is an F-constraint for every feature used in any human language and there is presumably a rather large set of W-constraints. Within its constraint class (faithfulness vs. well-formedness), we are not in possession of any evidence which would allow us to determine a unique ranking for these constraints.

[32] We must remain agnostic on the question of whether the functional considerations of "saving storage space" actually drive lexicon optimization, or whether such consolidation is merely a result of the automatic behavior of pattern recognition in linguistic stimuli by humans.

does is to license the elimination of predictable information from the lexicon. If we do not believe in such reduction, we do not need W-constraints (or, indeed, any constraints) at all. This is because having no phonology is the equivalent of having only F-constraints. With each elimination of redundant information from lexical entries, a W-constraint must come into play to "resupply" that information. The W-constraints do nothing else in standard models of OT phonology.

Children are innately sensitive to all possible phonological contrasts. This is dictated by every child's ability to learn any human language, as well as by experimental evidence from the study of infant speech perception, regardless of which subset of the universal feature inventory is used in that language, or what the distribution of those features in that language might be. Lexemes must be initially stored in a fully specified phonetic form (i.e. specified to the degree allowed by the universal feature system used for human languages), since only language-specific information, deducible once a reasonably sized set of such forms has been stored, will tell the child which features are relevant within the target language and which are not.

Given a sufficient number of forms stored in this manner, a process of Grammar Optimization (which is assumed to be a constant constraint on the procedure of establishing underlying forms) will lead the acquirer to deduce that, for example, the aspiration of the $[k^h]$ in $[k^h\text{æts}]$ represents lexically redundant information. It will therefore no longer be necessary to store such information in the lexicon. The output target will not change because of this, of course—it was established on the basis of the child's interpretation of the adult target. Since the phonology represents the mapping between underlying representation and output target, a change in the underlying representation without a corresponding change in the target will require a simultaneous change in the computational component linking the two. Such changes will, necessarily, reduce the role of a particular F-constraint— adding aspiration to the /k/ represents "unfaithfulness" to the underlying representation—by the promotion of a W-constraint previously dominated by the F-constraint in question. Similar elevations of W-constraints over higher-ranked F-constraints will be triggered once the Grammar Optimization procedure has sufficiently clear evidence that it can posit morphophonemic alternations of the normal type.

Under this conception of acquisition, F-constraints must be ranked high within UG. The elevation of W-constraints takes place as a result of grammar optimization. The "emergence of the unmarked" is therefore to be seen as the result of learning, rather than the accidental by-product of the structure of UG or the nature of OT grammars as opposed to other types.

3.5 Conclusions

The competence/performance contrast is, of course, accepted in phonological circles in the study of adult phonology, where it is used to determine which aspects of adult output phonological theory needs to concern itself with and which aspects it does not. We have argued that Smolensky's criticism of theories which appeal to both competence and performance as relevant to the study of child speech production is not only idiosyncratic in its rejection of a fundamental tenet of generative linguistics but also self-defeating, since his own theory fails to account for the very cases he invokes. Furthermore, we claimed that Smolensky's model of the different nature of production and comprehension in OT does not allow for comprehension of both more and less "marked" underlying forms which are neutralized by the phonology in production. We sketched an alternative to the OT model of acquisition proposed by Smolensky, who posits that F-constraints are initially ranked low in UG. In our model F-constraints are initially ranked high. Because Smolensky's model does not account for "child phonology" and implies a more complex learning task than ours without providing any benefits, our model should be adopted as the null hypothesis. Finally, given Smolensky's model of the initial state of the grammar and his denial (in practice) of the distinction between performance and competence, we are left with no explanation for the intermediate "stages" in children's speech output on which Smolensky's approach is predicated. We attribute these to extralinguistic maturational development, both cognitive and physiological. When all these objections are considered, it is clear that Smolensky's model is not relevant to the evaluation of the relative merits of OT vs. rule-based phonology. Our theory of initially high-ranking F-constraints is trivially translatable to a rule-based theory where the initial state contains no rules. The crucial aspect of our theory is its orthodoxy: performance and competence are both needed to account for human speech behavior.

It is harder to maintain this distinction in L1 acquisition studies than in the study of adult native-speaker phonology because of the greater disparity between competence and performance, but it is necessary (cf. Epstein et al. 1996 for similar arguments regarding L2 acquisition). Figuring out what intervenes between the grammar and the "mouth" is difficult but, one hopes, not impossible.

As an example of how this problem has been approached in another domain of innate human behavior, consider the following result from a study of infants' "knowledge" of how to walk, discussed by Faber and Best (1994), following Thelen and Ulrich (1991): "if the needs for balance and for ankle extension are removed, by holding infants with their feet touching a backward-moving treadmill, some infants as young as one month old will stay in place by stepping forward in the alternating pattern characteristic of adult walking." Apparently, manipulation of their production system allowed for closer observation of their competence as walkers. In a sense, these babies *knew* how to walk like adults, but their performance was hindered by factors including physiological considerations like the relative weight of their heads to their bodies and the state of their musculature, as well as their cognitive inability to synchronize "input from the visual and vestibular systems". As the relative weight of head and body approaches that of adults, and as other cognitive and physiological systems mature, the child's performance system catches up with the innate knowledge of how to walk. We propose that learning to talk follows a parallel path.

Smolensky makes several claims, including those listed in (50):

(50) Major claims of Smolensky (1996)
    (a) The "markedness" phenomena described in the child phonology literature are paralleled by phenomena of adult phonology.
    (b) Speech output during direct imitation and the existence of chain-shifts in the mapping of adult language to child language argue for a competence- (or grammar-)based approach to child speech production.
    (c) An OT analysis can maintain that children possess a single grammar and still capture the comprehension/production discrepancy in child language (which is known to be difficult in a rule-based approach).
    (d) Faithfulness constraints (F-constraints) must initially be ranked below Well-formedness constraints (W-constraints).

We have demonstrated that points (50a–d) are untenable, providing new arguments based on evidence which is well known in the linguistic, psycholinguistic, and phonetic literature as well as on learnability considerations. Having challenged some widespread assumptions about the nature of phonological acquisition and its study, we have shown that the evidence actually supports the following claims:

(51) Our claims
    (a) The supposed parallels between child and adult patterns of "markedness" are illusory.

(b) Improved performance under imitation is predicted only by a theory which appeals to a performance basis; chainshifts are not a problem for theories which take a "competence *and* performance" approach (and, in fact, they remain unexplained in competence-only accounts, such as Smolensky's).

(c) The OT model of comprehension posited by Smolensky is empirically inadequate.

(d) Within an OT framework, learnability considerations favor an initial ranking in which F-constraints outrank W-constraints.

The failure of Smolensky's account also requires us to reject the claim that the proposed solution to the performance/competence debate in child phonology can be taken as evidence for the superiority of Optimality Theory over rule-based phonology.[33]

In response to some of the criticisms we have made here concerning the methodology used in many acquisition studies, we have been told that there would be nothing left for acquisitionists to do if we decide that the data is, in general, misleading. We think that this is an overly pessimistic view. There remain open several paths to a better understanding of children's phonological systems, if we are willing to devise ingenious experiments that force them to be revealed.

In order to interpret any data derived from speech behavior the distinction between performance and competence must be maintained: an explicit characterization of the boundaries between the two should be one of the primary goals of phonological theory, since it defines the sphere of inquiry with which we must concern ourselves. It is clear that a more explicit theory of performance (or rather several theories) is a necessity; however, that theory must itself be predicated upon a coherent theory of grammatical competence. These issues were raised more than thirty years ago with characteristic lucidity by Chomsky (1964: 35): "It seems that the attempt to write a grammar for a child raises all of the unsolved problems of constructing a grammar for adult speech, multiplied by some rather large factor." He goes on to emphasize the complexity of issues regarding competence and performance in children, concluding by noting (p. 39) that there is:

a general tendency to oversimplify drastically the facts of linguistic structure and to assume that the determination of competence can be derived from description of a corpus by some sort of sufficiently developed data-processing techniques. My feeling

---

[33] This is not, we point out, the same as an argument that an OT model, *in general*, is not preferable to a rule-based model, it is merely that this particular argument does not support such a claim.

is that this is hopeless and that only experimentation of a fairly indirect and ingenious sort can provide evidence that is at all critical for formulating a true account of the child's grammar (as in the case of investigation of any other real system)...I make these remarks only to indicate a difficulty which I think is looming rather large and to which some serious attention will have to be given fairly soon.

We believe that, more than forty years later, the time has come to take these concerns seriously.

4

The Georgian problem revisited

4.1 What we now know about learning

What have we learned from the discussion up to this point? We have learned that we should expect there to be a correct model of each I-language and that it is the linguist's obligation to try and choose among competing, extensionally equivalent models. We also discussed ways to go about this—by looking at acquisition and by building a general linguistic theory, one that holds for all languages.

In Chapter 2 we demonstrated that the Subset Principle is to be interpreted as a requirement of maximal specificity in initial representations. Children are born with the full representational apparatus for phonology, and acquisition consists of learning which distinctions can be ignored or collapsed.

Chapter 3 critiqued much of the phonological acquisition literature for its overuse of impressionistic production data from children, and showed how acceptance of such data has led to the proposal of a logically incoherent model of learning within OT.

We are now ready to take our lessons and apply them to the problem of the distribution of laterals in Georgian, introduced in Chapter 1.

4.2 The solution to the Georgian problem

As we saw in Chapter 1, Georgian has a five-vowel system containing [i,e,u,o,a]. The language has two surface laterals which are in complementary distribution. Plain or clear [l] occurs before the front vowels [i,e]. The velarized back [ɫ] occurs elsewhere. Therefore, it is relatively straightforward to set up a rule of the form in (52).

(52) Georgian
    a. Vowels: [i,e,u,o,a]
    b. /ɫ/ → [l] before i and e

But if we try to formalize this, how general/concise should we make the rule? Should it be stated to apply before [−back] or before [−back, −low] vowels?

How could we possibly decide? No empirical language-internal evidence can tell us, since the language has no [−back] vowels that aren't [−low], so we have to rely on what a principled learning algorithm will tell us. Another relevant question is "Why do we care?" The answer is that we get paid to care—phonologists are supposed to explain the nature and content of phonological knowledge, a matter of "individual psychology", as we argued in Chapter 1.

Assuming that we have convinced the reader to care, let's proceed to a demonstration of what an explicit learning algorithm will lead us to. First of all, where does such a rule "come from"? The answer is that it is generated on the basis of some kind of positive evidence, that is on the basis of tokens of the rule's application. Let's gloss over some difficult details and imagine that the learner somehow comes up with the generalization that "/ɬ/ > [l] before i" and also with the generalization that "/ɬ/ > [l] before e". The final rule which is acquired is just the result of generalizing across these two "subrules". This process is achieved, of course, by finding the representation which subsumes the two cases—for our purposes, the intersections of the triggering environment will suffice. An early (i.e. rich, highly specified, restrictive) representation of the two subrules is given in (53).

(53)   "Subrules" of lateral fronting
    a. /ɬ/ → [l] before i

$$\begin{bmatrix} +\text{lateral} \\ +\text{son} \\ \vdots \end{bmatrix} \rightarrow [-\text{back}] \text{ before} \begin{bmatrix} +\text{hi} \\ +\text{ATR} \\ -\text{back} \\ -\text{low} \\ -\text{round} \end{bmatrix}$$

        AND

    b. /ɬ/ → [l] before e

$$\begin{bmatrix} +\text{lateral} \\ +\text{son} \\ \vdots \end{bmatrix} \rightarrow [-\text{back}] \text{ before} \begin{bmatrix} -\text{hi} \\ +\text{ATR} \\ -\text{back} \\ -\text{low} \\ -\text{round} \end{bmatrix}$$

The only generalization (loss of specificity) driven by the data is the pruning of the features where the two subrules disagree. This is accomplished by taking the intersection of the two rules—the result is shown in (54).

(54)   /ɫ/ > [l] before i *and* e

$$
\begin{bmatrix} +\text{lateral} \\ +\text{son} \\ \vdots \end{bmatrix} \rightarrow [-\text{back}] \text{ before } \begin{bmatrix} +\text{ATR} \\ -\text{back} \\ -\text{low} \\ -\text{round} \end{bmatrix}
$$

The representation of the environment thus denotes a natural class that includes both [i] and [e], but not [æ]. Therefore, from an acquisition viewpoint, there is no reason to believe that the child does generalize beyond the data (by choosing a *less specified* statement of the rule). This prediction is testable (with certain caveats), e.g. by evaluating Georgian speakers' production of lateral-*æ* sequences.[1] Preliminary results based on a survey by our student Anna Chigogidze, a native speaker, confirm that Georgian speakers trained to pronounce [æ] will not produce a fronted lateral when presented with the relevant sequences. In other words, they do not generalize the lateral fronting rule to this non-native environment.

In order to fully develop the ideas here, it would be necessary to present a theory of how morphological parsing is achieved over forms that the learner initially stores in unanalyzed form. However, for the sake of explicitness, we can provide the preliminary statement in (55).

(55)   How general are rules? (Formulation 1)
       The correct statement of a rule arrived at by the LAD is the *most highly specified* representation that subsumes all positive instances of the rule.

There is obviously one thing missing from this formulation: a guarantee that it does not overgenerate with respect to attested data. In brief, (55) must be reformulated with a qualification, as in (56).

(56)   How general are rules? (Formulation 2)
       The correct statement of a rule arrived at by the LAD is the *most highly specified* representation that subsumes all positive instances of the rule, and subsumes no negative instances of the rule.

The positive and negative instances of the rule are the stored forms which the learner ultimately parses morphologically in the process of figuring out a phonology and a lexicon. Note that (56) is not a description of what the learning algorithm does, but rather a characterization of the rules it generates. In other words, the representation of the Georgian fronting rule

---

[1] If they front laterals before, say, [ɪ], this is not necessarily a problem, since [i] may stand for a vowel which includes the [ɪ] space (as we have argued in some detail in Ch. 2).

that contains specification that the trigger is [−low] is more highly specified than the representation which excludes the specification of [−low]. The
more specific, i.e. more restrictive rule is the one provided by the LAD. Of
course, this contradicts the common practice of finding the most economical
rule.

While our conclusion about Georgian might be surprising, it is worth
pointing out that the notion that children overgeneralize or choose the most
general rule possible is incoherent. We have already presented the dangers of
taking child speech data too seriously; but let's just consider what it would
mean to posit the most general rule possible. Faced with a just enough data to
see that ł/ → [l] before *i* AND *e* (and nothing else) what would be the 'most
general' rule? Some conceivable proposals would be:

- ł/ → [l] before i
- ł/ → [l] before any vowel
- ł/ → [l] before any segment
- every segment / → [l] before i
- every segment / → [l] before any vowel
- every segment / → [−back] before any segment

Even determining which of these should count as "most general" for an
acquirer driven by the learning algorithm to initially posit the "most general"
rule is a challenge. In our model, by contrast, the child initially posits the
most specific rule, and generalizes only subsequently, during the batch learning
(or "lexicon optimization") stage. Determining which rule is "most specific"
seems to us by far the simpler task.

When phonologists speak of general rules, they seem to have two things
in mind: one is "the most general rule that works", but this will be extensionally equivalent with more specific rules that work. Once we accept the
arguments that children must start out with restricted, highly specified representations of segments and rules, we have to acknowledge that the shortest
learning path to a grammar consistent with the data involves richly specified
rules.

The other notion of generality is based on the impression that children
"overgeneralize". As we have seen, the data cited from child speech in support
of this phenomenon makes no sense from an empirical or theoretical standpoint when we consider both the logic of learning and the evidence from
comprehension studies. Furthermore, it is now understood that even in the
best-understood domain of "overgeneralization", verb morphology in English
(see e.g. Pinker 1995), the explanation for such patterns is to be sought in the
domain of performance, and not competence. Children apparently produce

forms like *holded*, despite having heard, stored, and even produced *held*, because retrieval of stored forms is not fast enough to "block" generation of the productive form.

4.3 English "overgeneralization"

Are we to conclude from this that the rules of a grammar are never stated in a form which entails greater generality than that provided by a *list* of positive tokens? The answer, due to the nature of our algorithm, is clearly "no". Just how far beyond the listed data a given rule would go will depend on what representations are subsumed by the acquired representation of the rule. We turn now to a case where the rule is predicted to be more general than what might be predicted a priori from a list of positive tokens.

A standard argument for the existence of phonological rules formulated in terms of features is based on the intuition that English speakers will extend the rule that devoices /z/ after voiceless obstruents to apply even after voiceless obstruents that don't occur in English, such as [x] or [ɸ].[2] In other words, since speakers cannot have memorized that the [-s] form of the plural marker, underlying /-z/, occurs after these sounds, it must be the case that speakers generate the correct, voiceless form on the basis of a rule stated in terms of distinctive features. Let's assume that this intuition is in fact valid and that English speakers do pluralize *Bach* as [baxs]. This result is trivially predicted by the learning algorithm which creates rules via intersection.

In (57, 58) we have broken down the problem in a manner that is meant to aid exposition and not to reflect, for example, stages of development. Leaving aside the sibilants, English has the following voiceless obstruents, all of which devoice a following /z/ to [s]: [p, t, k, f, θ]. For simplicity, consider what happens when the contexts of devoicing after various stops are compared. These stops all agree in being [−son], [−cont], [−voice], etc. They disagree in place features such as [ant], [lab], and [cor]. So the representation that subsumes all the stops that trigger devoicing does not contain these place features, but does contain the features for which the stops agree. Note that certain features that are typically assumed to be irrelevant, such as [−lat], are also specified, since there is no mechanism to remove them.

---

[2] Let's keep things simple and not worry about the plurals of words ending with coronal stridents, like *bushes, glasses, beaches.*

(57)   Collapsing place of articulation in stops.

$$
\begin{bmatrix}
-\text{son} \\
-\text{cont} \\
-\text{voice} \\
+\text{ant} \\
+\text{lab} \\
-\text{cor} \\
\vdots \\
-\text{lat} \\
\vdots
\end{bmatrix}
\cap
\begin{bmatrix}
-\text{son} \\
-\text{cont} \\
-\text{voice} \\
+\text{ant} \\
-\text{lab} \\
+\text{cor} \\
\vdots \\
-\text{lat} \\
\vdots
\end{bmatrix}
\cap
\begin{bmatrix}
-\text{son} \\
-\text{cont} \\
-\text{voice} \\
-\text{ant} \\
-\text{lab} \\
-\text{cor} \\
\vdots \\
-\text{lat} \\
\vdots
\end{bmatrix}
=
\begin{bmatrix}
-\text{son} \\
-\text{cont} \\
-\text{voice} \\
\vdots \\
-\text{lat} \\
\vdots
\end{bmatrix}
$$

Place features can be similarly factored out across the fricatives, generating a representation which is [−son, +cont, −voice ...] without place features. Finally, the general rule is found by collapsing cases for both stops and fricatives, that is, by eliminating [+/−cont].

(58)   The trigger of the devoicing rule

$$
\begin{bmatrix}
-\text{son} \\
-\text{voice} \\
\vdots \\
-\text{lat} \\
\vdots
\end{bmatrix}
$$

Since the resultant representation of the triggering environment is [−son, −voice] but not specified for [cont] or place features, this representation describes a natural class that includes [x] and [ɸ]. That is, the most highly specified representation that subsumes the actually occurring cases also subsumes the plurals of constructed nonce form introduced with final [x] and [ɸ].

To summarize, the LAD constructs a rule R whose representation subsumes the description of all positive examples of the rule and no negative ones. Presented with a string (a representation) S which is not identical to any previously encountered string, then R will be appear to be generalized (of course, it is just "applied") if and only if S is subsumed by the representation of R. This is of course what it means to have a rule. If rules did not work this way, then phonology would not show the kind of productivity that the *wug* test manifests.

4.4 A note on other work

A reviewer bemoans our "continued failure to acknowledge the work of Albright and Hayes on minimal generalization learning", saying that our "solution to the Georgian problem is very reminiscent of Albright and Hayes' work on rule learning" and that we do ourselves "a great disservice by not properly acknowledging the parallelism (and/or differences) between the two models". We obviously encourage the reader to consult the body of research generated individually and jointly by these two important scholars; however, we shall not enter into a full discussion of their work here for a number of reasons.

One reason to distinguish our work from that of Albright and Hayes is that our goals are much less ambitious than theirs. For example, a survey of their recent (solo and joint) work indicates that they consider the nature of historical change within an Optimality Theory framework, accounting for variability in speaker judgements and productions, and also statistical aspects of behavior to fall within the purview of phonological theory. Our own approach, as we hope to make clear throughout this book, is much more narrow and modest in its aims.

Second, the approach to initial restrictiveness or minimal generalization adopted here evolved from Reiss's 1995 Ph.D. thesis, which Hale supervised. Aspects of this approach were presented in numerous conference presentations as early as 1995, for example Reiss's "Stepwise assimilation and Optimality Theory", at *The Derivational Residue in Phonology*, Tilburg University, the Netherlands. Bruce Hayes was present at this conference and kindly provided comments on the version of restrictiveness advocated in this work. He did not find the arguments convincing, and we would be hesitant for this reason alone to equate our views on restrictiveness in acquisition with his. Related work of ours on initial restrictiveness was initially developed in 1996, and has been presented in Chapter 2 of this book and the published articles on which that chapter draws.

Finally, we are hesitant to offer an analysis of the research program of Albright and Hayes because of our own lack of clarity concerning their assumptions and goals. Much of their work is couched within OT, whereas the minimal generalization discussions appear to be set in a derivational, rule-based model of grammar. We are not sure if anything crucial hinges on this flexibility, or if it is just a matter of expository convenience; but without this understanding we are loath to either criticize their work or claim significant parallels to our own, beyond those shared with any number of other recent approaches, such as Culicover's (1999) Conservative Attentive Learner model or the work of Fodor and Sakas (2005).

Part II

Resisting substance abuse in phonology

5

Isolability and idealization

5.1 Galilean-style phonology

Before proceeding to the remaining issues to be treated in this book, it will be useful to establish some terminological and conceptual clarity regarding the range of phenomena for which the theory of phonology we are attempting to construct is going to be responsible. We hope to have shown in the last chapter how a failure to address fundamental questions in this domain has led to a great deal of confusion respecting the nature of first language acquisition. In this chapter we extend that discussion to the domain of "adult" phonology (a.k.a. "phonology").

As in the case of any attempt to comprehend some aspect of the world scientifically, a primary difficulty arises in deciding which of the myriad apparent facts which can be established by an examination of the world should actually be construed as relevant to the task at hand. The challenges which confront one in pursuit of this task lead, understandably, to a high likelihood that scholars will differ in their resolution of the definitional problems which arise. In this chapter we survey some approaches to the "grammar" which differ from our own, in the hopes that a contrastive sketch of a variety of positions will make it clear to the reader where exactly we stand on these matters.

We cannot overemphasize that we do not pretend of offer a demonstration that those adopting other approaches to the study of phonological knowledge are wrong. No one, including ourselves, knows the "right" way to conceive of matters in this domain. We focus on exploring the logical and empirical implications of the assumptions being made by others, and those being made by us, and argue that the particular approach to phonology which we advocate here leads to questions we find interesting and likely to be productive. Given the history of discourse regarding the pursuit of phonology in the twentieth century, it would appear that others are likely to share our opinion.

In general, we support an approach which could be sensibly labeled "Galilean-style Phonology".[1] This term is derived loosely from the following passage from Chomsky (2002: 98):

---

[1] For an earlier discussion of these matters, in part parallel to that we present here, see Hale (2007: ch. 4).

What was striking about Galileo, and was considered very offensive at the time, was that he dismissed a lot of data; he was willing to say "Look, if the data refute the theory, the data are probably wrong"... But the Galilean style... is the recognition that it is the abstract systems that you are constructing that are really the truth; the array of phenomena is some distortion of the truth because of too many factors, all sorts of things. And so, it often makes good sense to disregard phenomena and search for principles that really seem to give some deep insight into why some of them are that way, recognizing that there are others you can't pay attention to.

No one will be surprised, we assume, when it turns out that matters are more complex than superficial, pre-scientific consideration might lead one to suspect—this is, of course, a normal property of scientific investigation which, throughout its history, has taught us that things are not as simple as they generally seem to be under pre-theoretical consideration. Thus we expect that matters of considerable complexity will be hidden behind the relatively trivial and seemingly uncontroversial definition of "phonology" as the study of "the sound systems of languages" found, for example, in Crystal (2003).

It might seem that the fact that the "speech sounds" with which phonology is widely alleged to concern itself are highly concrete, measurable objects, with a large number of empirically determinable properties, would make them ideal candidates for scientific investigation. Indeed, the science of phonetics, coupled with numerous significant engineering breakthroughs in the acoustic and, perhaps just as importantly, computational domains, has been able in recent decades to provide a far richer body of quantitative material regarding human speech than has ever been available to scientists before. Interestingly, this increasingly sophisticated understanding of the physical nature of "speech sounds" has taken place largely independently of, and without direct impact on, the development of models of human phonological systems. For example, movement towards "underspecified" phonological representations in the mid-1980s (see e.g. the collected papers in *Phonology* 5—a special issue dedicated to this topic) was not in any significant sense a product of what was by that time a massive increase, relative to the state of the matter in the early days of generative phonology, in the sophistication of phonetic tools—nor, indeed, has the recent development of Optimality Theory been so motivated. Research into the architecture of the phonological system appears to have developed on its own, in spite of the enrichment of our knowledge of the phonetics of human speech during the relevant period.[2] It turns out that this separation

---

[2] There are some apparent exceptions to this doubtless overly broad claim. In rule-based phonology, "feature geometry" was often conceived of as arising directly from phonetic facts. However, the relevant "phonetic facts" were well known, basic aspects of articulatory phonetics, not recent discoveries about acoustic or auditory phonetics. Similarly, so-called "phonetic grounding" in the work of Archangeli

between the detailed measurements of the phoneticians and the development of phonological theory is appropriate and necessary, in our view. We will try to show this in what follows.

In Figure 5.1 we present a sketch of certain aspects of an event in which a speaker—one with a linguistic system much like that of the authors—utters the word *cat* and is heard by another individual who possesses a grammatical system similar to that of the speaker in the relevant respects. In spite of the highly convoluted nature of this figure, it represents a gross oversimplification of what is involved in any actual speech event, though it is designed so as to capture those aspects most relevant to our present concerns. It will be helpful to go through the diagram with some care, beginning with the "speaker" on the left.

In the upper left-hand corner of Figure 5.1 (at ❶) we see a (partial) lexical representation, /kæt/ (note that the listener has stored in his or her mind the very same lexical representation, see ❾, to the extent details are provided in the figure). In keeping with normal practice in the field, a "phonemic" representation of this type is given between "slashes". Also in keeping with widespread practice in the field, the phonological feature bundles which are assumed to actually be used in the mental representation of phonemic segments have been abbreviated into symbols of the International Phonetic Alphabet.[3] Lexical representations such as this, in adults, are assumed to consist of only that information required to generate all the allomorphs of a given morpheme. They are stored in long-term memory, in what is generally called the "lexicon", to which items may be added throughout the lifetime of the speaker.

This underlying representation is subjected to, or serves as the input for, phonological computation (which may be any one of various types—ordered rules, an Optimality Theoretic system, etc.), the result of that computation being a generated phonetic output, or surface, representation, usually included within square brackets (❷). The "representational alphabet" (i.e. the entities used in the construction) of these output representations is, it appears, the same as the representational alphabet of underlying forms.[4] Such

and Pulleyblank, and subsequently in Optimality Theory, is orthogonal to the machinery introduced by that theory, and to the motivation for the development of its apparatus. We discuss these matters in some detail in Ch. 6.

[3] This latter practice introduces the possibility of serious confusion—confusion which can be observed with regularity in the phonological literature, in our opinion—in that one and the same IPA symbol may, and far more frequently than is generally assumed does, represent what are in fact distinct phonological feature bundles. The matter will arise in some detail below, so we will postpone consideration of it at this time.

[4] This is not to say that a *particular* output representation may not contain information not present in the specific input form which gave rise to it, obviously. A typical output representation will contain e.g. an indication of the position of primary stress and syllable structure, both of which, if predictable,

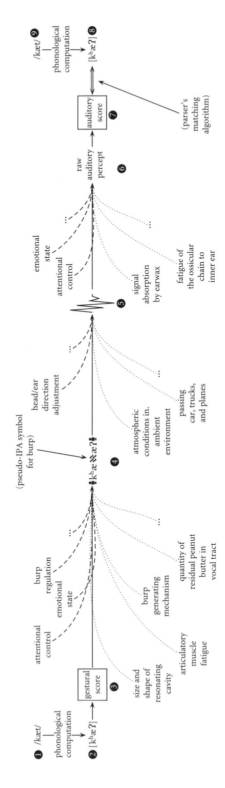

FIGURE 5.1 Saying *cat*

output representations should thus consist of phonological features, metrical/prosodic structure representations, and the like.

In discussing Figure 5.1 we will attempt to distinguish carefully between "computation", such as that seen in the mapping from phonemic representations to phonetic representations, and what we will term "transduction".[5] Computation involves the manipulation (reordering, regrouping, deletion, addition, etc.) of the elements present in the input *without a change in representational alphabet*. By contrast, transduction involves the mapping of an entity in one form onto a distinct form—the classic example is the transduction of (mechanical) air pressure differentials ('sound waves') into a stream of electrons by a microphone (electrical).

The distinction between computation and transduction provides a useful means of conceptualizing the broadly assumed modularity of the computational mind. A "module" can be thought of as a device which takes input representations (in some representational alphabet) and computes over these representations, generating thereby an output in the same representational system. The modules of the computational mind must be linked by a set of "transducers", which convert material in one form into a form required by the computational module fed by the conversion process. We will see a concrete example of transduction when we turn to details of articulation and speech perception below.

The "phonetic" output representation (❷) is then subjected to transduction to a distinct representational system: the so-called gestural score (❸). This representation maps out, much in the manner of a musical score, the *relative* durational and dynamic properties of the intended articulatory target. The actual timing and e.g. loudness will arise through a combination of this relative information and other aspects of the behavior-generating system (e.g. the emotions of the speaker), as we shall see. It is assumed, as indicated by the fact that this mapping has been labeled a "transduction", that the gestural score does not consist of sets of phonological features bundled into abstract segments.

The process of getting from this "gestural score" to an actual articulatory act is one of tremendous complexity, involving numerous factors which arise in what we would assume to be a rather large number of intervening computational systems. Little is known about the modules involved and no exhaustive

---

may be absent from the relevant input representation. However, in principle—i.e. as a property of the architecture of the system—such representational properties are not precluded from underlying representations (e.g. when not predictable, including perhaps in early stages of acquisition).

[5] The term "transduction" as used here is extended somewhat from its use in cognitive science by e.g. Zenon Pylyshyn, his use itself an extended version of the way the term is employed in physics.

listing of relevant factors is possible, so we have satisfied ourselves with giving a list of a relatively small number of factors, which, however, cover considerable conceptual range, and which must in some manner be involved. Doubtless some of the intervening modules involve computation; others certainly must involve transduction (since the output is some set of electro-chemical neuromuscular signals). We have attempted to separate what one might think of as "cognitive", as opposed to more purely physical, factors, placing the former above, the latter below, the line which indicates the course of the computation.

For example, it is clear that the degree to which a speaker successfully focuses his or her attention on the act of articulation itself will affect quite directly certain aspects of the actual physical act. The modules of the mind responsible for attentional control (as well as all aspects of the mind/brain which interact with that module—e.g. the electro-chemical effects of alcohol consumption) thus must play a role in what ultimately befalls the "gestural score" representation. Similarly, the emotional state of the speaker will have an effect, as well as, as indicated in Figure 5.1, whatever strategies the speaker uses to attempt to control an imminent burp ('burp regulation')—which may involve increasing the muscular tension in the vocal tract, for example. The reader can doubtless trivially expand the set of such cognitive factors which play some role in determining the properties of the ultimate bodily output of the speaker.

In addition to being embedded in this cognitive context, the generation of an actual physical signal will be determined in part by the non-cognitive, physical context within which the utterance event takes place. At this point, we are concerned with physical effects *internal* to the speaker. These include relatively stable properties of the speaker (e.g. the size and shape of his/her resonating cavities, tongue, vocal folds, and lungs) as well as more transient physical properties (e.g. the current degree of fatigue of the relevant muscles, or quantity of saliva or peanut butter or whatever in the vocal tract). Such factors thus vary both from individual to individual and from moment to moment within the same individual. That these variables will play a role in the acoustic shape of the output is not a matter of linguistic speculation, but is rather given by the nature of the physical universe, of which the speaker's body forms a part.

The combined effects of these various factors is a *potential* acoustic output—the *actual* acoustic output, as we shall see, is a function of yet further factors. The form in "human body" brackets (❹) is meant to represent what the output of the speaker's body would be, ignoring all external influences. This is much like the notion of the rate of a falling body in a perfect vacuum— actual falling bodies will match this only to some vague approximation, since they are not in a perfect vacuum; but to understand how such bodies fall *outside* the vacuum, it is worthwhile to formulate a hypothesis about how they *would* fall, absent the accidental effects of being in an atmosphere (this is the "Galilean style" referred to above). It is just such an idealized representation that the symbols between the "human body" brackets is intended to represent. This representation differs significantly in its basic properties from that of the "gestural score" (e.g. it includes, which the latter excludes, speech rate information, speaker-specific acoustic effects, and the like); the overall process of getting from the gestural score to the idealized bodily output is thus one of transduction, rather than computation.[6]

At this point in the figure our concerns shift from the speaker—from whom the signal has now become fully independent—to the listener. For example, an actual acoustic wave (indicated by the vaguely wave-like graphic in Figure 5.1) will differ on the basis of the listener's orientation relative to, and his/her distance from, the speaker. The acoustic wave (❺) is thus a *listener-specific* entity, as are all following representations in our figure.

The actual factors influencing the form of this acoustic wave are again too complex to list in any detail. As with the speaker-specific considerations, we have attempted to separate cognitive from more purely physical considerations. In the latter category, it is again a matter of physics that the properties of the medium through which the signal is being transmitted (the "atmospheric conditions in the ambient environment") must influence the form of the acoustic wave which reaches the listener—as indeed must the interference patterns produced by other ambient acoustic waves. On the cognitive side, the listener has attention control systems which include the ability to manipulate the orientation of his/her auditory receptors relative to the sound source (e.g. by tilting or turning his/her head), which may be invoked at this point. The combined effect of these various factors will be some waveform reaching the ear of the listener—that waveform is indicated by the wavy graphic at (❺).[7]

This waveform is then subject to a range of physical and cognitive effects within the auditory system of the listener. The cognitive factors again include how much of his/her attentional resources the listener gives over to this

---

[6] Of course, since this process actually consists of numerous mapping events, any number of these mappings may in fact be computations, as long as at least one of them involves transduction. The point is merely that if we collapse these into a single "system", and even one of them involves transduction, then the representational alphabet of the output will be different from that of the input and the entire simplified and collapsed "system" will thus perform a transduction.

[7] We abstract away from the fact that binaural listeners get, in fact, two distinct acoustic waves and exploit the difference between them in the course of processing. Binaural input is of course not *required* for speech perception.

acoustic signal, the emotional state of the listener, and the like. On the physical side, the signal will be modified by the ambient environment of the outer and inner ear, as well as by response fatigue in the relevant movable parts of the auditory system. The representation which results from the effects of these various auditory physical and cognitive factors we have called the "raw auditory percept" (❻). This representation must then be broken down into its component elements. This decomposition includes not only separating those aspects of the representation which are taken by the listener to be due to a speech signal component in the input waveform (as opposed e.g. to the sound of a passing truck), but also an analysis of the speech signal itself into "speaker voice quality", "speech rate", "speaker emotional state", and "linguistic content" components.[8] We are concerned at this point only with the "linguistic content" component of the "raw acoustic percept", which we will assume takes the form of an "auditory score" (❼)—similar, in many respects, to the "gestural score" on the production side. For example, the "auditory score", like the "gestural score", does not include rate information (but will include *relative* temporal durations, since these may be linguistically relevant), nor speaker-identification cues and the like.

Parsing involves the establishment of a link between this auditory score and an appropriate output representation of the grammar, the parser being the device which evaluates matched pairs for suitability. Numerous complications arise at this point, most of which lie well beyond our narrow concerns here, as well as well beyond our competence; but the rough approximation in our figure should suffice for our relatively limited purposes. In Figure 5.1, candidate output representations (❽) are generated by the grammar from the listener's stored phonemic representations (❾) and checked against the auditory score,[9] presumably by means of an algorithm, which produces an auditory score from the grammar's output representation, not unlike that which generates the gestural score from the grammar's output representation.[10] As we saw on the speaker side of the figure, the relationship between the 'phonetic' representation and the auditory score is assumed here to be one of transduction. This follows from some basic properties of the auditory score—e.g. the fact that

---

[8] As with most of the matters discussed regarding our seemingly elaborate figure, this list is not intended to be exhaustive, nor are the factors necessarily independent of one another.

[9] This is an "analysis by synthesis" model. Other possibilities exist; the details are not critical for our concerns here.

[10] Again, countless other possibilities exist. To give just one example, it may be that a gestural score is generated from the linguistic output representation, just as is done when one is speaking, and that this gestural score is then "converted" to an acoustic score by some transductive and/or computational process(es). To name just one more possibility, it may be that the "gestural score" is in fact the same (mode-independent) representation as the "acoustic" score, and that this score can be transduced to each system.

it encodes information about relative temporal duration and timing relations (matters which a bundle of features do not directly encode).

The result of this process is the establishment in the mind of the listener of a phonemic/phonetic pair, linked by the grammar.[11] The phonetic representation having been selected for its ability to transduce to an appropriate "auditory score", the phonemic representation for its ability to map, via phonological computation, to that phonetic representation. The phonemic representation thus posited can then be exploited by "higher-level" grammatical analysis.

Armed with this sketch of what could go on when one utters /kæt/— a sketch which on the one hand seems almost ridiculously over-detailed but which, on the other hand, falls far short of an even vague claim to comprehensiveness—we can turn to the question of which aspects of this figure fall into the domain of linguistics proper. It is important to bear in mind that there is a distinction between the sources of evidence which a scientific enterprise may make use of and the *object of study* of that field. Physics is not *about* linear accelerators, but understanding of and access to linear accelerator data has played a key role in the progress of modern physics. The question we are interested in at this point is that of what the object of study of linguistics, in the phonological domain, is.

Answering this question involves attempting to isolate narrowly linguistic concerns from the many and diverse factors which play a role in speech behavior. As linguists, it is not within our domain of responsibility to investigate why one speaker talks a great deal about dogs and another less so, or why one individual yells more than the average and another whispers, as interesting as these questions may appear. Nor are such questions answerable within the context of the types of explanation linguists are prepared to provide: the *grammar* does not tell you whether now is the time to tell that amusing anecdote about your favorite pet or loudly chastise your children. There is a difficulty, widely recognized in the philosophy of science literature, with conceptually isolating systems for investigation which do not in fact function in isolation. Nevertheless, as Lawrence Sklar (in part, paraphrasing Stephen Weinberg) has recently argued, there is reason to believe that the systems which interact to give us the world are isolable as a matter of fact, rather than simple methodological convenience. He notes:

…without a sufficient degree of isolability of systems we could never arrive at any lawlike regularities for describing the world at all. For unless systems were sufficiently independent of one another in their behavior, the understanding of the evolution of

---

[11] As noted in the previous chapter, there will in actual fact often be a *set* of such pairs in a given phonological parse. We abstract away from this complication here.

even the smallest part of the universe would mean keeping track of the behavior of all of its constituents. It is hard to see how the means for prediction and explanation could ever be found in such a world ... it can be argued that unless such idealization of isolability were sufficiently legitimate in a sufficiently dominant domain of cases, we could not have any science at all. (Sklar 2000: 54–5)

The determination of what the "object of study" of linguistics is, in the phonological domain, thus requires that we examine our figure for some object or objects which could be subjected to serious scientific investigation *as if isolated*, i.e. without regard for "extralinguistic" considerations. No "isolation" lines are given for the phenomena pictured in that figure by the world itself, nor indeed are we provided by nature with a division between what is narrowly "linguistic" and what is "extralinguistic". As a result, these issues are essentially definitional, though, following Sklar, it seems sensible to assume that the most useful system of breaking up our figure into isolated subsystems will be that which corresponds most closely to actual computational independence of the real-world systems involved.

5.1.1 *What is a "phonological object"?*

From Crystal's very standard definition of "phonology" cited above—which explicitly mentions "sound"—it might appear that we should select, as the part of our figure which contains "phonological objects", something one could in principle hear (i.e. a "sound'). There is in fact only one such entity in Figure 5.1—the waveform representation (for a specific listener) indicated by the wavy graphic (❺). It would appear, as well, that there would be some concrete advantages to adopting this representation as the relevant one—e.g. it is, to a reasonable approximation, amenable to measurement.[12] However, in establishing just what one would have to attempt to remove from the waveform to achieve "isolability", it seems clear that the factors which lead from the "idealized bodily output" form, ⫯kʰæ𝚆æ?⫯, to the waveform are precisely *not* linguistic factors: the cognitive processes by which one may adjust one's head position to optimize audition are psychologically interesting, but there is certainly no reason to believe—and no linguist has ever advocated—that such adjustments result from *grammatical computation*. After all, precisely the

---

[12] We say "to a reasonable approximation" because, on the one hand, acoustic measurements of a speech signal may contain far more information than a human can or will use in acoustic processing (and thus may contain irrelevant information), while on the other hand, these measurements generally fail to capture in any detail effects due to binaural audition, head/ear orientation, attention, and the like. Finally, such measurements are usually, at least in linguistic studies, taken in contexts quite different from those of normal speech transmission (e.g. the signals involved are produced in anechoic chambers, using head-mounted microphones, and testing is often done in relatively distraction-free environments using headphones and other state-of-the-art equipment, etc.).

same types of adjustment take place in an individual directing his/her auditory attention to non-speech acoustic events.

In addition, it seems clear that the ambient atmospheric conditions and interference from passing sound-wave-producing entities should play a role in our investigations only insofar as being something we want to *exclude* from consideration in determining the linguistic properties of a waveform. But if the factors which get us to the waveform from the "idealized bodily output" form (at ❹ in Figure 5.1) are precisely non-linguistic ones, then in the interest of isolating those components of our figure which are linguistic objects we would surely be better off targeting the idealized bodily output form. Selecting this as our object of study would already eliminate many factors which we want to exclude from narrow linguistic consideration in any event.

However, if we examine the factors that got us to the idealized bodily output form from the gestural score in ❸, those factors appear once again to be precisely of the type which we would not want to include within the scope of our *linguistic* investigation. It is doubtless fascinating just what computational and memory systems are leveraged to try to get yourself *not* to burp while saying "cat", and someone should surely be investigating such matters, but just as surely that someone is not the phonologist.[13] The same holds for the physical, rather than cognitive, level of the mapping from ❸ to ❹: peanut butter/saliva ratios in the vocal tract are, again, fascinating topics for scientific study, but they are not phonological topics.

So, if the factors which give rise to the "idealized bodily output" from the "gestural score" are non-linguistic, then we do not want to include them within the scope of our object of study. This leaves only the phonemic representations (in ❶ and, for the listener, ❾), the phonological computation system (which isn't blessed with a number in our figure), the phonetic output representation (at ❷ and, for the listener, ❽), and the gestural and auditory scores (❸ and ❼). Since the "speaker-oriented" phonemic and phonetic representations are assumed to be the same formal object as the "listener-oriented" phonemic and phonetic representations, we'll ignore the listener side in what follows.

There is, we assume, no real controversy over whether or not it falls within the purview of the phonologist to concern him/herself with the phonemic

---

[13] Again, although we've probably already said it too many times, this does not mean that the phonologist may not need or want to take into consideration the gains we've made in understanding the "burp regulation mechanism", if any, when considering the masses of empirical data which enter into his/her considerations. It just means that if we called a book about the burp regulation mechanism in Mark's home town Ypsilanti—where it seems a little less active than it does in some other communities—*A Survey of Ypsilanti Phonology*, there'd be something incredibly disingenuous about that title.

representation, the phonological computation system, and the (epiphenom-enal) phonetic representation. The only remaining issue in the delimitation of phonology thus concerns the "gestural" and "auditory" scores. For this ques-tion, our competence in this domain falters, so we will have to satisfy ourselves with a mere statement of the issues. Let us take the "gestural score" as our example, though presumably parallel arguments hold for the auditory side of things. We can envision two distinct possibilities. Under the first, the gestural score is generated by the same type of "action plan" process which gives rise to any coordinated physical activity. Imagine someone has formulated some intent—presumably a mental representation of some type—to scratch his/her nose. Some systems of the mind/brain must convert that representation into a "nose-scratching" score, which contains the relevant key inflection points for the planned action, the relative timing of those inflection points (so that the slight lowering of the head, to which the nose is conveniently attached, will be timed to meet the rising hand, thus avoiding overly rough contact between the relevant objects), and the like. Similar considerations would hold for raising an arm, rolling over, and other useful and willfully incited physical acts. If the gestural score arises from the same modules of mind which are responsible for, in general, converting intentional representations into coordinated "scores", then the fact that they happen in this instance to be operating over linguistic, rather than nose-scratching, representations is of no scientific import, and the "gestural score" would remain outside the scope of the definition of a "linguistic object".

If, on the other hand, the process of generating the "gestural score" from the phonetic representation involves considerations that are unique to language—not unique because of properties of the phonetic representation, but unique because of the manner in which the transduction to a gestural score treats the objects of such a representation—then the gestural score would fall within the scope of linguistics proper.

The distinction may be of little practical significance, in any event, for it would appear unlikely that the transduction processes involved in giving rise to the gestural score involve linguistic *learning*. We know that the acquirer must construct underlying representations and a phonological computation module in the course of the acquisition process. The evidence for this con-struction operation comes from data which has been made complex and messy by the intervention of "too many factors, all sorts of things". The learner must attempt to correct for these various factors (e.g. not take too seriously the acoustic output of people with a mouth full of crackers), but the target of learning in the phonological domain is limited to the relation-ship between two representations, the phonemic and the phonetic, and that relationship is heavily constrained by the restricted set of possible human phonological systems. Imagine that we were to assume that the conversion of the phonetic representation to a gestural score also required learning on the part of the acquirer. We would then have three elements which the learner must link by his/her positing of (1) an underlying representation, (2) a phonological computation system, and (3) a transduction-to-gestural score system. Without a prioristic knowledge of (3), the acquirer cannot know what the output of the phonological computation should be, and without that information, the acquirer cannot construct an underlying representation and computation system pair. Perhaps there are ways around this problem of which we are unaware, but we do note that, at least in Minimalist circles in syntax, the argument that the articulatory/perceptual interface systems are invariant is a common assumption. Further support for this position comes from general considerations regarding the foundations for positing specific modules of the computational mind, an issue to which we turn in the next section.

5.1.2 *Transduction and computation*

Let us direct our attention (Figure 5.2) to the relationship between what we have labeled "phonological computation" and the gestural and auditory "scores" in Figure 5.1 above.

In attempting to determine just how one might divide up the world in a productive manner, it seems crucial (as we mentioned above) to distinguish between transduction and computation. Transduction, to repeat, is a process which converts the form of an input entity to a different form (e.g. the conversion of air pressure differentials to a stream of electrons by a microphone), i.e., one which changes the representational alphabet over which computation is taking place. It contrasts, then, with computation, which involves the manipulation (modification, reordering, deletion, insertion, etc.) of a set of entities, maintaining their form (or their "representational alphabet").

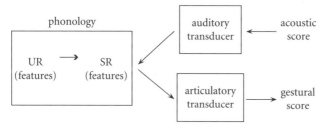

FIGURE 5.2 Computation and transduction

The conversion of a phonological input representation (a so-called "underlying representation" or UR) to an output representation (a so-called "surface representation" or SR) is performed by the phonological computation system. The phonological computation system is a device which converts a representation made up of phonological entities (features, syllable structure, etc.) to a different representation made of the same primitives—that is, URs may contain any of the properties which one may find in an SR.[14] In other words, in the course of phonological computation there is no change of representational alphabet, and thus the label "computation" is justified.

By contrast, the articulatory transducer in Figure 5.2 takes a phonological output representation and converts it to a "gestural score"—itself made up of elements from a non-phonological representation system (including non-featural properties like relative duration). In a similar manner, the auditory transducer takes the acoustic score of an input stream—generated by the acoustic perception system and expressed in elements relevant to that domain—and converts it to a phonological representation. Both of these modules introduce a change in the representational alphabet of their input data, and thus represent transducers in our sense.

We mentioned above how the contrast between transduction and computation can be used to establish on general grounds a structure for the modular mind—with major modules being distinguished in that movement of a representation *across* modules requires a transduction event, while movement of a representation *within* a single module would require only computational events. This conception of things establishes a module boundary between the phonetic output representation and the gestural score—it seems useful to label the module within which phonological computation takes place "the grammar". The transduction to the gestural score would thus involve extralinguistic factors, by definition.

In conclusion, it would seem that the object of study of phonology should be the underlying, phonemic representations and the phonological computation system (which are together responsible for all of the properties of the phonetic output representation). Valuable evidence regarding the nature of these entities and processes can come from a wide range of sources, including the study of phonetics, the study of sound change, and the study of acquisition. It will become apparent in the rest of this part of the book how this definition impacts the pursuit of phonological theory.

---

[14] Again, we do not mean that every element in a *given* UR will be found in that element's corresponding SR, but rather that the *representational capacity* of the two levels is the same.

5.2 The "gradedness" of linguistic objects

Several issues concerning this relatively restrained notion of the object of linguistic study were addressed recently at a conference in Potsdam, at which scholars presented a variety of ways in which one might dissent from arguments such as those presented above. The conference announcement encouraged this dissent:

The kind of grammar typically employed in theoretical linguistics is not particularly suited to cope with a widespread property of linguistic objects: gradedness." (?-??-???-*? Conference Announcement, Potsdam, October 2002)

The organizers of the Potsdam conference were interested in both of the following, rather distinct notions of "gradedness":

a. Variability in production and perception (i.e. variation in the "quantitative phonetic details for realizations of phonological units" (Pierrehumbert 2001: 196)) for both "languages" and individuals.
b. Variability in well-formedness judgements (e.g. the "*" vs. "?" notations often used in the syntactic literature, as well as variation in the assignment of same).

In the rest of this chapter we will argue for the position articulated at the end of the last section, which holds that a coherent place to draw the line between what is "linguistic" and what is "non-linguistic" (and thus, to determine what is a "linguistic object")—a line which must be drawn *somewhere*—is at the end of the computational (as opposed to transduction) processes. This is the general argument for modularity in any domain of human cognition. To support the claim made by the Potsdam organizers, and in much other recent work (e.g. the collected papers in Bod et al. 2003), that "linguistic objects" have "gradedness" as a property, one would need to show that:

a. there is no level of computation within which phonological (or, in syntax, syntactic) features and structures are stored and manipulated categorically (i.e. in a non-gradient manner);[15]

It is not sufficient to show that:

b. speakers' and hearers' *judgements* about "language behavior" display gradedness (since the content of these judgements is not, in the relevant sense, a linguistic object);

---

[15] Since otherwise *that* level of computation could represent a categorically functioning "grammar" in the traditional theoretical sense.

c. observed "language behavior" (whether output behavior or behavioral reaction to inputs) displays gradedness, since observed "language behavior" is not a linguistic object (in the relevant sense).

We will examine, after a brief digression, two attempts to establish that the grammar itself is responsible for generating and/or computing over "gradient" objects (in some of the senses above), arguing that the conception of grammar these approaches entail is not likely to represent a successful way of dividing up the messiness of the world alluded to in the Chomsky and Sklar quotes above. We append a brief consideration of variability in grammaticality judgements, a matter which has become quite important in current research in phonology and about which we have serious misgivings. We will focus on the history of well-formedness judgements in syntactic research, though the problems we see in that field, where the notions have been more explicitly discussed over a much longer span of time, seem to us to bedevil similar research in the phonological domain.

5.2.1 *A brief digression: the granularity problem*

Both types of gradedness above give rise to what we call the "granularity" problem. This can be summarized as follows. How much variation one detects is a function of how finely tuned a metric one employs. For example, if one forces a speaker to assign an analysis of either "well-formed' ('grammatical') or "ill-formed" ("ungrammatical") to a given set of strings, one may find invariant behavior, all examples of some particular type giving rise to a judgement that they are ungrammatical, let's say. However, if one allows three degrees of freedom (perfect, marginal, bad) one may discover some variation. If one forces speakers to use a scale with 10 (or, just to be silly, 1,000) degrees of grammaticality, *even more* variation will be detected. Similarly, if one measures VOT in msec. to the sixth decimal point one will almost certainly find much more variation than if one measures VOT to the second decimal point.

The "granularity problem" is just this: measured with some arbitrary degree of coarseness, any phenomenon may display categorical behavior. On the other hand, measured with some arbitrary degree of fineness, any phenomenon may appear to display variability. But how fine-grained should the analysis be?[16] The goal, presumably, should be to discover just how fine-grained an analysis the speaker-hearer actually uses—but how do we discover what that is? Developing a statistical model which directly encodes the variability of the output of a speaker, or the well-formedness judgement of a listener, to an

---

[16] This is in some sense identical to the question of just what the "equivalence classes" for the given domain are.

arbitrarily fine degree may impede, rather than promote, our understanding of the phenomenon under investigation.

5.2.2 *A probabilistic approach*

In this section we survey some recent claims about phonetics and phonology of morphologically complex words in English presented in Hay (2000). Hay is particularly concerned with the relationship between lexical frequency and morphological decomposition. She presents a model in which access to words which seem to be morphologically complex can be affected either through the "whole word" (i.e. undecomposed) or through the "decomposed" route. Which procedure the listener[17] uses is said to be a function of the statistical frequency of the simplex involved, relative to the frequency of the complex entity. Thus, to take one of Hay's examples, *sane* has a frequency in the CELEX Lexical Database of 149/17.4 million. By contrast, *insane* has a CELEX frequency of 258/17.4 million.[18] From these statistics, Hay (2000: 14) draws the following conclusion:

> it is clear that the whole word route has an advantage. The higher *relative frequency* of *insane* speeds the whole route, relative to the decomposed route.

We leave to one side here our serious concerns regarding the representative nature (or lack thereof) of CELEX probabilities and other empirical issues to focus on the conceptual matters at hand. It is interesting, in that regard, to consider the contrasting case offered by Hay—i.e. the case in which the decomposed route is to be preferred:

> [i]nsane can be compared with a word like *infirm*. *Infirm* is fairly infrequent (27/17.4 million), and, importantly, its base *firm* is highly frequent (715/17.4 million). As such, we predict the decomposed route should have a strong advantage over the whole word access route.

The problem which this passage introduces exists already in the "insane" discussion, but becomes more blatant in the "infirm" case: the method being used by Hay seems to allow both "morphological" decomposition and "whole word" storage for complex materials, or, indeed, to require both (?); but the principles of morphological segmentation, as well as what types of element that segmentation gives rise to, and what their status is relative to grammatical

---

[17] It is difficult to determine whether Hay's arguments are intended to hold of the speaker as well, though we note that to the extent they do not, she is proposing a model with different "production" and "perception" grammars—a serious expansion of the power of the grammar which should not be advocated lightly.

[18] The cultural significance of these statistics goes uncommented upon by Hay, and we too will restrain ourselves.

computation, is left seriously vague. We have found no native speakers who seem to support, through introspection, Hay's assumption that *infirm* means "not firm", but, of course, perhaps Hay does not require that to be the case. Under vaguely connectionist models it becomes incredibly difficult to figure out what the elements over which processes are defined actually might be.

These problems recur in Hay's discussion of a more narrowly phonological problem: the alleged "variable" length of /t/ in *swiftly* and *softly*. In this discussion Hay presents the results of an experiment designed to show that the statistical frequencies of complex elements and their bases need to be represented at the *grammatical* level. The experiment is specifically designed to show that such frequencies affect segment-level production properties. We hardly need point out that if Hay is correct, fundamental aspects of the model being advocated here cannot be valid. (Indeed, Hay points out regularly how serious a challenge her data is to more traditional generative assumptions regarding phonology.) It is important to evaluate Hay's claims in some detail, and to regularly consider as we walk through her evidence precisely where the differences from our own model lie in terms of the entities and processes assumed to be at work in a grammar.

The experiment involves the production by native speakers of a "midwestern variety of English" of a set of lexemes (masked by distractors to keep the subject from catching on, in the usual way), grouped into what Hay calls "paradigms" (using the term in a non-canonical—at least within linguistics— sense). The words are selected so as to have the following properties:

a. "Word A of each paradigm is more frequent than the base it contains." (Hay 2000: 180)
b. "Word B of each paradigm is of approximately the same frequency as Word A. In Word B, however, the base is of much higher frequency." (Hay 2000: 181)

An example should make this clearer. In Table 5.1 below, *swiftly* and *softly* form a "paradigm" as do *exactly* and *directly*. We can see that the conditions on item selection are (roughly) satisfied: *swiftly* and *softly* have approximately the same frequency, but *swiftly* is more common than its base and *softly* significantly less so.[19] Hay then goes on to argue that her model would predict that speakers will use "less /t/" in *swiftly* than in *softly*. It is worth providing her arguments for believing this:

---

[19] The contrasts here, with the statistical frequency of *softly* vs. *soft* being much more divergent than that of *swiftly* and *swift*, are not commented upon by Hay, nor do we know whether it may have impacted the results of the experiment in any way.

TABLE 5.1 Base and derivative frequencies

Word A	Frequency	Base freq.	Word B	Frequency	Base freq.
swiftly	268	221	*softly*	440	1,464
exactly	2,535	532	*directly*	1,278	1,472

- "First, if *swiftly* has a robust whole-word representation which is not very decomposed, then the /t/ is enclosed in a true consonant cluster, and highly prone to simplification. *Softly*, on the other hand, if it is more decomposed, has a boundary inside the consonant cluster (*soft#ly*). As such, the degree of gestural overlap may be somewhat reduced." (pp. 179)[20]
- "Second, the *-ftl* transition is unattested morpheme-internally in English, and so is a strong cue to decomposition. Upon encountering such a transition, we predict the Fast Phonological Preprocessor to hypothesize a boundary. Such a hypothesis will facilitate recognition of any form which is parsing-route dominant, but hinder recognition of any form in which the whole-word representation is more robust ... This may lead the speaker to be more likely to reduce the /t/ in *swiftly* than *softly*." (pp. 179–80)
- "And third, the /t/ is an important part of the base word. It will obviously be easiest to recognize *soft* in *softly*, if *soft* is fully contained therein. The presence of the /t/ is therefore important for any word in which the identity of the base word is important. If, on the other hand, a derived word tends toward whole-word access, then the identity of the base word is not important for recognition. For this reason, too, we expect the /t/ to be more likely to be produced in *softly* than *swiftly*." (p. 180)

We note that there is some unclarity here as to what exactly is being measured—on the one hand, Hay seems to be discussing variation in the *durational* properties of a pronounced *t*, on the other, the probability that there will be a *t* in the target representation for the word in question at all. We might expect the experimental techniques used by Hay to establish whether there is "less t" in a given case to reveal what what she has in mind here, however they do not do so. The procedure for measuring "how much *t*" was used by a given speaker is outlined by Hay as follows:

---

[20] This appears to assume that morpheme boundaries have direct phonetic effects, somewhat contrary to the usual assumptions.

- "For the *swiftly/softly* set, the ranking was based solely on the duration of any characteristics associated with the /t/. That is, the period from the offset of the fricative to the onset of the lateral was measured. If the stop was released, then the period of release was included in the measurement . . . There were several cases in which there was no stop present, but the fricative was clearly geminated (as in *swif-fly*). Such cases were ranked below any tokens which contained stops, but above cases which contained a simple, non-geminated fricative." (p. 183)
- "Measurement in the *exactly/directly* word-set included the complete duration from the offset of the vowel to the onset of the lateral, to avoid the difficulty associated with discerning any boundary between the two adjacent stops."[21] (p. 188)
- "The analysis resulted in a ranking in terms of the presence of /t/, for each of the word-sets . . . , for each of the six speakers." (p. 189)

These procedures for establishing a numerical estimate of the "amount of *t*" are somewhat convoluted and, in our view, questionable (from the point of view of statistical methods), but need not detain us any longer here in our pursuit of more "big picture" questions. The results Hay got, from six undergraduates, are given in Table 5.2 below, where the labels *swiftly, softly*, etc. represent classes of words which fit the selection criterion given above. Thus the *softly* column stands for a set of words containing two morphemes, the first ending in *-ft* and the second being *-ly*, for which it is true that the frequency of the root to which *-ly* is added is lower (in the CELEX database) than the frequency of the morphologically complex word. The column labeled *swiftly* represents similarly derived words for which, however, the frequency of the adjectival base is significantly greater than the frequency of the derived adverb. The *briefly* column is, in some sense, control data—there being no *t* in either the base or the derived adverb. The last three columns represent precisely the same relationships, holding, however, over bases in *-kt*. Hay's predications for the data are quite clearly spelled out by her, and we have quoted some of them above. Since a low number represents a *greater* quantity of *t* in the complex word and a high number a lesser quantity, Hay predicts that, reading across in each set of three columns, the numbers should steadily increase. That is, the numerical values should in the columns should look like this: *softly* < *swiftly*

---

[21] This represents a rather unfortunate "drunk and the lamppost" phenomenon, often seen in psycholinguistic experimentation. The actual required measurement is difficult to get (although, in this case, not *that* difficult given our sophisticated machinery for assessing production phenomena), so one substitutes a different measurement, i.e. not the right measurement, and treats that new, ill-founded measurement the same as all the valid measurements in subsequent discussion.

TABLE 5.2 Coded experimental results

Subject	*softly*	*swiftly*	*(briefly)*	*directly*	*exactly*	*(quickly)*
1	2.25	3.25	(3.25)	2	2.25	(4)
2	3	3	(3)	2.5	3	(2.5)
3	2	2.75	(3.75)	2.75	2.25	(3.5)
4	2.5	3.125	(3.125)	2.75	2.25	(3.75)
5	2.875	2.25	(3.375)	1.75	3.75	(3)
6	2.125	2.375	(3.25)	2.25	2.25	(3.5)

< *briefly* for the first three columns, and *directly* < *exactly* < *quickly* for the last three.

It is difficult to get a precise sense of what is going on this data—I've given the figures for each subject for all of the trials, which average to the values above—but Hay makes a strong argument that they support her hypothesis because, when summed and averaged, the results show significantly less *t* for the *swiftly* and *exactly* columns than for the *softly* and *directly* ones.

In turning to a consideration of how this data looks to us, let us remind the reader that the explicit prediction of Hay is that the numbers should steadily increase as one crosses the three columns for each type of lexeme. Any instance of a decrease in numbers, *or any tie* in numerical values, is counter-predicted. The reader might wonder why we think the requirement that there be no "tie" is so important. It is precisely the status of the *t* in the "middle set" of forms which is at issue in establishing the "gradience" of the phenomenon under investigation. Since we can safely assume that there is no *t* in *briefly*, and we might assume (as Hay clearly does) that there *is* a *t* in *softly*, if *swiftly* "ties" with *briefly*, the *t* can be treated as categorically, rather than "gradiently", absent, and if *swiftly* ties with *softly* (and *softly* in fact has a *t*), then the *t* can be treated as categorically *present*. No gradience will have been established in such a case.

For three of Hay's six subjects, neither the -*ftl*- data nor the -*ktl*- data fit her prediction. Subject 2 does not distinguish any of the -*ftl*- cases (including *briefly*) as far as quantity of *t* goes, and has "more *t*" in *quickly* than in *exactly*![22] For Subject 4 *swiftly* and *briefly* tie, counter to Hay's prediction, and *directly* has "more *t*" than *exactly*, again, counter to prediction. Finally, for Subject 5, *softly* has "more *t*" than *swiftly*, and, once again, *quickly* has "more *t*" than *exactly*, both counter to prediction. Of the remaining three subjects, none performs according to prediction. Subject 1 has no more *t* in *swiftly* than

[22] This is a pretty good hint, also seen in subject 5, that the metric being used by Hay is not measuring what she is actually interested in. She fails to take the hint.

in *briefly*, but, if the .25 difference beween *directly* and *exactly* is statistically significant (which we doubt), performs as Hay predicts on the -*ktl*- data. The remaining two subjects fail to perform as expected on the -*ktl*- data (Subject 3 has more *t* in *exactly* than in *directly*, and Subject 6 treats the two forms identically), but, again, if we accept a .25 difference as significant in the case of Subject 6, do distinguish the -*ftl*- cases as predicted. To summarize, two of the subjects perform as expected on the -*ftl*- data,[23] four do not. On the -*ktl*- data, one subject performs as Hay predicts, five do not.

Hay concludes from the fact that the *summed* and *averaged* behavior of the six subjects appears to match her predictions that her experimental results support her model of lexical access. We have several concerns about this. First, the factors she appears to be invoking seem to be intended to capture psychologically real aspects of the processes which go on in a given speaker's mind during the course of articulating elements of the type she investigated. However, it is precisely in the behavior of the *individuals* investigated that her hypotheses find their weakest support. Second, it is not clear that it is at all safe to assume that all midwestern college students have a *t* in words like *soft* and *swift*, as her experimental design appears to do.

This leads directly to our third, and major, concern. Hay appears to have given no attention to the question of what the actual *representations* of the set of lexical items involved in her study might in fact be, for any of her subjects. It seems to us that many possibilities exist within the midwestern dialect area: for example, there may be speakers with no *underlying* /t/ in one or more of the "base" forms (thus some speakers may have /sɔf/ as their underlying representation for *soft*, but /swɪft/ as their UR for *swift*). The /-li/ forms in the study may or may not be derivationally (in purely synchronic terms) generated from a base which itself may or may not have an underlying final /t/. Final /t/ may undergo phonological deletion either word-finally or in certain internal clusters as a matter of categorical phonology. Many other possible scenarios can be imagined, and there is certainly no reason to believe that all midwestern speakers have the same system with respect to this data. In short, Hay fails to even ask, let alone seek to answer, the question as to what the actual representations are for each of the speakers in her study of the forms she is investigating. The possibility that she is, thereby, misconstruing purely diachronic events (such as the historical loss of /t/ in the relevant context in some of the word-forms for some of her speakers) with sophisticated and psycholinguistically complex "realization strategies" on the part of those speakers seems very real to us. Experimental results such as those offered by Hay cannot

---

[23] This is true only if the .25 difference in Subject 6 is treated as statistically significant.

be construed as relevant to the "gradience" issue unless these concerns are explicitly addressed.

5.2.3 *Stochastic Optimality Theory*

One of the main assertions of Hay's model is that the kind of low-level variation she claims to have found regarding the realization of *t* is a property of the grammar itself, which is said to generate its output probabilistically. A rather more explicit model of variable output being generated by a single grammar is provided by recent work in Stochastic Optimality Theory (StOT). While such a model is not inconsistent with our notions of the nature of "linguistic objects" *per se*, it is often seen as a challenge to the more traditional "categorical" output grammars of the type we are advocating here. It is thus worth our time to explore the properties of this model in some detail.[24] Although formalized somewhat more explicitly than earlier "variationist" approaches to linguistic phenomena (e.g. those of traditional sociolinguists), Joan Bresnan and her colleagues working in the domain of Stochastic OT have developed a model of morphosyntactic computation which shares many of the underlying assumptions about the nature of the "grammar" with earlier sociolinguistic work. While the specific paper we will discuss here concerns morphosyntax rather than phonology proper, the fact that phonology is the original domain of OT research should make the discussion quite easy for phonologists to follow, and the implications for the architecture of the grammar itself transcend narrow modular concerns.

We will not predominantly concern ourselves with the specific analyses presented in the Stochastic OT literature on morphosyntactic variation, but rather on the theoretical underpinnings of the framework itself. Particularly interesting in this regard is the analysis of some forms of English dialectal *be* presented in Bresnan and Deo (2001). The general framework developed by these authors can be explored without fully considering the range of English dialect data they treat in their paper—we will focus here for expository purposes on their treatment of Standard English, the dialect they call "Kent", and the one they call "Kent Variable". We will sketch only most perfunctorily the structure of the OT model itself, assuming that by this time virtually all phonologists have enjoyed some exposure to the basics of the model. In any event, it is not the machinery of the model that will concern us here, but rather the interpretation of that machinery—in particular, we will focus on

---

[24] This model is treated also in Hale (2007), upon which the following discussion is largely based.

	Standard		Kent		Kent variable	
	SG	PL	SG	PL	SG	PL
1	am	are	are	are	am, are	are
2	are	are	are	(are)	are	(are)
3	is	are	is	are	is	are

FIGURE 5.3 Some English *be* conjugations (present, non-inverted)

the questions of what the framework is modeling and whether that is, in fact, what our theory of "grammar" should model.

Let us first examine the data, extracted by Bresnan and Deo from the Survey of English Dialects (SED) materials. The forms in question are those of the present tense of the verb "to be" in non-inversion contexts. The relevant data can be seen in Figure 5.3.

The forms labeled "Standard" are presumably familiar to the reader of this book. The dialect called by the authors "Kent' differs from the Standard only in the first person singular, where we find the form *are* where the Standard has *am*. The variety of English which the authors have called "Kent variable" shows both the "Standard" and the "Kent" forms of the 1SG form of *to be*. Although one might want to subject the precise characterization provided by Bresnan and Deo (2001) to some scrutiny, as well as their use of these particular sources of evidence, for the time being we will accept that the generalizations which form the foundation for the table in Figure 5.3 are valid and require some type of linguistic (in a very broad sense) explanation.

Bresnan and Deo (2001) present their analysis in terms of Optimality Theory, whose basic structure is quite straightforward. Following Bresnan and Deo, we will ignore issues like "non-inversion context" and the like and focus on the fact that we are seeking to find a mechanism to generate the 1SG form of the verb *to be*. In the framework developed and used by the authors this will involve an input form (let's say [1sg], assuming the universe of discourse to be non-inverted forms of *to be*), a set of candidate output forms (again, for simplicity, we'll limit the forms we consider to potential expressions of *to be* actually found in English dialects),[25] and a set of ranked constraints. The constraints perform two important tasks in the model: they can penalize output forms which ignore specified aspects of the input (or, as an alternative way of saying the same thing, favor those output forms which are faithful to

[25] This "simplifying assumption" is very difficult to interpret in any coherent manner. The learning issues involved, in particular, seem insurmountably complex.

[1sg]	*PL	ID(N)	*SOC	ID(P)	*2	MAX(P)	*1	*3	*SG	MAX(N)
☞ am[1sg]							*		*	
art[2sg]				*!	*				*	
is[3sg]				*!			*	*		
is[sg]						*!			*	
are[pl]	*!	*				*				
are[]						*!				*
are[1pl]	*!	*				*				
are[2pl]	*!	*		*	*					
are[3pl]	*!	*		*				*		

FIGURE 5.4 Tableau for "Standard" variety 1SG *am*

the input in the relevant respect) or they may penalize output forms which violate universal markedness requirements, in the manner familiar to the reader from the nature of these constraints in the phonological domain.

The ranking of these so-called Faithfulness Constraints for individual features of the input against the so-called Markedness Constraints for those features determines to what extent marked structures are allowed to surface and to what extent universal markedness considerations are able to block the surfacing of particular forms. The evaluation function is simple: as candidate output forms violate highly ranked constraints which other candidate output forms respect, they fall out of the running for "winning candidate" status. In the end, there will be a candidate which has run least foul of the more highly ranked constraints and that candidate will be the actual output form. A concrete example should make this quite clear. Figure 5.4 gives Bresnan and Deo's "tableau" of candidates and ranked (left-to-right) constraints for the "Standard" variety of English. We will walk through the evaluation process.

Let us first consider the Constraint Set, which runs across the top of the tableau.[26] The first constraint says *PL, which means merely that it is marked to have contrastively plural output forms. Forms such as *are[PL]* violate this constraint in that they are specified as distinctly plural. A violation of this constraint is indicated by a * symbol in the column under *PL. In addition, since this constraint is not violated by at least one other output candidate (in

---

[26] The form in the upper left corner, to the left of the double bar, is the relevant portion of the Input representation, and not a constraint.

fact, it is not violated by several other candidates), the violation incurred by forms such as *are[PL]* is fatal for these output candidates, which can now never win. This fact is indicated informally by placing a ! in the column as well. The next constraint, ID(N), is a Faithfulness constraint, favoring output forms which are faithful (stand in IDentity with) the Number (N) specification of the input candidate. Since the input candidate represented in this tableau is 1SG, forms which have a different specification for Number (such as, again, *are[PL]*) incur a violation mark in this column. It is worth noting that the form *are[]*, which is a morphological form not specified for number at all (an "unmarked" or "default" output form, if you will) does not violate the constraint ID(N) because it does not contain a conflicting number specification. In this particular tableau, which is for the first person singular, the second constraint does not actually get rid of any candidate output forms not already eliminated by the *PL constraint.

The constraint which Bresnan and Deo call *SOC is defined by them as follows: "SOC: Avoid singular expressions for second person inputs. That is, mark a candidate if the input PERS value is 2 and the candidate NUM value is SG" (Bresnan and Deo 2001: 11). This constraint is designed to capture the fact that it is common, cross-linguistically, for speakers to "avoid too direct reference" to the second person, a tendency which, the authors note, "may become crystalized in grammars". This constraint plays no direct role in the tableaux we will be considering here.

The constraint ID(P) favors output candidates which respect the input form's specification for Person. Obviously forms such as *art[2SG]* violate this constraint. In fact, at this point in the evaluation process the only surviving candidates are *am[1SG]*, *is[SG]* (which is underspecified for Person, and thus does not violate ID(P)) and the massively underspecified *are[]*.[27] The next constraint, which is a markedness constraint against having distinct specified second person forms, does not get rid of any of the surviving candidates in this particular tableau. The MAX(P) constraint is a Faithfulness constraint, like the Ident constraints we saw earlier; however, in order not to violate it, an output candidate must be as fully ("maximally") specified along the Person dimension as the input form. Underspecified forms such as *are[]* which do not violate ID constraints, do violate MAX constraints, since they do not maximally encode a Person (or whatever) specification like the input form does. Since this holds of both *are[]* and *is[SG]*, but not of *am[1SG]*, at this point in the tableau

---

[27] It is important for the general assessment of work in Optimality Theoretic syntax that one try to understand just how the output candidate set is arrived at, but that matter lies outside the scope of our critique here. We will assume, though it is far from obvious that this assumption is valid, that an appropriate mechanism exists.

[1sg]	*PL	ID(N)	*SOC	ID(P)	*2	*1	MAX(P)	*3	*SG	MAX(N)
am[1sg]						*!			*	
art[2sg]				*!	*				*	
is[3sg]				*!				*	*	
is[sg]							*		*!	
are[pl]	*!	*					*			
☞ are[]							*			*
are[1pl]	*!	*				*				
are[2pl]	*!	*		*	*					
are[3pl]	*!	*		*				*		

FIGURE 5.5 Tableau for "Kent" variety 1SG *are*

am[1SG] becomes the winning candidate. Every other candidate has violated some higher-ranked constraint than has *am[1SG]*. For the standard language this is, of course, the correct result. Note that the fact that the winning candidate, *am[1SG]*, violates lower-ranked constraints against specified first person forms (*1) and specified singular forms (*SG) is of no significance—all of its competitors have already violated constraints which were more highly ranked and thus have been eliminated; the violation of the lower-ranked constraints is completely irrelevant.

How does the Optimality Theoretic grammar of the "Kent" variety differ from that of the "Standard" variety? If we were just worried about these two varieties of English (recall that Bresnan and Deo 2001 attempt to include a broader range of data in their model), we could readily represent the constraint rankings for "Kent" as in Figure 5.5.[28] The only difference between the constraint ranking in this tableau and that in the "Standard" tableau above has to do with the relative ranking of the constraints *1 and MAX(P). In the "Standard" variety tableau, MAX(P) outranks *1, whereas in the "Kent" variety tableau, the reverse holds. Let us now turn to a consideration of how the re-ranking changes the winning output candidate for the 1SG form.

Since the first five constraints have maintained their ranking status in Kent, we find that when we get to the sixth constraint we have the same three surviving candidates as we had at that point in the "Standard" tableau (Figure 5.4):

[28] In Bresnan and Deo's analysis, there are many differences between the "Standard" constraint ranking and that seen in the "Kent" tableau—these have to do with getting the entire paradigm to come out in numerous dialects. The issues arising from that approach need not detain us here.

am[1SG], *is[SG]* and *are[]*. In the "Standard" tableau, the next constraint to be considered was MAX(P), which served to eliminate *is[SG]* and *are[]*, leaving *am[1SG]* as the winning output form. In the Kent tableau (Figure 5.5), by contrast, the next constraint to be considered is *1, which of course eliminates *am[1SG]* from the output candidate pool, since it favors forms which are not specified for first person. This leaves only *is[SG]* and *are[]* as potential output candidates.

The next constraint, MAX(P), which served to eliminate these candidates from the "Standard" tableau, can now no longer perform that function. Since *both* surviving candidates violate MAX(P) it fails to select an optimal output form from between them, and the evaluation process continues by checking the candidates against the next most highly ranked constraint. The constraint *3, which favors forms which are not specified for third person, also fails to distinguish between our two surviving output candidates, since neither is so specified. It is only when we get to the next constraint, *SG, which favors forms which are not specified as singular, that the grammar allows us to eliminate *is[SG]* as a potential output candidate, leaving only the massively underspecified "default" form *are[]* as our winning candidate, and thus the optimal output form. As you will recall, this is correct for the Kent variety.

The third variety treated by Bresnan and Deo (2001)—and the variety which allows us to explore their model of morphosyntactic variation in detail, is that which they call "Kent variable". To account for this output, which shows (as you will recall) variation between *am* and *are* in the first person singular, Bresnan and Deo expand the computational power of the Optimality Theoretic grammar by adding one more component to it: "stochastic perturbation" of real number-based rankings. In traditional OT, as described above, the constraints are simply rank-ordered—the distance between any two adjacently ranked constraints is always the same (one "step", if you will). Under the constraint-ranking system envisioned by Stochastic Optimality Theory, each constraint is assigned a numerical value, so that the distance between any two adjacently ranked constraints could be a very large one or a very small one.

Imagine, for example, in the Kent tableau given in Figure 5.5 that the numerical ranking value of the constraint *2 is .75, that that of *1 is .60, and finally that the numerical ranking value of MAX(P) is .58. The relative ranking of these constraints will be just as in the non-stochastic version sketched above: *2 will outrank, at .75, *1 (whose value is .60), which will in turn outrank MAX(P) (at .58). However, crucially, *2 outranks *1 by a much greater amount than that by which *1 outranks MAX(P). To this more explicitly detailed constraint-ranking model, Stochastic Optimality Theory then adds the notion of "stochastic perturbation", whereby the rankings are, on any given computational "run" through the grammar, each multiplied by a random, i.e. "stochastic", factor. Those constraints which are ranked one above the other, but with a considerable distance between them, will not be affected in their ranking by the relatively slight changes in numerical ranking value induced by the stochastic factor (so in the example just outlined the constraints *2 and *1 will not be likely to change their ordering under stochastic perturbation). However, those constraints whose separation is relatively small, such as the constraints *1 and MAX(P) under the assumptions sketched in this paragraph, can have their values "perturbed" to such an extent that their ranking comes to differ.[29] That is, if we imagine that due to the stochastic factor, the ranking value of *1 (which starts out at .60) were to be decreased by .05, while that of MAX(P) were to be kept constant, the resulting values would be .58 (the initial value) for MAX(P), but .55 for *1, resulting in MAX(P) being perturbed to ranking position above that of *1. On the other hand, if the effects of the stochastic factors were reversed, such that MAX(P) was reduced by .05 and *1 were kept constant, the values would be .60 for *1 and .53 for MAX(P). This would mean, of course, that the "base' ranking would be unaffected (for these two constraints, anyway) by the stochastic perturbation.

To construct a Stochastic OT grammar of "Kent variable", one would need to do two things. First, ensure that the ranking distance between the constraints in the tableau in Figure 5.5 was sufficiently great for all of the constraints *other than* *1 and MAX(P), so that the stochastic perturbation (which is small enough to only modify constraint rankings which are close to one another in numerical ranking value) could not lead to their reranking. Second, provide *1 and MAX(P) with numerical ranking values which were sufficiently close that the stochastic perturbation *could* lead to reranking of these two constraints. In the unperturbed order (i.e. when the stochastic perturbation did not lead to reranking) we would get the constraint ranking seen for Kent, and thus a 1SG form of the shape *are[]* would be the winning candidate. In those instances, by contrast, when the stochastic perturbation did lead to a reranking of *1 and MAX(P), we would get the constraint ranking seen in the tableau in Figure 5.4, with MAX(P) ranked above *1. The result would be that on those occasions, the grammar in question would select *am[1SG]* as the optimal output form.

The formal device of stochastic perturbation, when combined with real numerical ranking values for constraints, thus provides a mechanism for directly generating variable output from a single formal grammatical device,

---

[29] Remember that each constraint is *independently* perturbed by the stochastic factor.

an accomplishment which Bresnan and Deo recognize as a clear advantage for this model:

> Recall that all of our variable inventories, like the categorical ones, represent the outputs of individual speakers or groups of speakers with shared responses. Given that a single StOT grammar can produce both variable and categorical outputs and explain their shared grammatical structuring, we can hypothesize that variation is part of the internalized knowledge of language—the linguistic "competence"—of speakers. (Bresnan and Deo 2001: 37)

Models such as this, which assume that grammatically significant variable output can be generated by a single computational system (the grammar, or "linguistic competence'), raise serious challenges for our understanding of the nature of the grammar. It is therefore crucially important that we understand the nature of these systems, in particular which of their mechanisms allow them to generate "variable" output. Unfortunately, it is precisely upon this point that it seems very difficult to pin down the Stochastic OT scholars. For example, in the quote immediately above this paragraph, it seems quite clear that Bresnan and Deo intend for a Stochastic OT system to have the same status as a "grammar" in other modern linguistic frameworks: such entities represent our attempt to model the "linguisic competence" referred to at the end of the quotation above.

However, whereas many elements of the Stochastic OT model correspond to aspects of grammatical systems of a familiar type (constraints, features such as sg or 2, for "second person', inputs and outputs), the element of the model which is singularly responsible for giving rise to variable output—the "stochastic perturbation" of numeric ranking values for constraints—does not. If an operation such as "stochastic perturbation" captures a real fact about human grammatical competence, then other models which lack such a component are seriously flawed and in need of revision.

Unfortunately, figuring out the status of the stochastic perturbation in the model itself proves to be a seriously confusing affair. In the passage just quoted, the Stochastic OT grammar was claimed to be a model of the linguistic competence of the speaker. The stochastic perturbation is clearly included within the model, both since it is a key component of *stochastic* OT (as opposed to other Optimality Theoretic frameworks) and because it is responsible for generating the variable outputs which are under discussion in the paragraph. This would lead one to believe that the process which leads to the stochastic perturbation of the numeric ranking values of the constraints is a valuable part of an appropriate model of human linguistic competence. However, a little later in the same paper, in response to an expressed concern that "if alternative outputs are randomly generated, the speaker cannot know what she is going to say!", Bresnan and Deo (2001: 37) write the following:

> This objection stems from the misconception that a stochastic process involving a probability distribution represents something intrinsically random and unknowable. We refer to it as THE FALLACY OF REIFIED IGNORANCE. In fact, the stochastic models represent gaps in our knowledge of the world, not gaps in the causal structure of the world. The speaker does of course know what she is going to say. The specific choice of variant outputs is *not* determined solely by the grammar, and stochastic evaluation provides an explicit model of this fact.

This passage presents the stochastic perturbation as an element added to the model to capture "gaps in our knowledge of the world". But, of course, a gap in our (i.e. linguists') knowledge of the world cannot be part of the linguistic competence of an individual. If it were, and scientific research were to allow us to close one of these gaps, the grammatical knowledge of individuals would suddenly have to change (since there would no longer be a "gap in our knowledge of the world")! Note in particular the striking contrast between the earlier claim of these authors that "variation is part of the internalized knowledge of language—the linguistic 'competence'—of speakers" with the claim above that "[t]he specific choice of variant outputs is *not* determined solely by the grammar, and stochastic evaluation provides an explicit model of this fact". Stochastic perturbation must be either, as the first quote would indicate, part of the internalized linguistic competence of the speaker, or a way to tweak our models because of gaps in our knowledge of the world—but it cannot be both.

The following passage is somewhat more explicit about the details of the model, building on Boersma and Hayes (2001). Note, however, the frequent use of some crucially undefined concepts.

> It is well known from sociolinguistics that macro-level factors—such as the social meaning of an expression in a certain context—affect variation. While some aspects of social meaning could be grammaticalized into the contents of expressions and constraints (morphological markers of politeness levels, for example), other social aspects could be independent of the grammar fragment/partial theory in question, constituting "noise" to the syntactician, perhaps. A third way that sociolinguistic factors could affect variation is by systematically boosting or depressing selected constraints. A model of this effect is given in (16) (adapted from Boersma and Hayes, 2001: 82–3):

(16)   effective ranking = constraint ranking$_i$ + *styleSensitivity*$_i$ · *Style* + noise

> Here *styleSensitivity* is a constraint-specific value added to the constraint ranking: when positive, a constraint's ranking is boosted; when negative, the ranking is depressed; and when zero, the ranking is unaffected, or stylistically neutral. *Style* is a continuous variable ranging from 0 (for most casual style) to 1 (for most formal).

According to this model, the rankings of various "style sensitive" constraints may covary (directly and inversely) with the speech style. These covarying subgrammars could be viewed as representing SOCIOLINGUISTIC COMPETENCE. (Bresnan and Deo 2001: 37–8)

The passage defines some terms mentioned in a quotation from a somewhat later paper by Aissen and Bresnan (2002) to be given momentarily, but, as mentioned above, gives rise to a number of unclarities. What is a "grammar fragment/partial theory" and who cares what is independent of it?[30] What are "covarying subgrammars"? Are these the same, or different from, Kroch's "dual base" systems? What is "sociolinguistic competence' and how do "covarying subgrammars" represent it? Is it different from the authors" earlier mention of "linguistic" competence (which 'variable output" was also taken to be a hallmark of)?

A rather clear sketch—though one that is not consistent with many of the quotations given above—of how these issues come together for some proponents of Stochastic OT can be seen in slide 47 from Aissen and Bresnan (2002). In response to the self-posed question "Does it make sense to derive frequencies of usage from grammar?", they note the following:

Knowledge of the grammatical structure of a particular language is represented by the (mean) ranking values of the constraints. Extra-grammatical factors affecting language use are represented by the variables that perturb the rankings. So each "competence" grammar (= set of ranking values) is embedded in a "usage" grammar (the style and noise variables). This embedding enables a much richer array of evidence to be used in studies of grammar than with classical approaches. (Aissen and Bresnan 2002: slide 47)

The first sentence of this passage stands in stark contrast to the claim by Bresnan and Deo (2001) that a Stochastic OT grammar represents the knowledge of language ("linguistic competence") of a speaker. In this discussion, the OT grammar *without* any stochastic perturbation is taken to represent grammatical knowledge, and the stochastic perturbation is an "extragrammatical" factor.

As we have had occasion to argue extensively at several points in this chapter, no one to our knowledge has ever maintained that all aspects of human behavioral output in the language domain are the result of grammatical computation. Grammars do not tell one what to say, how loud to say it, how fast to talk, which language to use on a particular occasion, nor do they control many other fascinating dimensions of human behavior. That the output of the

---

[30] After all, "phonology" could be absent from a "grammar fragment/partial theory" of English, but does that tell us anything?

grammar is subjected to post-grammatical transduction and computational processes is quite clear. What is unclear is what advantage might arise by labeling some or all of these processes elements of a "usage" grammar.[31] Expanding the term "grammar" in this way only makes seemingly intriguing statements, such as "This embedding enables a much richer array of evidence to be used in studies of *grammar* than with classical approaches" (emphasis added)—statements which are repeated like political slogans—incredibly mundane. It is, after all, fairly obvious that if we link some number of additional formal systems to that of the "competence" grammar (i.e. the "grammar" as that term has been used in late twentieth-century linguistics), e.g. that of planetary motion (call it a "planetary grammar"), a "much richer array" of evidence will be used to study "grammar" (which term now has been expanded to include the systems which underlie planetary motion). But have we learned anything by taking distinct systems, each of which could (and, as we have seen, almost certainly must) be studied independently, and treating the diverse evidentiary foundations for their study as a unitary body? We fail to see how we do.

Some amount of the "rich array of evidence" must be used to construct the "competence grammar", which does not generate variable output. This is, of course, the type of evidence exploited by "classical approaches" to the study of linguistic competence. The rest of this "much richer array of evidence" is to be "accounted for" by positing a stochastic perturbation of the "competence" grammar's constraint ranking—but if the "stochastic perturbation" is simply an admission that, for the relevant phenomena, we have a "gap in our knowledge of the world", then are we actually *using* this new kind of evidence in any meaningful sense?

If we ask ourselves what the Stochastic Optimality Theory approach has gained us over an approach which posits only categorical grammars for the case of the "Kent variable" variety of English whose analysis by Bresnan and Deo we have sketched in some detail above, it is not difficult to see, in our opinion, that we have gained very little indeed. After all, a perfectly plausible explanation of the "Kent variable" data, one that—unlike the Stochastic OT approach—doesn't separate such variation from the real sociolinguistic context in which the data was gathered, can be readily constructed. The "Kent" variety has, as noted above, a first person singular present tense non-inverted form of the verb to be *are*, where the "Standard" variety of English has *am*. It seems not at all implausible that many if not all "Kent" speakers are aware of this difference between the English they experience in the media, in books, and

---

[31] Note that the passage from Aissen and Bresnan (2002) starts out calling the factors which are now being said to be part of the "usage grammar" "extragrammatical". So why call it a "usage *grammar*"?

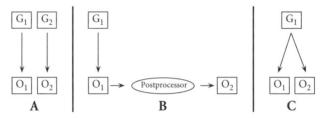

FIGURE 5.6 The natures of sociolinguistic variation

from non-Kentish anglophones they meet on a day-to-day basis and their own dialect. It would not be at all surprising if the choice of which form to use in a particular context carries social significance. Some Kentish speakers, plausibly, have experienced more exposure to the standard than others; some, doubtless, feel less comfortable using Kent dialect forms with non-Kentish individuals than others, etc. If a speaker in Kent occasionally used the Standard form instead of the Kentish one, or if a speaker who generally, in her/his day-to-day life, speaks the Standard a great deal were to provide the linguistic field worker with Kentish forms with less than perfect consistency in the course of the Survey of English Dialects interview, who would be astonished? The mixture of forms from different dialects for social effects is a well-known attribute of poly-dialectal speakers; that it occasionally worked its way into the SED materials is to be expected. "Kent variable" is variation *between* grammars, not "covarying subgrammars", nor a "single Stochastic OT grammar" producing variable output. There is simply no compelling reason to complicate our understanding of the pursuit in which we are engaged with such notions, nor with "usage grammars" next to "(competence) grammars". Ripping the subtle and complex sociolinguistic processes which give rise to variable linguistic *behavior* by individuals out of their social context is emphatically *not* the way to develop a richer understanding of this interesting phenomenon.

Finally, let us make a general point about positing grammars which give rise to multiple outputs. There is no denying (and to our knowledge, it has never been denied) that the output of humans is variable. This variability is certainly not limited to what one might term "subgrammatical" variation (e.g., in the precise height of an [æ] within the æ-space), but includes variation along dimensions normally regulated by grammatical knowledge. There are several possible explanations for this phenomenon, the most plausible of which we sketch in Figure 5.6.

At the leftmost portion of the figure we find Explanation A. As in all the scenarios to be discussed, the speaker generates two distinct forms of output for "the same" communicative intent, let's say.[32] The outputs are labeled O_1 and O_2. Under scenario A, each output is generated by a different grammar. The speaker in question is bidialectal or bilingual, so, of course, produces two types of *behavioral* output. Type A phenomena must exist, barring quite bizarre assumptions about the mental states of e.g. Chinese-English bilinguals.

Under the model in B, by contrast, the speaker is getting variable behavioral output out of a single mental grammar. This is done by direct modification of the grammar's output by what we may term a post-grammatical processor which "translates" the speaker's output forms into a new shape, usually for prestige reasons. Basically, the speaker is feigning bidialectal or bilingual competence. Type B can be experimentally distinguished from Type A because the post-processor requires higher-order cognitive engagement than does grammatical computation, and thus falters under distraction or other performance impediments in ways in which the grammar itself does not. Again, Type B phenomena must exist, since we can fake an unfamiliar English accent after an hour's training. Of course, we cannot fake it *well* after so little exposure, but, after all, that's kind of the point.

In the Type C scenario, there is again a single (relevant) grammar in the mind of the speaker, and that speaker is not using a post-processor to modify the output of that grammar. Instead, the grammar itself directly generates doublets, much like the Stochastic OT model we considered earlier in this chapter. The question naturally arises as to whether we should supplement our theory of the nature of grammars by expanding them such that they have this capacity—i.e. do Type C phenomena necessarily exist? We already have two ways of explaining the relevant type of variant behavioral output, and each of these two, it seems, must exist. We can't imagine what evidence could not be accounted for by one of the already necessary types of explanation (Types A and B) such that we should make our theories more powerful in order to have a *third* mechanism for getting variable data. Doing so would appear to be a blatant violation of Occam's Razor.

5.3 "Gradedness" of grammaticality judgements

Is grammaticality a categorical or "graded" phenomenon? It is of some interest to note that Chomsky (1957) argues both sides of this question. Early in the book, he states:

---

[32] It's a matter of some difficulty to know what to label the relationship between what people call "variants", so we will leave it in this rough form.

That is, we may assume for this discussion that certain sequences of phonemes are definitely sentences, and that certain other sequences are definitely non-sentences. In many intermediate cases we shall be prepared to let the grammar itself decide, when the grammar is set up in the simplest way so that it includes the clear sentences and excludes the clear non-sentences. (Chomsky 1957: 14)

It is fairly clear that this is a temporary, methodological move (rather than a claim about the substance of the matter). We can contrast Chomsky's position some pages later in *Syntactic Structures*:

The most reasonable way to describe this situation would seem to be by a description of the following kind: to form fully grammatical sentences by conjunction, it is necessary to conjoin single constituents; if we conjoin pairs of constituents, and these are major constituents..., the resulting sentences are semi-grammatical; the more completely we violate constituent structure by conjunction, the less grammatical is the resulting sentence. This description requires that we generalize the grammatical-ungrammatical dichotomy, developing a notion of degree of grammaticalness. It is immaterial to our discussion, however, whether we decide to exclude such sentences as "John enjoyed and my friend liked the play" as ungrammatical, whether we include them as semi-grammatical, or whether we include them as fully grammatical but with special phonemic features. In any event they form a class of utterances distinct from "John enjoyed the play and liked the book," etc., where constituent structure is preserved perfectly... (Chomsky 1957: 35–6, n. 2)

Chomsky's position on the matter remains stable, as the following quote from *Aspects* reveals:

A descriptively adequate grammar must assign to each string a structural description that indicates the manner of its deviation from strict well-formedness (if any). A natural terminological decision would be to say that the grammar *directly generates the language* consisting of just the sentences that do not deviate at all (such as (3)), with their structural descriptions. The grammar *derivatively generates* all other strings (such as (1) and (2)), with their structural descriptions. These structural descriptions will indicate the manner and degree of deviance of the derivatively generated sentences. (Chomsky 1965: 227)

No formal explication has ever been offered, to our knowledge, for the notion "derivatively generates". The powers (and responsibilities) of the grammar are expanded further by the time of *Knowledge of Language*:

The system of knowledge attained—the I-language—assigns a status to every relevant physical event, say, every sound wave. Some are sentences with a definite meaning (literal, figurative, or whatever). Some are intelligible with, perhaps, a definite meaning, but are ill-formed in one way or another ("the child seems sleeping"; "to whom did you wonder what to give?" in some dialects; "who do you wonder to whom gave the book?" in all dialects). Some are well formed but unintelligible. Some are assigned a phonetic representation but no more; they are identified as possible sentences of some language, but not mine. Some are mere noise. There are many possibilities. Different I-languages will assign status differently in each of these and other categories. (Chomsky 1986: 26)

The system envisioned by Chomsky would seem to have the following properties (at least):

- The grammar generates (including now both "direct" and "derivative" generation) not simply output representations (as is widely assumed), but rather a pair OR,WF, where OR is a set of output representations (presumably one for each "module" of the grammar) and WF is the well-formedness "status" of the elements in that OR (or a set of statuses, one for each element of OR).
- The "status" in WF for an element of OR includes not only the well-formedness of the element but also in what ways that element deviates from well-formedness.
- Note that the actual contents of WF appear to be inaccessible to consciousness, since non-linguist speakers do not say, confronted by *John is likely Bill to leave*, that a theta-criterion violation has occurred, but rather something like "it doesn't sound right with 'Bill' there."
- Thus, even if the grammar were to generate a list of violations (Principle X violated here, Rule Y violated there, etc.), it appears that the *speaker's own account* of ungrammaticality does not contain this information (since that would require conscious access to the rules and mechanisms of grammar). It thus appears that the speaker generates a *conscious* judgement at least in part *independently* of this information.

We therefore can see no reason why one would want the *grammar* to do this work. This seems like a serious confusion between a module of the mind which provides as complete a parse as it can of a given input (linguistic, visual, olfactory, etc.) and the higher-order responsibility of determining the (possible) significance of the fact that you have been confronted by that particular input.

In conclusion, we would say that it much more likely to be useful to adopt a model in which:

- The grammar parses what it can of an input stream, spewing out the unparsable material as an "error" (or, perhaps, simply ignoring it).
- The *listener* may use a wide variety of higher-order cognitive processes to attempt to determine the source of the error. These would include at least: knowledge about the speaker (where is this person from? how

do people talk there? is the speaker intoxicated?); knowledge about the likely communicative intent of the speaker (s/he must have meant 'kicked Peter' when s/he said *picked Keter*; s/he was going to finish that sentence in some way like this, but got distracted by the fact that her/his hair was on fire ...); how does this string differ from an error-free one which is *like* it (e.g., if one just discards the error as a total mistake, is the resulting parsed string coherent, given the source of the string and his/her likely communicative intent), or must one interpret the error as an attempt to say something other than what was said? etc.

- Making these judgements may entail sending several alternative versions of the string heard—constructed by the listener by manipulating the string in light of the information considered above—through the grammar for parsing until a *minimally divergent* but *maximally coherent* (given the above considerations) string is generated.
- The grammar's outputs consist solely of the parsed string and any residual unparsed material (identified by the fact that it is not in the parse)—there is no gradedness in those representations.

Note that we have no formal theory regarding the various factors adduced above as playing a role in the listener's efforts to develop a coherent account of an ungrammatical string. More importantly, treating gradient grammaticality judgements as the direct product of the grammar—which surely does not contain the kinds of information mentioned above—(1) entails that such non-grammatical factors are not relevant (since the graded grammaticality judgement is given by the grammar itself) and (2) precludes discovering what role, if any, such factors play (since they are excluded a priori as explanatory principles). A theory which allows for *both* gradedness in the grammar *and* a role for the full range of factors sketched above in generating gradient grammaticality judgements suffers from an embarrassment of riches: since the factors above, on their own, would already generate gradedness in judgements, it violates Occam's Razor to construct a grammar which duplicates this work.

5.4 Conclusions

We hope to have provided compelling arguments in this chapter as to why we are resistant to modern tendencies within linguistics to move the variability of human behavior, whether that behavior involves the generation of linguistic output representations, the parsing of speech by the grammar, or the development of well-formedness judgements by the speaker, into the domain of linguistic competence—i.e., the domain over which we assume our models to be attempting to capture. We have tried to emphasize throughout, and we reiterate here, that in no way do we mean to imply that research into the observables of human speech behavior, including human judgements regarding speech input, should be shunned or avoided. Key insights into the nature of grammatical competence can be developed and sharpened only by a careful consideration of the role of performance systems in giving rise to properties of human speech. Linguistics, like other sciences, has a domain of inquiry, a part of the world of which it is attempting to present coherent, formal and insightful models. It has mounds of data, coming from a wide range of sources, which might bear on the nature of the models being constructed. But, just as we have found in other domains of scientific inquiry, none of the readily observable, superficial data sources provides *direct* evidence for the underlying isolable but interacting systems which give rise to that data. Instead, the observed data reflect the interaction of "too many factors, all sorts of things", and it is only through relatively sophisticated chains of reasoning that the relevance of any particular observation can be established.

6

Against articulatory grounding

6.1 Introduction

As can be seen from the following quote from Kager (1999: 421), Optimality Theory has given rise to a strong renewed interest in the question of the relationship between phonetics and phonology.

In work by Steriade, Flemming, Kirchner, Hayes, and others, it is argued that constraints should be able to refer to much more *phonetic detail* (including non-contrastive features and numerical values of acoustic parameters) than is allowed on classical generative assumptions, which maintain a strict separation between phonology and phonetics ... This blurring of the phonology-phonetics boundary goes hand in hand with an increased role for *functional explanations* ... No doubt, real progress can be made by this approach. An increased role for functional explanations in grammatical theory matches well with a major goal of OT, which is to *encode directly* markedness in the grammar, an enterprise that has been crucial to OT's typological achievements.

This chapter explores the relationship between phonetics and phonology against the backdrop of what we take to be a particularly interesting "test case", that of Marshallese. It argues that several aspects of Optimality Theoretic approaches to the nature of this relationship are incoherent and that the generalizations these approaches are attempting to capture should not be accounted for by phonological theory at all, having an adequate explanation—necessary independent of the "phonetics" issue—in a technically "extralinguistic" domain, that of historical linguistics.[1]

6.2 A sketch of Marshallese phonetics and phonology

A basic sketch of Marshallese phonetics and phonology can be extracted from an impressive body of work by Byron Bender and his colleagues

---

[1] This chapter represents an expansion and development of Hale (2000). For a more systematic, though still incomplete, discussion of the diachrony of the Marshallese phonological system, see Hale (2007: ch. 5).

(Abo et al. 1976; Bender 1968; 1969). The rather startling conclusions regarding Marshallese vowels presented in these works have been confirmed, in their essentials, by the detailed acoustic analysis of Choi (1992). Bender divides the consonants of Marshallese into three classes: palatalized ("light"), velarized ("heavy"), and round velarized ("round"). We can conceive of these classes as being distinguished featurally: "light" consonants are [−back, −round], "heavy" consonants are [+back, −round], and "round' consonants are [+back, +round].

The Marshallese vowel system is striking. The "surface" vowels are given below, where the "tie" symbol (as in iu̯) represents a smooth transition from one vowel to another, e.g. in this case, *i* to *u*.

(59)

i	ɯ	u	i͜ɯ	i͜u	ɯ͜i	ɯ͜u	u͜i	u͜ɯ
ɪ	ʏ	ʊ	ɪ͜ʏ	ɪ͜ʊ	ʏ͜ɪ	ʏ͜ʊ	ʊ͜ɪ	ʊ͜ʏ
e	ʌ	o	e͜ʌ	e͜o	ʌ͜e	ʌ͜o	o͜e	o͜ʌ
ɛ	ɐ	ɔ	ɛ͜ɐ	ɛ͜ɔ	ɐ͜ɛ	ɐ͜ɔ	ɔ͜ɛ	ɔ͜ɐ

An example may make this clearer. Choi (1992: 68) presents a graph, sketched in (60) below, of an F2 trajectory for the Marshallese word /tʲeʌpᵚ/ "to return". F2 trajectory reflects movement of the tongue along the front–back dimension, with high F2 correlating with frontness, low F2 with backness.

(60)

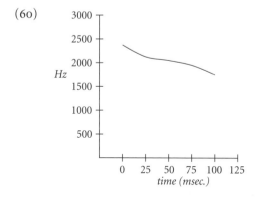

This graph shows quite clearly that there is no steady-state position for the tongue during the realization of this vowel: it moves gradually from a front position at time 0 to a back position at 100 msec. As Choi (1992) demonstrates, this lack of steady-state position holds for all the "tied" vowels above. Bender (1968) had already compellingly argued that the most coherent phonological analysis of the Marshallese vowel inventory is one in which the vowels themselves bear no features along the dimensions front–back and round–unround. That is, they differ from one another *only* along the height (or, in our view, height and ATR) dimensions.[2]

In order to present the resulting phonological inventory, we must confront a representational difficulty (one which is quite significant in the context of this chapter). It is common in phonological circles to use the symbols of the International Phonetic Alphabet (IPA) in a systematically ambiguous manner, and, indeed, for the most part we have followed that practice so far in this book. On the one hand, a symbol such as *i* is used to represent a bundle of features (both at the start of a derivation—i.e. features in an underlying representation—and at the end of a derivation, i.e. in a "phonetic" *representation*); on the other, this same symbol is used to represent the acoustic impression (or articulatory realization) of a segment. Since issues in these domains form a central concern of this chapter, and since in our view the constantly shifting use of a single symbol for these three distinct purposes ("phonological" input representations, "phonetic" output representations, and phonetic realizations) has created some confusion in the literature, we must try to clarify the matter. The highest vowel of Marshallese, in underlying representations, is neither front nor back, round nor unround, so there is in fact no appropriate IPA symbol which may be used to represent it. In order to keep this clear in the mind of the reader, we will use arbitrary non-IPA symbols for each of the Marshallese underlying vowels: the [+hi,+ATR] vowel will be indicated by ✿, the [+hi,−ATR] vowel by ☎, the [−hi +ATR] vowel by ✆, and the [−hi,−ATR] vowel by ☺.

How do we get the Marshallese surface realizations from these underspecified underlying representations? We owe to Bender (1968) the core descriptive insight; but the theoretical framework which permits this derivation is provided by the insightful proposal regarding "phonetic underspecification" in Keating (1988), which was adopted by Choi (1992) for Marshallese. In keeping with Keating's proposal we may distinguish between three types of representation: (a) a phonological representation, (b) an output representation, derived by the phonological system, which we may refer to as the "phonetic representation", and (c) an impressionistic representation by the linguist of the acoustic or articulatory realization (bodily output).[3] Keating's essential

---

[2] Bender proposes an analysis in which one of the height contrasts might be eliminable, given sufficiently abstract underlying representations. The particular type of abstractness involved, while current when Bender developed his analysis, is no longer widely practiced amongst phonologists. Obviously, this fact does not bear directly on the validity of his analysis. Since the height issues are orthogonal to our principle concerns here, we will not pursue the matter.

[3] It is important to bear in mind that we are following the standard, if confusing, practice of using "representation" to refer both to entities in the mind ("mental representations") and to objects constructed by linguists for heuristic purposes ("linguist's representations").

insight is that some representations of type (b) are underspecified for what are, in principle, featurally specifiable values. That is, just as we have phonological representations—like the Marshallese vowels—which do not have values assigned to all phonological features, so too do we have "phonetic representations" which leave unspecified some values for the phonological feature set. The "transducer", which is responsible for converting the "phonetic representation" into a set of articulatory commands, treats underspecified values just as it treats other underspecified aspects of the phonological representation (those not featurally specifiable, e.g. the transitions between consonants and vowels): it computes a shortest articulatory path between the target demands imposed by specified values.

Before turning to how phonetic underspecification works in Marshallese, we must first confront yet another confounding issue regarding representations. It is traditional in phonology to use two distinct "bracket" systems to distinguish between phonological and phonetic segments. Unfortunately, as we have seen above, it is necessary to distinguish, precisely in the matter under discussion, between phonetics as grammar output and phonetics as (impressionistic transliteration of) bodily output. We thus introduce a new set of brackets, retaining / for phonological representations and using square brackets, [ ], for the representation of phonetic strings as output of the grammar. As a mnemonic aide, we introduce the use of little human bodies to represent impressionistic transliterations of the output of the body. So, in the case of English *cat* we will have a phonological representation /kæt/, a phonetic (as output of grammar) representation [kʰæt], and a phonetic (as impressionistic rendering of the output of the body) representation ⫧kʰæt⫧. In this case, since the third representation does not involve any phonetic underspecification, the latter two representations look alike.[4] We will henceforth call the phonetic "as output of grammar" representation the "phonetic representation" and the phonetic "as (impressionistic rendering of) bodily output" representation the "bodily output".

In the case of Marshallese vowels, the phonetic representation diverges considerably from that of the bodily output because of the phonetic underspecification of the vowels. As pointed out above, the underlying representation of Marshallese vowels lacks specification for the features [back] and [round]. This lack is not modified in the course of the phonological computation; thus the vowels at the level of the phonetic representation are similarly underspecified. Obviously, they cannot remain indeterminate at the level of

---

[4] This representational identity should not be misconstrued as identity in any deep sense: an acoustic output can *never* be identical to a mental representation. One is a physical fact about the physical world, one is a cognitive construct.

physical realization: the tongue must be either more or less back during the articulation of an actual vowel, the lips must be either round or spread. In the realization of phonetically underspecified vowels in Marshallese, front–back tongue position and lip-rounding are determined not by features on the vowels themselves but by the values that adjacent consonants bear for these features. The front–back position of the tongue and the degree of lip-rounding during the duration of the vowel are simply "transitions" from the values of the adjacent consonants (Choi 1992), not unlike the transitions from e.g. *i* to *g* in English "league" (such transitions exist in any VC or CV sequence, in any human language, of course). This can be seen from the derivations in (61a–c).

(61) a. $C_{light}VC_{round}$: /nʲ✋kʷnʲ✋kʷ/ > [nʲ✋kʷnʲ✋kʷ] > ✝nʲiukʷnʲiukʷ✝ 'clothing'

  b. $C_{light}VC_{heavy}$: /nʲɘtᵚ/ > [nʲɘtᵚ] > ✝nʲeʌtᵚ✝ 'squid'

  c. $C_{light}VC_{light}$: /ʈʲɵʈʲ/ > [ʈʲɵʈʲ] > ✝ʈʲɛʈʲ✝ 'Lutjanus Flavipes'

Examples are given in (61) for vowels left-flanked by light consonants—parallel examples for vowels with heavy and round consonants on their left can easily be constructed (for a systematic list, see Choi 1992: 30).

   This analysis not only accounts for the typologically bizarre "tied" vowels of Marshallese but also provides interesting insights regarding the "normal" Marshallese surface vowels, such as *i* and *o*. Although these vowels sound like the vowels usually designated [i] and [o] in the phonetics literature, they have a decidedly different status with respect to the phonological system vis-à-vis the similar vowels of e.g. English. For example, the Marshallese word for "bark" (of a dog) is derived as follows: /rʷɘrʷ/ > [rʷɘrʷ] > ✝rʷorʷ✝ . By contrast, the English word *roar* shows the following derivation: /ror/ > [ror] > ✝rʷorʷ✝. The vowels present in the bodily output are roughly the same in the English and Marshallese examples. The English examples, however, represent the bodily realization of phonetic representations for which the front–back position of the tongue and the degree of lip-rounding are specified. In the Marshallese examples, by contrast, the bodily output *o* is the result of the same "transition" phenomenon found with the odd "tied" vowels—it just happens to be the case in this instance that the transitions are, for the example of *o*, from a back and round articulation to a back and round articulation. Such a "transition" gives rise to the *mirage* of a steady-state vowel in the output (see e.g. the relatively flat F2 trajectory in Choi's /ʈʲɵʈʲ/ graph, 1992: 67, fig. 4.8).

6.3 The phonetics–phonology interface

The considerations above give rise to an interesting question for recent Optimality Theoretic approaches to the relationship between phonetics and phonology. Imagine that there were a constraint against *o*, which we can call NoO.[5] The interesting question is this: Does the winning candidate for Marshallese underlying /rʷƏrʷ/ violate this constraint or does it not? That is, what is the "output" over which constraint evaluation takes place? Is it what we have been calling the phonetic representation, or is it what we have been calling the bodily output? If the former, then Marshallese [rʷƏrʷ] does not violate NoO. If the latter, then Marshallese ⁞rʷorʷ⁞ does.

Interestingly, we think there are two rather different answers to this question in the OT literature, though the approaches arising from these answers are marred in both cases by a certain degree of incoherence on the matter. We will call these approaches the "traditional" and the "phoneticist" approach.

6.3.1 *Traditionalists*

In the traditional approach, relatively standard generative assumptions about the nature of the grammar as a computation over representations (representations in, representations out) are maintained. For authors working within this approach, who appear to include Kager (1999), the "output" over which constraint violation is evaluated is what we have called the phonetic representation. This can be seen, even for authors who make no specific claim on the matter, from the nature of many of the constraints, including, but by no means limited to, FAITH[VOICE], ALIGN(STEM,RIGHT), and *VOICED-CODA. FAITH[VOICE] is evaluated, in traditional practice, by checking for the presence of the feature VOICE in the winning phonetic representation if there is a feature VOICE on the relevant segment in the input. Since the bodily output does not contain features, this particular interpretation of FAITH[VOICE] (or any of the other featural faithfulness constraints) is only coherent under an interpretation in which the output is a phonetic representation.[6]

---

[5] If "inventories" are a function of constraint ranking, as widely advocated in the OT literature, some such constraints—or a set of constraints which result in the same effect—will be necessary. For the issue which interests us, the precise characterization is of no relevance.

[6] One can imagine a "phoneticist" reaction to this issue: one can redefine FAITH[VOICE] as checking for the phonetic correlate of VOICE in the output. Note that this entails a straightforward correlation between features and their realization—which may run into problems of various sorts—as well as a mechanism, within the grammar, for evaluating whether the correlation holds. Under the traditional approach this is a simple matter: check for the presence of the feature VOICE. Under the phoneticist

In the case of ALIGN(STEM,RIGHT) we find in fact a minor deviation from the standard generative view of the nature of outputs: to evaluate this constraint, the output representation must contain information about (at least the edges of) stems. Since it is not possible for morphological entities such as "stems" to be present in the *bodily* output, positing morphological alignment constraints requires a representational, rather than realizational, conception of the output. *CODA[VOICE] combines both of the preceding arguments. This well-formedness constraint disfavors the presence of a specific feature in a specific structural position in the output—since features are representational entities, the output must be a representation. Moreover, since codas are not present in acoustic or articulatory realization—they are features of the abstract syllabification of a representation—such constraints could not be evaluated over bodily output. Thus, under "traditionalist" assumptions, the phonological computation is a mapping of the following type: *phonological representation* (featural) → *phonetic representation* (featural). As noted above, preserving the mapping as one between entities of the same type (features) makes the evaluation of FAITH constraints (MAX, DEP, IDENT, etc.) a trivial matter.

Under this view, the nature of the "output" of the phonological derivation is that of a representation—the phonetic representation (apparently containing morphological information inherited from the input). Given this fact, it is strikingly odd that proponents of this traditionalist OT view, having constructed a system which starts with a cognitive representation and ends with a cognitive representation, promote the notion that constraints should be articulatorily or perceptually "grounded" (Kager 1999: 11). Thus, for example, Pulleyblank (1997: 79) says, regarding a constraint which Kager (1999: 40) calls VOP (VOICED OBSTRUENT PROHIBITION), which states that "an obstruent must be voiceless", that "[t]he tendency for obstruents to be voiceless derives from the phonetic fact that it is more difficult to maintain the vibration of the vocal cords when there is a constriction of the type that produces a fricative or an oral stop". To fully appreciate the issues involved by the move to "phonetically motivate" OT constraints, it is worth considering the (relatively standard, at least for "traditionalist" OT practitioners) general conceptualization of the OT model. Kager (1999: 10) notes that it is one of the "major properties" of constraints that they are universal:[7] "In its strongest interpretation, by which

---

approach, the matter is of considerably greater complexity and this complexity is now *in the grammar*, rather than being left to the articulatory-perceptual transduction mechanism.

[7] This is "relativized", on p. 12, such that alignment constraints, while universal in form, are allowed to make reference to language-specific material. This relativization is not relevant to the issues under discussion here.

all constraints are part of UG, this implies that all constraints are part of the grammars of all natural languages."

Universal Grammar is a genetic endowment of humans, its features encoded in the human genome. If Kager's VOP is a universal OT constraint it is encoded in UG, itself part of the human genetic code. On the other hand, if we take Pulleyblank's assertion above at face value, then the relatively "unmarked" status of voiceless obstruents is to be explained not with reference to the human genetic code but rather by dint of some alleged fact of phonetic difficulty. Contrary, perhaps, to our intuitive sense of these matters, a scientific theory which presents two radically different explanations (the human genome *and* phonetic "difficulty") for a single phenomenon is not twice as good as one which presents a single coherent account for the phenomenon in question—it is, in fact, not nearly as good. It seems singularly odd to assert that constraints, which regulate, according to the traditionalist view, relationships between an input form (a featural representation) and a winning candidate (a featural representation), are "motivated" by what is (relatively, though apparently not very) difficult for an independent aspect of human life—the articulation which results from the transduction of the phonetic representation. The encapsulated nature of the phonological computation under the traditionalist view makes such explanations as unlikely as they are— in light of the available phonetic "explanation"—irrelevant. We will return to these issues below.

6.3.2 *Phoneticists*

The "phoneticist" view of OT departs from the traditional assumptions about the nature of the "output". This can be seen from some of the constraints which have been proposed in this tradition. For example, Steriade (1997: 17) proposes the following constraints:

- FORTITION: "Consonants must be realized with increased closure duration at the onset of stressed syllables."
- TAPPING: "Alveolar stops must be tapped in intervocalic contexts, where tap refers to: the extra-short duration of closure, the lack of concomitant jaw raising gesture and the absence of a glottal opening gesture."

To evaluate a given candidate against these constraints one must know, obviously, whether it shows an "increased" or "extra-short" duration of closure, whether it involves a "concomitant jaw-raising gesture", and whether it lacks a "glottal opening gesture". Compare also Hyman's (2001: 144) description of Flemming (1995), who, Hyman notes, "proposes various auditory constraints

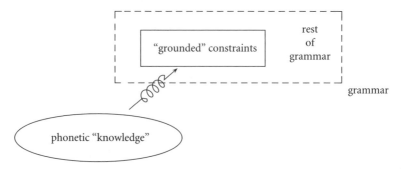

FIGURE 6.1 The origin of "grounded" constraints

within OT which refer directly to formant structure". To evaluate such constraints one needs to know the formant structure of the candidates.

It is clearly incoherent to hold that these constraints refer to bodily output in any direct sense. This would require, for the evaluation of the candidate set, the actual articulation of each candidate so as to determine what properties it manifests—e.g., whether the closure has an extra-short duration or what the formant structure of the articulated string is. Instead, what must be envisioned is a gestural (or, in the case of Flemming 1995, an acoustic) *representation* as output. The basic idea behind various versions of this model (which differs from author to author) is that some acquired or innate "phonetic knowledge"[8] gives rise to (a subset of) the constraints (which are not, therefore, themselves innate) used in the generation (via an Optimality Theoretic grammar) of output representations. Either through the uniformity of early ("prelinguistic") experience with one's articulators and the acoustic effects generated by their manipulation, or by virtue of the fact that they come into being through the (uniform) workings of innate "phonetic knowledge", the same set of constraints are generated by all humans (see (62) below). The precise nature of the mechanism involved in the origin of these constraints is not spelled out in the work under discussion (this motivates the rather non-direct arrow symbol in Figure 6.1).

Thus, under "phoneticist" assumptions, the phonological computation is a mapping of the following type: *phonological representation* (featural) ⤳ *gestural or acoustic representation*, where the gestural or acoustic representation is non-featural (or uses a set of features distinct from that used in the phonological representation). The fact that the basic alphabet of the

---

[8] Sometimes described as "knowledge of relative perceptibility conditions, knowledge of auditory consequences of gestural timing, etc." (Steriade 1997).

representation system undergoes a shift in this mapping—i.e., that it involves a transduction—is indicated by the wavy arrow.

Given that this theory is relatively new, there is much which has yet to be made explicit about how precisely it is supposed to work. The form of "phonetic knowledge" (how is it represented?), the mechanism whereby such knowledge generates output constraints (do we end up with explicit constraints to block everything that is physically impossible?), and the specific form the resultant constraints might take are all unclear at this time. However, some matters appear to be clear. The mapping done by the phonological component is a representation-to-representation mapping (as pointed out above)—it thus does not, and cannot, directly encode "the Bernoulli effect, Boyle's Law, etc." (mentioned by Steriade 1997). Indeed, once the "phonetic knowledge" generates the constraint set, that knowledge appears to be irrelevant to the process of computation itself in adult grammars.[9] That is, by some stage in the infant's development, a set of constraints exist. Under traditionalist assumptions this is because these constraints are innate, but under phoneticist assumptions the constraints are a direct function of innate properties (without themselves being innate). From that point on (and, it is assumed, under the phoneticist approach, that no language-specific learning has occurred by the time the constraint set is generated), the two theories are distinguished by the terms used in the constraints and in the types of output generated: featural, gestural, or perceptual under phoneticist assumptions, featural under traditionalist assumptions.

Here it is of some value to note, because it does not appear at all times to be entirely clear to advocates of the phoneticist approach, that gestural representations do not have the properties of gestures. In particular, while "phonetic knowledge" may include knowledge of the "auditory consequences of gestural timing" as well as knowledge of gestural interactions, the grammar does not include such knowledge. Or rather, if it does, then such knowledge must have some representation for each phonological computation. Under standard assumptions, the interaction of the various elements of an output representation—which will give rise to the actual gestures involved—is the result of the conversion of the output *representation* to a set of gestures (by the "transducer" which converts representational schemas into action). The output representation does not contain the results of this transduction process. To advocate the inclusion in an OT grammar of constraints which make reference to issues such as the "auditory consequences of gestural timing"

---

[9] Other, more physicalist versions of the theory exist—e.g., that of Flemming—which essentially deny the existence of the grammar as a module of human cognition at all. Such views will not be further considered here.

without explicitly discussing the nature of a GEN component that would generate representations of the type that would allow for the evaluation of such constraints is such a hopelessly vague notion that it is difficult to treat it seriously in a scientific context.

6.4 An unsavory thought experiment

We would like to present now a rather unsettling thought experiment. We apologize for its mildly disgusting nature. Imagine that, because of a nuclear power plant accident, a genetically transformed human-like species came into being. These humanoids are physiologically identical to humans in every way except the following: in their necks at the base of their oral cavities they have a thin but strong membrane which expands under sufficient pressure, not unlike the croaking membrane of the *rana catesbeiana*, or common bullfrog. In particular, imagine that the degree of pressure required to expand this membrane is sufficiently small that the well-known aerodynamic problems which arise in producing voiced stops (e.g.) disappear: voicing throughout the duration of the stop closure is no problem for these near-humans.

The argument concerning the phonetic grounding of the OT constraint *VOICED-CODA (Kager 1999: 325) or Pulleyblank's grounding of the VOP no longer holds of this species. Taking first what we have termed above the "traditionalist" approach, we can see that, since UG has remained invariant (*ex hypothesi*), the constraint against voiced obstruents in codas and voiced obstruents anywhere would continue to be properties of these humanoids— let's call them *homo collitumens* to distinguish them from ourselves, with our presumably sarcastic self-designation, *homo sapiens*. In the case of the *homo collitumens*, however, these constraints are no longer phonetically motivated, since their physiological "grounding" has been removed.[10]

The question—to which of course we do not *know* the answer—which arises naturally in such a thought experiment is this: suppose we were to take three infant *homo collitumens* and expose one of them to German-type data (which shows, in coda-obstruent devoicing, the effects of *VOICED-CODA outranking FAITH[voice]), one to English-type data (which does not have *VOICED-CODA ranked high), and one to Hawaiian-type data (which shows the effects of the VOP). Remember that we have not changed the formal properties of the learning algorithm (i.e. UG survived the mutation). What types of language would our three infants construct? In our view, the answer

---

[10] It doesn't really matter if you think the aerodynamic problem is the phonetic basis for these particular constraints—we can distort the bodies of our mutants however you like to make this example probative.

to this question is obvious, under any coherent theory of acquisition (e.g., that expounded upon in some detail earlier in this book), as well as under a whole slew of less coherent ones (e.g. Tesar and Smolensky 1998, or indeed any theory which incorporates LEXICON OPTIMIZATION: Kager 1999: 32–3). The children would learn the relevant properties of the languages involved: the infant exposed to German would generate [rat] : [radəs] 'wheel', the infant exposed to English would say things like [kæt] and [dɔg], and the child exposed to Hawaiian would not have any voiced obstruents in his or her output. If some "traditionalist" disagrees that this would be the outcome, it is incumbent upon that person, it seems to us, to present the details of a learning algorithm that would generate some other outcome.

In any event, the point we think is clear: precisely the same set of grammars would result whether or not any "phonetic motivation" exists for the constraints in question. It is obvious why this is the case: the "phonetic motivation" plays no role in the acquisition process, no role in the computation of output representations, indeed, no role in the phonology at all. It is simply irrelevant. While we are fully in favor of restricting the current embarrassingly rich power of OT by imposing some limitations on the types of constraint we can attribute to UG, these limitations should be motivated by some *relevant* factors, rather than by phonetics. These would include consideration of issues in learnability, universality, and computational power and/or redundancy.

What would happen to our infants under what we have termed above "phoneticist" assumptions? We need only consider those "phoneticists" who believe that the constraints are *learned* by early "experimentation" by the infant— those who hold that the constraints are universal face the same problem in our thought experiment as did the "traditionalists". Under the assumption that constraints are posited by the infant on the basis of acquired "phonetic knowledge", the *homo collitumens* infants will *not* end up with constraints against coda obstruent voicing, nor against obstruent voicing generally, since we have modified the physical basis (the "equipment" if you will) upon which their early experimentation is performed. What types of grammar will our three thought-experiment infants construct?

The *homo collitumens* infant exposed to English-type data will presumably construct something English-like in the relevant respects: neither *VOICED-CODA nor the VOP play any criterial role (as far as we know) in the generation of English-type output forms. Similarly, the infant exposed to Hawaiian-type data will construct a grammar which lacks voiced obstruents in its output— after all, there are no voiced obstruents in the infant's input and the principle of Lexicon Optimization would not permit such an acquirer to posit any. It should be clear from this experiment that constraints motivated with reference to inventories are quite irrelevant to both acquisition processes (which must posit "inventories" based on the data received, regardless of any prejudices introduced by the constraint set) and phonological computation (there is no role for an "inventory" in the evaluation of candidate sets). Our *homo collitumens* infant exposed to Hawaiian ends up with no voiced obstruents in his/her output for precisely the same reason the *homo sapiens* infant does— there are none in the relevant Primary Linguistic Data (PLD).

Interestingly, the *homo collitumens* infant exposed to German is going to have a problem. We assume that *Voiced-Coda is *necessary* to generate German-type output—indeed, if it is not, then it isn't clear why we need the constraint at all. Since our mutant baby won't have added this constraint to his or her system during the "phonetic experimentation" phase of acquisition, are we to conclude that (s)he won't acquire German? Clearly, not having a particular constraint could hardly preclude the learner from *noticing* a particular mophophonemic alternation (we "notice" *go : went*). The answer to this acquisition riddle comes from the phoneticists themselves. For example, Hayes (1999) has the following to say regarding "ungrounded constraints":[11]

It has often been emphasized that a language's phonological structure is not always sensible. A language may have a system that is synchronically odd, as a result of a conspiracy of historical circumstances such as borrowing, or a peculiar sequence of changes, each one natural...if grammars really do permit [ungrounded constraints], then they must have some source. I would conjecture that the source is induction, in this case not over the learner's phonetic experience but over the input data...

It seems clear that even the "phoneticist" phonologists recognize that the mutant baby learning German will, via "induction over the input data", discover *Voiced-Coda on the basis of its obvious presence in numerous morphophonemic alternations.

What this thought experiment tells us is that *we get the same set of grammars with or without "phonetic grounding".* The costs incurred under the "phoneticist" approach—two transduction processes (the conversion of a representation in the "phonological" alphabet to one in a "phonetic" alphabet *within* the grammar and the conversion of the "phonetic" alphabet to actual articulation) and two distinct learning procedures (induction over "early phonetic experience" and induction over the "input data")—buy us nothing.

---

[11] Marshallese provides a good example of the type of "a peculiar sequence of changes" giving rise to an 'unnatural' system alluded to by Hayes: vowels assimilated (partially) to consonantal place (e.g. fronting of back vowels adjacent to coronal stops—ProtoMicronesian), then consonants assimilated (partially) to the rounding/backness of adjacent vowels, leading to uniformity in [back] and [round] values throughout the syllable. Each change is sensible in itself, but the result is the typologically strange set of vowels in (59).

6.5 The (seeming) importance of phonetics

Let us extend our thought experiment a bit. Because of their sexy necks, *homo collitumens* breed extensively, eventually pushing the homely-necked *homo sapiens*—who occupy the same ecological niches—out of existence. The human world now consists of billions of *homo collitumens*, speaking different languages, including some which have coda obstruent devoicing. Do we expect to find linguistic descendants of these mutants which show innovative coda obstruent devoicing? That is, would acquirers be expected to show coda obstruent devoicing when exposed to data from a target grammar which lacks this property? We think we would not, and we suspect that our "phoneticist" friends would believe the same. Coda obstruent devoicing could of course be lost in the course of transmission of grammars which possess it (as it is now, amongst us regular humans). Isn't this fact—that we would end up with a different cross-linguistic distribution of coda-obstruent devoicing than we presently find—evidence in support of the "phoneticist" position?[12]

This thought experiment relates directly to the widespread practice of using cross-linguistic statistical generalizations to establish features of the synchronic computation performed by the grammar. Aside from the well-known problem of knowing precisely how to count when making such generalizations, we will accept that there are certain synchronic linguistic phenomena (coda-obstruent devoicing, intervocalic lenition, etc.) that we all expect to find a lot, and other phenomena which we expect to be quite rare. In fact, we can think of a continuum here: Unattested > Rare > Frequent > Universal.

It is clear—indeed, it follows by definition—that UG can be invoked for the extreme right side of this continuum, and perhaps for the extreme left. But how are we to account for the "middle"? Why are some processes computationally possible but rare, and others computationally possible and frequent? In OT terms, the middle part of this continuum is typically explained with reference to the initial ranking of the constraints. If well-formedness (or "markedness") constraints are initially ranked higher than faithfulness constraints (as is widely assumed), the grammar has a "prejudice" in favor of avoiding marked structures. It presumably takes extraordinary evidence to support the construction of a grammar which will generate marked structures, whereas the default, unmarked structures will emerge from ambiguous (or clearly unmarked) evidence in the PLD. There are, unfortunately, learning

[12] We don't think the "traditionalist" approach would predict this result—the constraints, under this view, are innate and therefore should show the same diachronic effects as any well-formedness constraints are alleged to do. That is, markedness relations have not changed under traditionalist assumptions, only under "phoneticist" ones. The matter will be discussed further in the final section of this chapter.

theoretic difficulties with the assumption that well-formedness constraints start out ranked high, as we have argued in some detail in Chapter 3.

We accept that it is part of the responsibility of linguistics to account for the middle portion of the continuum cited above. It is, we think, understandable that linguists have sought the explanation for these statistical facts in the phonological component of the grammar—it appears to be a phonological continuum, after all. However, we would like to propose that the middle portion of the continuum can be coherently accounted for without reference to the synchronic phonological system at all.

6.6 Resolving the dilemma: historical phonology

We can use the fact that humans are capable of constructing only certain types of phonological computation systems to account for the "impossible" end of the scale alluded to above. Similarly, those phonological systems which are possible will, because they are built upon innate knowledge of the species, share certain properties. This makes it inevitable that there will be a "universal" end of the scale as well. Concerning the mysterious middle portion of the scale, consider the following diachronic principle, based on experimentally confirmed facts of human perception: "an acquirer cannot attend to a cue in a context in which it is relatively difficult to parse and ignore it in a context in which it is relatively salient" (Hale 1995). Given that, for example, the saliency of obstruent voicing in codas is less than in onsets, it follows from this principle that an acquirer may fail to perceive such voicing in onsets *only* if s/he does so in codas as well. Since the failure to perceive obstruent voicing contrasts is clearly a possible event (thus its existence as a type of sound change), it is clear that we predict that we will find (a) languages with voicing contrasts in both positions (e.g. English), (b) languages with a voicing contrast in onsets, but only voiceless obstruents in codas (e.g. German), and (c) languages with no obstruent voicing contrast (e.g. Hawaiian). The nonexistence of languages with a voicing contrast *only* in codas is thus a simple function of (1) the initial conditions (no language initially had the contrast only in codas) and (2) the acquisition/change principle under discussion.[13]

The relative rarity of a given phonological process, cross-linguistically, is a simple function of how likely the misperception (or sequence of misperceptions) required for the coming into being of that process is. Some particular sequences of misperceptions are extremely rare, giving rise to such "marked" systems as the vowels of Marshallese, in which the originally *articulatory*

---

[13] For a more extensive consideration of this conception of change as acquisition, see Hale (2007).

effect of vowels on adjacent consonants was misparsed as being due rather to inherent features of those consonants. Other simple misperceptions are essentially accidents waiting to happen, broadly attested in the languages of the world because the grammar is an imperfectly replicating system. It is essentially the *flawed* nature of "induction over the input data" which gives rise to historical change and, through that mechanism, to cross-linguistic "markedness" patterns. It is precisely *not* the grammar itself, whether or not its constraints are "phonetically grounded", that gives rise to these patterns. This follows trivially from the universality of constraints (whether they are universal because of early phonetic "learning" by the acquirer or because they are innate): a universal constraint cannot cause one individual to construct a grammar which differs from that of his/her linguistic ancestors, who, by hypothesis, possessed precisely the same constraints as that individual now does when they began their own acquisition task.

The most important point of this discussion is a simple methodological one. Hayes notices that, even under strongly "phoneticist" assumptions, learning through inductive generalization about the data itself is necessary. Any scientific theory which attempts to expand the set of explanatory principles beyond this, e.g., through the addition of "induction over early phonetic experience", must demonstrate that there is an aspect of the *synchronic computational properties* of the phonological system which cannot be attributed to the mechanism of which they already recognize the necessity in any event: inductive learning over the data. No such demonstration exists, or has even been attempted. Instead, facts which readily follow from any reasonable model of change—not facts about synchronic phonological computation, but facts of statistical distribution of phonological phenomena—have been invoked to justify this otherwise unmotivated expansion of our explanatory tools. We do not *need* phonetic grounding and therefore we may not use it.

6.7 A final note on "traditionalist" OT

As noted above, the "traditionalist", confronted by a world inhabited by *homo collitumens*, would assume that e.g. *Voiced-Coda would continue to be a constraint in the grammars of these mutants. If we assume that the diachronic factors which give rise to systems with coda devoicing (such as German) disappeared with the genetic innovation of this subspecies, it seems clear that, given sufficient time, the statistical foundation which forms the basis for the claim that voiced stops are "marked" in codas would disappear. Kager (1999: 11) notes that such a "typological" argument is circular in any event, pointing out that "a second (non-circular) criterion of universality should ideally accompany typological criteria: phonological markedness constraints should be *phonetically grounded* in some property of articulation or perception". However, it is precisely in the case of *homo collitumens* that the phonetic grounding of *Voiced-Coda has, through physiological evolution, disappeared. But remember that since, in Kager's system, the constraints are given *genetically*, i.e. are part of UG, the mutants *must* have the constraint *Voiced-Coda (since the grammar genes are not involved in their mutation, by hypothesis), in spite of its lack (in this thought experiment) of both typological and "phonetic grounding" support.

Note that Kager's position is not improved if he denies the diachronic assumption we have made in section 6.5 above that systems with coda devoicing would cease to come into being in the *homo collitumens* population. If, because of the presence of *Voiced-Coda in the grammar, such systems continued to come about (an assumption which requires some not-presently-available coherent learning theoretic support), Kager is still left in the uncomfortable position of recognizing that a constraint which is not phonetically grounded is still necessary, with only the "circular" typological argument to lean on.

The most intriguing question arising from the traditionalist's position that, in spite of the cognitive encapsulation of the phonological computation, constraints must be "phonetically grounded" may be a simple evolutionary one. The innate knowledge which we refer to as "Universal Grammar" must have come into being at some point in the prehistoric evolution of the species, although which precise point that was cannot at present be ascertained with confidence. How are we to know that, relative to these evolutionary ancestors of ours, we are not like the imaginary *homo collitumens*, with UG-given innate constraints encoded in our genes, but no longer "grounded" in our modern physiology? Given the requirement that all acquirers must in any event be able to make "inductive generalizations over the input data", the question is, fortunately, academic. A scientific model of human phonological competence will, with a simple reference to Occam's Razor, make no reference to "phonetic grounding".

6.8 The irrelevance of the past

In our discussion of the diachrony of the *homo collitumens*, we have touched upon the potential relevance of diachrony to resolving issues of synchronic grammar. We are in general skeptical of most attempts to exploit diachrony in synchronic work. Let us return to Catalan briefly to explain why.

One might propose adopting the analysis of Catalan that posits underlying /g/ in *sek–seɣə* because we know enough about the history of the Romance languages to know that the alternating velar reflects Latin *g*. The Latin *g* is well documented in archaic texts; it is probably the segment that a historical linguist would reconstruct on the basis of comparative evidence with other Romance languages; and it is the segment that a historical linguist would posit for an earlier stage of Catalan (in the sociopolitical sense of "language", obviously) using the methodology of internal reconstruction. This is not the place to question the methodology of historical linguistics (see Hale 2007); however, even if we assume that these methods are flawless, the extrapolation from "historical *g*" to "synchronic *g*" is unwarranted. Acquirers have *no* access to the history of their "language" beyond the data presented by their caretakers and peers. Grammars that were in other minds in different places or different epochs from that in which the acquirer lives cannot be relevant to a model of how the child represents his or her language. Any claim to the contrary depends on a set of assumptions so incompatible with our own that we do not think it is useful to pursue this issue further.[14]

---

[14] This is not to say that a confusion, or even conscious decision to not differentiate, between synchonic and diachronic issues is not rampant in the literature. For example, consider the number of textbooks that present sound change and dialect comparison problems alongside phonology problems in their exercise sections, as examples of *grammatical* computations. This practice just reflects a confusion based on notation, discussed in several places by both of us, especially Hale (2007).

7

Against typological grounding

7.1 The irrelevance of segment markedness

All phonologists will be familiar with the following argument: one should select underlying /g/ for the root morpheme in the Catalan [sek–seɣə] pair since [g] is a *less marked* segment than [ɣ], and one should only posit marked segments in a language if one is unambiguously compelled by the evidence to do so. That is, since one can develop an analysis of the Catalan data without resorting to an underlying /ɣ/, why not do so? We think that this argument holds no water, and we devote this chapter to a general discussion of the validity of the notion of markedness being invoked in such a proposal.

7.2 Form and substance in phonology

This chapter continues the development of ideas discussed in the previous chapters concerning the purview of grammar vis-à-vis other domains such as processing and acquisition. We will continue to treat phonology as a branch of the study of mental representation, the psychology of mind. In order to develop this "phonology of mind" we need to understand the relationship between form and substance in linguistic representation. A clear and compelling account of this distinction has, in our view, not yet been proposed for either phonology or syntax. In this chapter we attempt to contribute to this necessary inquiry in the domain of phonology by first defining "form" and "substance", then critiquing some recent work which implicitly or explicitly touches on the relationship between the two. We will argue that current trends in phonology fail to offer a coherent conception of form and substance and are also inconsistent with basic principles of science. Since we are not proposing a complete alternative model of phonology, we invite the reader to reflect on how our proposals could be implemented or on how our assumptions (which we believe are widely shared in principle, if not in practice) should be modified.

It has proven quite useful for linguists to conceive of a grammar as a relationship between (i) a set of symbols—entities such as features and variables, constituents like syllables, feet, NPs; and (ii) a set of computational operations (whose operands are drawn from the set of symbols), such as concatenation and deletion. The set of symbols and relations together describe the formal properties of the system. Relevant questions in discussing formal properties include "Is the system rule- and/or constraint-based?"; "Do operations apply serially or in parallel?"; and "Are there limits on the number of operands referred to in the course of a given phonological computation?"

The issue of substance essentially arises only with respect to the set of symbols, the central concern being the extent to which their behavior in phonological computation is driven by what they symbolize. For the sake of simplicity we restrict ourselves in this discussion to the set of phonological primitives known as distinctive features and to the representations which can be defined as combinations of distinctive features.

We will concentrate in this chapter on this notion of substance in phonological representation. In brief the question we are interested in is the following:

(62)   Do the phonetic correlates (i.e. the substance) of a particular distinctive feature or feature bundle have any non-arbitrary bearing on how that feature or feature bundle is treated by the computational system?

It is trivial to show that languages differ in that their computational systems treat specific features or feature bundles in a distinct manner—for example, Standard German has coda obstruent devoicing (a computational operation defined over the feature [+voice] in a particular configuration) and English does not. From this we can conclude that languages *can* treat the same symbols differently. A more challenging problem arises when we find an apparent example of cross-linguistically universal, seemingly non-arbitrary treatment of a feature or feature bundle. In such cases we must ask ourselves the following:

(63)   Is the observed pattern a reflection of substantive constraints on the computational system (i.e. the grammar), or is the pattern due to other causes?

Other a priori plausible causes include, as we shall show in what follows, the process of language change, the nature of the language acquisition device, and sampling errors. From the standpoint of grammatical theory, factors such as sampling errors are obviously uninteresting. However, language change and the nature of the learning path are also, strictly speaking, not part of grammatical theory (as we have attempted to show in earlier chapters). The modular approach to linguistics, and to science in general, requires that we both model the interactions between related domains and also sharply delimit one domain with respect to another. Occam's Razor demands that, in doing so, we avoid redundancy and the postulation of unnecessary factors.

Even before proceeding to our argument that generalizations that bear on patterns of phonetic substance are not relevant to phonological theory as we define it, we can see that there is potentially much to gain from this modular approach, in that it posits that universal phonology should be studied not just across languages but also across modalities. What is shared by the phonologies of signed and spoken languages? We believe that phonology consists of a set of formal properties (e.g. organization into syllables and feet, feature-spreading processes) that are modality-independent and thus not based on phonetic substance. The goal of phonological theory should be to discover these formal properties. Failure to appreciate this goal has resulted in rampant "substance abuse" in the phonological community. We believe that this abuse arises, at least in part, from the fact that the mnemonics used as labels for the entities over which phonological computations are stated have been defined in articulatory (or, earlier in the field, acoustic) terms. We note the striking similarity in the computational properties of phonological analyses developed by, e.g., those working in Slavic linguistics (where the use of features with acoustic labels still predominates) and those developed by scholars using features bearing labels from the articulatory domain. This similarity seems to provide strong support for a "substance-free" conception of the nature of the relevant entities.

We discuss various instances of substance abuse in the following sections, including a discussion of the putative phenomenon of phonetic enhancement in grammars. We draw on these topics for general arguments against functionalist "explanation" in linguistics. We argue that *dysfunctionalist* reasoning fares as well as its better-known rival. We conclude with a plea for a modular approach to the study of sound patterns in human languages.

7.3 Three examples of substance abuse in grammatical theory

7.3.1 *Positional faithfulness in Beckman (1997)*

Beckman (1997) proposes the constraints in (64a, b) as members of the universal constraint set:

(64)   a.   IDENT-σ_1(hi)

A segment in the root-initial syllable in the output and its correspondent in the input must have identical values for the feature [high].

b.   IDENT(hi)

Correspondent segments in output and input have identical values for the feature [high].

As Beckman explains, this set of constraints allows faithfulness to a feature, like [high], to be maintained in some contexts but not others, since the context-sensitive constraint (64a) can be ranked above a markedness constraint that is violated by, say, the presence of high vowels, *HIGH, which in turn is ranked above the general constraint in (64b). In other words, the ranking in (65) will allow surface high vowels only in root-initial syllables.

(65)   IDENT-σ_1(hi) $\gg$ *HIGH $\gg$ IDENT(hi)

This is assumed to be a welcome result:

The high ranking of positional faithfulness constraints, relative to both the more general IDENT constraints and markedness constraints, yields the result that features and/or contrasts in *just those positions which are psycholinguistically or perceptually salient* are less susceptible to neutralisation than in other locations which are not protected. (Beckman 1997: 8; emphasis original)

Beckman (1997: 5) cites more than ten psycholinguistic studies to support her claim that word-initial material is more salient than medial or final material.[1] We believe that the correct conclusion to be drawn from this psycholinguistic evidence is the exact opposite of that which Beckman draws.[2] Encoding the findings of psycholinguistic experimentation in the grammar is a mistake, because it is possible to achieve the same empirical coverage without positing new mechanisms like positional faithfulness.[3] Consider the following alternative account.

We know that children acquire spoken language primarily on the basis of acoustic input from speakers in their environment, with UG determining the hypothesis space.[4] We also know that phonological contrasts are best distinguished (perceptually) and recalled when occurring in certain positions. Imagine a child exposed to a language $\mathcal{L}_1$ which allows high vowels in all syllables—initial, medial, and final. Imagine further that $\mathcal{L}_1$ has initial stress and that stress is realized as relatively increased duration and intensity. Given this scenario, it is easy to see that a child constructing $\mathcal{L}_2$ on the basis of ouput from $\mathcal{L}_1$ could consistently fail to acquire a contrast between mid and high vowels in relatively short, quiet syllables (those that are non-initial and thus

---

[1] It is unclear whether this generalisation would hold, say, in a language with non-initial stress. It is also unclear whether Beckman's extension of psycholinguistic findings concerning word-initial syllable to *root*-initial syllables is justified. However, we will assume, for purposes of this discussion, that Beckman has stated the relevant generalizations correctly.

[2] We wish to stress that we are not singling Beckman out for any reason except for the fact that her paper appeared in a widely read journal and is well written and clear in its arguments and assumptions.

[3] For other arguments against context-sensitive faithfulness, see Reiss (1996: 315).

[4] It is a useful idealization to assume that UG does not just constrain the learning path but completely determines it. We suspect that such a position will prove most fruitful in sketching an explicit theory of acquisition, but justification for this goes beyond the scope of this discussion.

unstressed), but succeed in acquiring this distinction in initial syllables, which are stressed and thus longer and louder. This type of relationship between $\mathcal{L}_1$ and $\mathcal{L}_2$ is known as "sound change" (in particular, as a "conditioned merger"). On the other hand, it is highly implausible that an acquirer would consistently fail to correctly analyze the mid/high contrast in longer, louder (stressed) syllables, yet successfully analyze the contrast in relatively short, quiet syllables. Note that this implausibility is independent of our view of the nature of UG.

We see therefore that the existence of positional faithfulness phenomena can be understood as merely reflecting the nature of the learning situation and not a reflection of any grammatical principle:[5]

(66)   If the acoustic cues of a given contrast in the target language are correctly analyzed by the acquirer in a context where they are relatively weak, they will also be analyzed correctly in a context where they are relatively strong.

Note that (66) is essentially definitional, since the strength, or acoustic salience, of a contrast is just a measure of how easy it is to perceive. What is most important to understand is that the theory proposed here is not meant to *replace* a synchronic account of the data. So, the best synchronic analysis must somehow be able to generate vowel neutralization in noninitial syllables. The statement in (66) is meant to guide us in choosing a theory of grammar in which to couch that synchronic account, but (66) is not part of the grammar. Whatever theory of phonology one adopts, it must be able to synchronically generate the type of pattern that Beckman describes; but the predictions generated by the correct theory, *qua* phonological theory, need not replicate the predictions derivable from (66).

By adopting the view of sound change proposed here, we see that many supposedly phonological tendencies, or markedness patterns, are actually emergent properties, i.e. epiphenomenal. "Positional faithfulness" is due, not to the nature of *phonology*, but to the "sifting effect" of acquisition on the incidental, arbitrary nature of the phonetic substance. Since effects such as those observed by Beckman already have a coherent extragrammatical account within acquisition theory (and it is necessary, in any event, to have an acquisition theory), building positional faithfulness into a theory of universal phonology is a misuse, or abuse, of phonetic substance in theory construction.

---

[5]   This idea is discussed more thoroughly in Hale (2007).

7.3.2 /r/-insertion in McCarthy (1993)

McCarthy's (1993) discussion of intervocalic *r*-insertion in Massachusetts English is fairly well known, so an example should be sufficient for illustration. In this dialect, an underlying sequence, like *Wanda arrived*, is realized with a "linking" [r]: *Wanda[r] arrived*. As McCarthy himself notes (and as discussed by LaCharité and Paradis 1993 and Halle and Idsardi 1997), "r is demonstrably not the default consonant in English" (p. 189). That is, it is not the maximally unmarked consonant that an OT account predicts would emerge in such a situation. In order to account for the insertion of [r] McCarthy proposes a special *rule* of *r*-insertion: "a phonologically arbitrary stipulation, one that is outside the system of Optimality" (p. 190). There are several problems with this proposal, many of which are insightfully discussed by Halle and Idsardi. However, we propose that one of their criticisms requires elaboration. Halle and Idsardi rightly point out that "reliance on an arbitrary stipulation that is outside the system of Optimality is equivalent to giving up on the whole enterprise" (p. 337), but these authors do not discuss what we consider to be the most important aspect of McCarthy's analysis: grammars do contain arbitrary processes. McCarthy's grammar has an arbitrary component (containing rules like *r*-insertion) and a non-arbitrary component (containing the substantive OT constraints). Such a theory is empirically non-distinct from the theory we propose below, which posits that *all* grammatical computations are arbitrary with respect to phonetic substance. This is because the set of phenomena predicted to exist by our theory (with only arbitrary processes) is identical to the set of phenomena predicted to exist by McCarthy's theory (with both non-arbitrary and arbitrary processes). Since McCarthy must adopt a model which allows arbitrary phenomena (like *r*-insertion), the addition to the theory of a special subcomponent to account for alleged "non-arbitrary" phenomena violates Occam's Razor.

The diachronic source of *r*-insertion is transparent—the relevant dialects also exhibit *r*-deletion in codas, so insertion reflects rule-inversion triggered by hypercorrection. Again, the diachronic facts do not make a synchronic account unnecessary, but they show us that basically idiosyncratic historical events affect the construction of specific grammars—and, in part, how they may do so.

7.3.3 *Structural constraints on non-structures*

Perhaps one of the most problematic cases of substance abuse we have come across is McCarthy's (1996) appeal to parameterized constraints to account for opacity effects in Hebrew spirantization by invoking the notion of constraint schema. McCarthy makes some reasonable simplifying assumptions in this first attempt:

I will assume that every constraint is a prohibition or negative target defined over no more than two segments, α and β. That is, the canonical constraint is something like $*\{\alpha, \beta\}$, with appropriate conditions imposed on α and β. These conditions are as follows:

(i) a specification of the featural properties of α and β as individual segments.
(ii) a specification of the linear order relation between α and β ($\alpha < \beta$, $\beta < \alpha$, or both in the case of mirror-image rules...
(iii) a specification of the adjacency relation between α and β (e.g., strict adjacency, vowel-to-vowel adjacency...

The decomposition of the conditions imposed by a phonological constraint will be crucial in accounting for the range of opacity phenomena. Even more important, though, is this: each condition—the featural composition of α, the featural composition of β, linear order and adjacency—must also name the level (underlying, surface, or either) at which it applies. Correspondence Theory allows us to make sense of conditions applying at one level or the other. As a bookkeeping device, I will state the constraints in the form of a table...

We reproduce here the schema-based constraint that McCarthy proposes to account for Tiberian Hebrew Post-vocalic Spirantization.

(67)   Constraint for opacity in Hebrew spirantization (McCarthy 1996: 223)

*	Condition	Level
α	V	Indifferent
β	$[-son, -cont]$	Surface
Linear order	$\alpha > \beta$	Indifferent
Adjacency	Strict	Indifferent

As McCarthy says, "In correspondence terms, the meaning of this constraint is this: the constraint is violated if a surface stop β or its underlying correspondent is immediately preceded by a vowel."

This powerful constraint type has several problems. First, it compromises the OT notion of a universal, innate constraint set by allowing apparently language-specific parameterized constraints. This may not be a serious problem, since it represents an attempt to define the form of possible constraints. In other words, McCarthy could be interpreted as presenting a theory in which the intensional description of the set of constraints is universal, but languages vary in which constraints they actually incorporate (based on evidence presented to the learner).[6]

Most relevant to our present purposes, however, is the fact that such constraints undermine implicit and explicit appeals to phonetic grounding of well-formedness constraints in McCarthy's work. For example, McCarthy and Prince (1995: 88) refer to a constraint *VgV as the "phonologization of Boyle's Law". It is incoherent to argue that a constraint is motivated by the facts of phonetics, when the structures which violate this constraint need not be surface structure strings. In fact, they need not exist as strings at any level of representation.

7.4 Neo-Saussureanism

The conclusion we wish to draw from the above examples and many others like them is that the best way to gain an understanding of the computational system of phonology is to assume that the phonetic substance (say, the spectral properties of sound waves) that leads to the construction of phonological entities (say, feature matrices) *never* reflects how the phonological entities are treated by the computational system. The computational system treats features and the like as arbitrary symbols. What this means is that many of the so-called "phonological universals" (often discussed under the rubric of markedness) are in fact epiphenomena deriving from the interaction of extra-grammatical factors like acoustic salience and the nature of language change. It is not surprising that even among its proponents, markedness "universals" are usually stated as "tendencies". If our goal as generative linguists is to define the set of *computationally possible* human grammars, "universal tendencies" are irrelevant to that enterprise.

We therefore propose extending the Saussurean notion of the arbitrary nature of linguistic signs to the treatment of phonological representations by the phonological computational system. Phonology is not and should not be grounded in phonetics, since the facts which phonetic grounding is meant to explain can be derived without reference to *phonology*. Duplication of the principles of acoustics and acquisition inside the grammar constitutes a violation of Occam's Razor and thus must be avoided. Only in this way

---

[6] McCarthy does not explicitly make this argument, but it seems to us to be a better theory than the standard OT claim that all constraints are literally present in all grammars. Of course, adopting our suggested interpretation will force OT practitioners to revise their views on acquisition and, especially, *emergence of the unmarked*. This view of OT would also make it much closer to a theory of learned rules.

will we be able to correctly characterize the universal aspects of phonological computation.

John Ohala (e.g. 1990) has done the most to demonstrate that many so-called markedness tendencies can be explained on phonetic grounds and thus should not be explained by principles of grammar. Examples discussed by Ohala include patterns of assimilation and the contents of phonemic inventories. For an extensive bibliography on this topic, see Ohala (1998). We differ from Ohala in our use of the term "phonology" (which for him covers *all* aspects of the sound systems of human language), but wholeheartedly endorse his approach to explaining certain aspects of phonological typology.

7.4.1 *Substance in* SPE

It is obvious that our proposal runs contrary to most of the discussion in Chapter 9 of the *Sound Pattern of English* (Chomsky and Halle 1968). Chapter 9 starts out with an "admission" that the theory developed in the earlier chapters of SPE is seriously flawed:

The problem is that our approach to features, to rules and to evaluation has been overly formal. Suppose, for example, that we were systematically to interchange features or to replace [aF] by [−aF] (where a is +, and F is a feature) throughout our description of English structure. There is nothing in our account of linguistic theory to indicate that the result would be the description of a system that violates certain principles governing human languages. To the extent that this is true, we have failed to formulate the principles of linguistic theory, of universal grammar, in a satisfactory manner. In particular, we have not made use of the fact that the features have intrinsic content. (Chomsky and Halle 1968: 400)

Later in the chapter Chomsky and Halle themselves seem to acknowledge that, with the above-quoted assertion, they are on the wrong track:

It does not seem likely that an elaboration of the theory along the lines just reviewed will allow us to dispense with phonological processes that change features fairly freely. The second stage of the Velar Softening Rule of English (40) and of the Second Velar Palatalization of Slavic strongly suggests that the phonological component requires wide latitude in the freedom to change features, along the lines of the rules discussed in the body of this book. (Chomsky and Halle 1968: 428)

In other words, Chomsky and Halle ultimately recognize that the significant aspects of the computational system which makes up the phonological module are those which cannot be derived from functional considerations of naturalness. This conclusion is echoed elsewhere: "Where properties of language can be explained on such 'functional' grounds, they provide no revealing insight into the nature of mind. Precisely because the explanations proposed here are 'formal explanations,' precisely because the proposed principles are not essential or even natural properties of any imaginable language, they provide a revealing mirror of the mind (if correct)" (Chomsky 1971: 44).

We propose that switching the feature coefficients as described in the first quotation might lead to the description of systems that are *diachronically* impossible human languages (ones that could never arise because of the nature of language change), but not to ones that are *computationally* impossible. The goal of phonologically theory, as a branch of cognitive science, is to categorize what is a computationally possible phonology, given the computational nature of the phonological component of UG.[7]

7.4.2 *A place for substance*

It is important to note that the preceding discussion is not meant to imply that the mapping of sound to features is arbitrary. It is only the treatment of phonological representations *within* the computation that is arbitrary. Articulatory and acoustic substance *are* related to the representations we construct, but not within the grammar. The nature of this relationship is part of the theory of the process we have discussed in some detail in earlier chapters, transduction—the mapping between the physical and the symbolic (Pylyshyn 1984). As Bregman (1990: 3) points out, "In using the word representations, we are implying the existence of a two-part system: one part forms the representations and another uses them to do such things as calculate." In discussing language, we will also need to model output transducers that map from surface (featural) representations to articulatory gesture. For our purposes, Bregman's distinction corresponds to speech perception (construction of featural representations, ultimately from auditory signals) and grammar, which performs symbolic computation. We know from the existence of visual and auditory illusions that the transduction process is not simple. The perceptual system does not just form a direct record of physical stimuli. As Bregman repeatedly pointed out, we know that representations are being constructed, because only then could they be constructed incorrectly, leading to illusions.

Pylyshyn (1984: 152) provides the following discussion:

This, then is the importance of a transducer. By mapping certain classes of physical states of the environment into computationally relevant states of a device [*e.g.* a human], the transducer performs a rather special conversion: converting computationally arbitrary physical events into computational events. A description of a

---

[7] This argument, as well as some other ideas in this chapter, was anticipated by Hellberg (1980). See also Burton-Roberts (2000: section 5).

transducer function shows how certain nonsymbolic physical events are mapped into certain symbolic systems.

Pylyshyn points out that the "*computationally relevant* states are a tiny subset of [a system's] physically discriminable states" and that the "former are typically a complex function of the latter" (1984: 150). In (68) we paraphrase Pylyshyn's criteria for a psychological transducer, i.e. a transducer from physical signals to representations.

(68)   Criteria for a psychological transducer
   • The function carried out by a transducer is itself *nonsymbolic*; it is part of the functional architecture of the system.
   • A transducer is stimulus-bound, operating independent of the cognitive system.
   • The behavior of a transducer is described as a function from physical events to symbols:
      a. The domain of the function (the input) is couched in the language of physics.
      b. The range of the function (the output) must be computationally available, discrete atomic symbols (for example, feature matrices).
      c. The transformation from input to output must follow from the laws of physics.

This is where issues of substance arise: the physical aspects of the acoustic signal serve as the input into the transducer function. From that point on, in the manipulations of the constructed symbolic representations, substance is irrelevant to computation. Only the *formal* properties of such representations are accessible, and thus relevant, to the computational system.

It is worth contrasting Pylyshyn's well-articulated modular approach to that of Prince and Smolensky (1993), who directly reject the kind of extreme formalist position we advocate here.

We urge a reassessment of this essentially formalist position. If phonology is separated from the principles of well-formedness (the "laws") that drive it, the resulting loss of constraint and theoretical depth will mark a major defeat for the enterprise. (Prince and Smolensky 1993: 198; see also 1993: 3)

This view of the goals of phonology stems from a failure to observe the critical transducer/grammar distinction, i.e., from extensive "substance" abuse. It is also at odds with the well-established goals of cognitive science in general:

[I]f we confine ourselves to the scientific and intellectual goals of understanding psychological phenomena [*as opposed to predicting observed behavior*—MH&CR] one could certainly make a good case for the claim that there is a need to direct our attention away from superficial "data fitting" models toward deeper structural theories. (Pylyshyn 1973: 48)

As our discussion of markedness below will indicate, we do not believe that any "principles of well-formedness" exist, aside from those that constrain the set of possible representations. That is, we find the evidence for markedness-based constraints to be unconvincing.

The "principles of well-formedness" that Prince and Smolensky refer to and adopt as the basis of OT constraints are merely derived from the heuristic devices that constitute the intuitions of an experienced linguist. For example, we may intuitively believe that a sequence like [akra] will more likely be syllabified as [a.kra] rather than as [ak.ra] in a random sample of grammars, although both syllabifications are found, for example, in the Ancient Greek dialects. Lacking information to the contrary, it may be useful to assume that the more common syllabification is present in a new, unfamiliar language. This will allow the formulation of hypotheses that may then be tested; and the guess will turn out to be correct more often than not, if our intuitions have any basis. However, it is a mistake to assume that our intuitions reflect the nature of the system we are studying in any direct manner. The intuition that heavy things fall faster than light things is very useful when someone drops something from a window, but the intuition needs to be transcended to understand the workings of gravity. Heuristics are used by the analyst to make useful guesses about data, and guesses can be wrong. This is why OT constraints need to be violable, unlike all other scientific laws.

The pervasiveness of such "data-over-principles" approaches to phonology can be appreciated by the following quote from an influential pre-OT paper: "The goal of phonology is the construction of a theory in which cross-linguistically common and well-established processes emerge from very simple combinations of the descriptive parameters of the model" (McCarthy 1988: 84). By concentrating on what is "common", rather than on what is possible, phonology will provide (or rather has provided) plentiful material for descriptive work at some level of sophistication; but it is clear that no science should be concerned with making it particularly simple to express that which happens often. The goal of any science is to define a coherent domain of inquiry and to establish a common vocabulary for *all* events in that domain. This involves reducing the common *and* the rare events (e.g. planetary motion and the Big Bang) to special cases of an abstract set of primitive notions. All of this suggests that while a change of course for phonological theory was definitely needed in the early 1990s, certain aspects of the Optimality Theory model represent a change in the wrong direction.

7.4.3 *Acoustophilia: a warning*

Sapir (1925: 37) points out that "it is a great fallacy to think of the articulation of a speech sound as [merely] a motor habit". A corresponding error is committed in many of the studies (e.g. Flemming 1995) that argue for the increased use of acoustic information to model human phonological computation. This work tends to establish units of analysis in terms of measurements taken over the acoustic signal itself. We believe that this technique shows the negative effects of "acoustophilia"—the mental state arising from the deep and abiding satisfaction which comes from having *something* concrete to measure, in this case the acoustic signal. There is, we believe, a fairly serious difficulty with such an approach: we know with a great deal of confidence that human perception does not show the kind of direct dependency on the signal which the methodology of the acoustophiliacs requires.[8] This attitude towards the study of language echoes the overly positivist brand of empiricism adopted by the behaviorists, an attitude that was already discredited in the 1950s.

An example may make this clearer. Flemming (1995) argues from an examination of F_2 interactions in an experimental setting that it is necessary to have the grammar generate a statistical pattern which forms a reasonable match to his experimental results. A parallel from the field of the cognition of vision would examine the properties of an image as measured with, e.g., a photometer, and require of us that our "grammar of vision" generate a representation like that measured on the page. So, in Figure 7.1 below, it would require—since the triangle we see is of precisely the same color and brightness as the background (as can be verified by the use of a photometer)—that we construct a human visual system that does *not* see the triangle projecting from the page. This is of course the wrong result: the human visual system, given the input in Figure 7.1, constructs a "percept" which is very different from the patterns we might infer from photometric readings (for extensive and insightful discussion, see Hoffman 1998).

---

[8] Since phonetic substance provides the raw material for phonological theory construction, selective use of fine-grained acoustic data can give rise to insights into the nature of phonological computation. We recognize the significant body of work done on the phonetics/phonology interface with reference to acoustic studies. Keating (1988), which uncovers interesting phonetic regularities but maintains a theory of phonology which makes no direct reference to this phonetic substance, is a brilliant example.

FIGURE 7.1 Triangle constructed by visual system

The difficulty that this presents to more acoustically oriented approaches to *phonology* is fairly obvious: it is often claimed, on the basis of some physical measurement of the signal, that something is "difficult" or "easy" to perceive (auditorily), "salient" or not so salient. Again, note that the edges and inside of the perceived triangle have absolutely no physical properties to distinguish them from the background. What the visual example in Figure 7.1 shows us is that measurements taken over the raw data presented to the human auditory system should not be taken as direct evidence for what kind of data actually arrives at the *linguistic* processing system.

Turning to the domain of auditory perception, it is a well-known result of psychoacoustics that the relationship between, say, intensity of a signal and *perceived* loudness is non-linear: doubling the physical intensity of a signal does not create a signal that is judged to be twice as loud. As we move further from the physical signal, to auditory perception and on to the construction of linguistic representations, things become even less clear. In particular, when several distinct and independent cues interact in the signal (as in the cases discussed by Steriade 1997), we cannot conclude without detailed and extremely difficult studies of the nature of auditory perception that we understand the way these cues interact to form an auditory percept. It is yet more difficult to then determine how these auditory percepts get organized into *linguistic* (i.e. featural, symbolic) representations. These topics will provide psychologically oriented phoneticians and their colleagues with challenging research projects for years to come. However, the questions and the answers we hope to get are only distally related to the subject matter of phonology.

Part of the confusion in this area stems from the fact that discussion of "output" forms almost universally fails to exercise sufficient sensitivity to the contrast we introduced in earlier chapters of this book between the output of the grammar (a feature-based representation) and, say, the output of the speaker (an acoustic or articulatory event). As demonstrated most clearly by our ability to construct 3-D representations based on a black and white pattern on a printed page, there is a vast gap between physical stimuli/outputs and the internal (cognitive) representations that relate to them. Therefore, even if phonologists had a metric for the complexity or difficulty inherent in interpreting or creating certain physical stimuli or outputs (which they do not), it is apparent that there is no reason to believe that such a scale would translate straightforwardly to a markedness scale for representations. There is no reason to believe that the *representation* of the act of pushing a bar of gold is more difficult or complex or marked than the representation of the act of pushing a feather (cf. Burton-Roberts 2000). Indeed, it is important, as Pylyshyn (2000: 8) notes, to resist "the temptation to make the mistake of attributing to a mental representation the properties of what it represents".

7.5 Explanatory inadequacy

What are the implications of our view that phonology should be all form and no substance? In particular, does this conclusion about the nature of phonological operands have any positive implications for phonological theory? We think that there is one clear conclusion to be drawn. Since, as we have argued, languages appear to vary in some arbitrary ways (e.g. inserting [r] and not, say, [t]), it is necessary to develop a theory which allows for such variation. In other words, the child should be equipped with a universal computational system and a set of primitives whose precise relationship can be modified upon exposure to positive evidence. For this reason, we believe that current versions of Optimality Theory, which assume a universal set of (phonetically) substantive constraints (e.g. *VoicedCoda, Lazy), do not shed light on the nature of grammar. A set of constraint templates, with principles of modification from which the learner can construct the necessary constraint inventory for the target language, may prove to be more useful. Similarly, a rule-based theory equipped with a set of principles for defining possible rules would also allow for the type of stipulative, cross-linguistic variation we have argued is necessary. Note that, given an explicit theory of acquisition, such a "nativism *cum* constructivism" view of phonology is well constrained: UG delimits the set of possible rules or constraints; the data determines which rules or constraints are actually constructed.

In order to appreciate the fact that positing the type of substantive constraint found in the the OT literature adds nothing to the explanatory power of phonological theory, recall our discussion in the previous chapter regarding the situation in which a learner finds him/herself. Equipped with an OT type UG, a child born into a Standard German-speaking environment "knows" that voiced coda obstruents are "marked". However, this child never needs to call upon this knowledge to evaluate voiced coda obstruents, since there are none in the ambient target language. In any case, by making use of positive evidence the child successfully acquires a language like German. Born into an English-speaking environment, the child again knows that voiced coda obstruents are marked. However, the ambient language provides ample positive evidence that such sounds are present, and the child must override the supposed innate bias against voiced coda obstruents in order to learn English. So, this purported UG-given gift of knowledge is either irrelevant or misleading for what needs to be learned.

Our substance-free theory of phonology shares with OT-type theories a reliance on positive evidence. The two theories have the same empirical coverage, since we also assume that both English and German are acquired. The difference is that we leave out of the genetic inheritance "hints" that are irrelevant or misleading. We find our solution to be more elegant. Once again, note that this argument is equally applicable to markedness theories of all types, not just those couched within OT. Since markedness cannot have any bearing on learnability it is probably irrelevant to any explanatorily adequate theory of grammar. We thus propose eliminating markedness from consideration in future linguistic theorizing unless some compelling learnability argument which justifies adding it to the innate arsenal provided by UG can be coherently formulated.[9]

7.6 Discussion

Pylyshyn proposes the following thought experiment (1984: 205ff.). Consider a black box that outputs signals of spikes and plateaus. When a two-spike pattern and a one-spike pattern are adjacent, it is typically the case that the former precedes the latter, as on the left side in Figure 7.2. However, we occasionally see the order switched, but only when the two- and one-spike patterns are preceded by the double plateau-spike pattern on the right side of

---

[9] In fact, there are two distinct types of markedness in the phonological literature. Here we are concerned with substantive markedness. Simplicity or evaluation metrics of the *SPE* symbol-counting type can be seen as measuring "formal" markedness. We believe that the best approach to such formal requirements is to build them into the language acquisition device (LAD). Under this view learners never compare extensionally equivalent grammars for simplicity or economy; they just construct the one that is determined by the LAD. There is, then, no reason to introduce the terms "simplicity" and "economy" into the theory, since they are contentless labels for arbitrary (i.e. not derivable) aspects of the LAD.

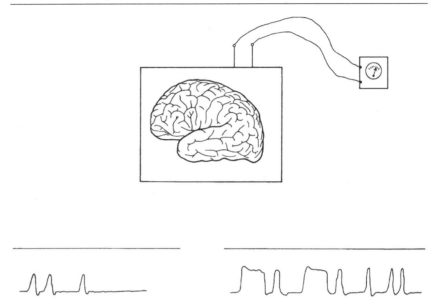

FIGURE 7.2 How do we figure out the computational capacity of the system inside the box? (Reproduced from Pylyshyn 1984 , by permission of MIT Press)

Figure 7.2. Pylsyhyn asks what we can conclude from such observations about the computational capacities of the system in the box. His answer, perhaps surprisingly, is that we can conclude almost nothing from such observations. This, he explains, is because "we would not find the explanation of the box's behavior in its internal structure, nor would we find it in any properties intrinsic to the box or its contents".

Pylyshyn's claim is based on what he designed his imaginary black box to be doing. The spikes and plateaus in Figure 7.2 correspond to the dots and dashes of Morse code, and the observed regularities reflect the English spelling rule "*i* before *e*, except after *c*". In other words, the system is processing English text. If we fed it German text, with *ie* and *ei* clusters freely occurring in overlapping distribution, we would no longer observe the same output patterns.

Pylyshyn explains:

The example of the Morse-code box illustrates … that two fundamentally different types of explanation are available for explaining a system's behavior. The first type appeals to the intrinsic properties of the system … The second type of explanation appeals, roughly, to extrinsic properties … of real or imagined worlds to which the system bears a certain relation (called *representing*, or, more generally, *semantics*). The example illustrates the point that the appropriate type of explanation depends on more than just the nature of the observed regularities; it depends on the regularities that are *possible* in certain situations not observed (and which may never be observed, for one reason or another). (Pylyshyn 1984: 205ff.)

In linguistic terms, the explanation for the patterns we see in the data (actually, either patterns we see or patterns in what we don't see, systematic gaps) may not reflect intrinsic properties of the language faculty, but instead reflect properties of the kinds of information the language faculty has access to.

We can clarify this by asking what Universal Grammar (UG) should be a theory of, and considering the relationship between this theory and available data. A rather naive first proposal would be that UG should account for all and only the attested languages. Obviously, we do not want our theory to just reflect the accidents of history, everything from genocide and colonialism to the decisions of funding agencies to support research in one region rather than another. So, the purview of UG must be greater than just the set of attested languages.

It would be an error in the other direction to propose that UG should be general enough to account for any statable language. For example, we can describe a language that lengthens vowels in prime-numbered syllables, but there is no reason to think that the human language faculty actually has access to notions like "prime number".[10] To make UG responsible for all of formal language theory would reduce biolinguistics to a branch of mathematics, with absolutely no empirical basis.

A tempting intermediate hypothesis between the set of attested languages and the set of all statable languages is the suggestion that UG is responsible for all *attestable* languages. In other words, we know that there are extinct languages, and languages that have not yet come into being, and these are attestable in principle.[11] However, even this middle-of-the road compromise turns out to be insufficiently broad, for reasons that relate to Pylyshyn's point that "the appropriate type of explanation depends on more than just the nature of the observed regularities; it depends on the regularities that are

---

[10] Actually, the notion of prime number appears to have no relevance in any empirical field. This point leads to an issue that has arisen in numerous discussions of the proposal that phonology is pure computation and thus substance-free. It has been objected that our claim is uninteresting, since it appears that we are proposing that the phonology is basically a Universal Turing Machine. This is not a valid conclusion, since our position is that phonology is all, i.e. only, computation; not that all computations can be used by the phonological faculty of the mind.

[11] Of course, in the context of mentalistic, I-linguistics, we have to recognize that only an infinitesimal number of attestable languages have been described in any detail.

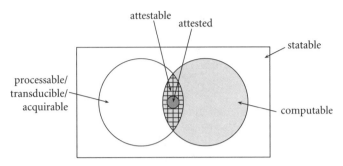

FIGURE 7.3 Attested, attestable, computable, processable, and statable grammars (repeated)

possible in certain situations not observed (*and which may never be observed, for one reason or another*)" (emphasis added).

Why should we have to account for classes of languages that can never be observed? Consider that grammars are embedded in humans and that they partially learned. It follows from this that the human transducers (input and output systems), the language acquisition inference systems, and performance systems place a limit on the set of attestable languages beyond the (upper) limits determined by S_0, the initial state of the language faculty.

Let's look again at a figure which we first presented in Chapter 1, which we repeat here as Figure 7.3. In this figure we can see, as discussed above, that the set of attested languages, corresponding to the small dark circle, is a subset of the attestable languages, shown as the hatch-marked region. Obviously, this latter set is a subset of the statable languages, the box that defines the universal set in our diagram. However, there are two remaining regions defined in the diagram that need to be explained. Note that the set of attestable languages corresponds to the intersection of two sets, the set of humanly computable languages, the large gray circle, and the white circle labeled as "processable/transducible/acquirable".

In order to be attestable, a language must be acquirable on the basis of evidence presented to a learner; an attestable language must also not overload the processing capacity of a human; and finally, an attestable language must be able to be presented to the language faculty via the perceptual and articulatory transduction systems. If a language failed to meet any of these criteria, it would not be attestable, even if it made use only of the representational and computational primitives of the human language faculty—i.e., even if it were a member of the set represented by the large light gray circle.[12]

---

[12] The careful reader will notice that the diagram in Figure 7.3 has to be interpreted as fairly informal, since the languages represented are sometimes conceptualized as grammars, sometimes as

An example of an unprocessable language, one falling outside the white circle, would be one in which all words contained at least 98 syllables—word recognition memory buffers would presumably not be able to handle such input. An example of an untransducible language would be one presented in a signal outside of the range of human hearing. We would not want to explain the fact that such a language is unattested or unattestable by appealing to properties of the language faculty *qua* computational system.

Languages that fail to fall inside the white circle may or may not fall inside the large gray circle. Those that do fall within the gray circle would fall in the part that is not hatch-marked. It would take us too far afield to present an example here of a computable language that is nonethless not acquirable— in other words fails to be attested specifically because no evidence could lead a learner to posit such a language—but the stress computation example discussed at the end of section 1.2 would qualify.

Pylyshyn's example raises the question of whether constraints are appropriate elements for the construction of grammars at all. By defining grammars via constraints, that is in negative terms, we are drawn into the problem of *inductive uncertainty*. In general, science works in terms of positive statements. A physical or formal system is defined in positive terms by a list of primitive elements, operations, relationships, etc. The set of impossible chemical or physical processes, for example, is infinite, and so is the set of impossible linguistic structures.

Consider the question of hierarchical structure in syntax. Let's imagine that we want to express the claim that all structure is hierarchically organized as a trait of UG. How should this proposal be formulated? If one seeks to characterize UG by listing constraints on the set of possible languages, then one might say something like "Flat structure is not possible". Since UG is instantiated in real brains, it must consist of a finite set of characteristic features. Note, however, that using such negative constraints, we would actually need an infinite set of statements to characterize UG. This is because it is also the case that "No language marks past tense by having the speaker eat a banana after uttering the verb", and "No language requires that listeners look at a square to interpret iterativity", etc. are also true statements about human language. In other words, there are an infinite set of constraints on the set of possible languages.

These examples are of course preposterous, because in practice the constraints are stated in terms of a (usually implicit) universe of discourse.

sets of sentences or even utterances. We think the expository usefulness of the diagram outweighs this inconsistency.

For example, the universe of discourse of linguistic theory does not include bananas, eating, seeing, and squares. Therefore, a constraint is only inter- pretable in the context of a list of positive statements (such as a list of primitive elements like phonological distinctive features, and primitive oper- ations like *Move*) which define the universe of discourse of any formal system.

The approach advocated here seems to be consistent with that used in science in general. If a physicist observes a constraint on the behavior of a particle, say, then s/he posits a set of properties for that particle from which the observed behavior emerges. The constraint thus has the status of a derivative and not primitive aspect of the theory.

The issue of "substance abuse" is closely tied to the use of constraints in phonological theory. Despite the fact that phonologists tend to characterize current debate concerning OT as a question of "rules vs. constraints", this is misleading. Many rule-based analyses make use of constraints such as the Obligatory Contour Principle (OCP). Constraints in otherwise rule-based phonologies serve two main purposes. Either they define certain structures as disfavored or ill-formed, and thus subject to modification by rule; or they are used to block the application of a rule just in case the rule's output would be disfavored or ill-formed. Work by Paradis (1988) and Calabrese (1988) are typical of the use of constraints as diagnostics for repair of certain structures. The rule-based account of stress systems presented by Halle and Idsardi appeal to "Avoidance Constraints" (1995: 422ff.), which prevent the application of rules in cases where the rules' output would be a "disfavored" structure. The OCP has been invoked for both of these purposes in a number of papers, most notably McCarthy (1986) and Yip (1988), who makes the following remark: "The main contribution of the OCP is that it allows us to separate out condi- tion and cure. The OCP is a trigger, a pressure for change..." (p. 74).

Given the problems with markedness theory alluded to above, note that in the absence of a theory of disfavoredness, this approach is slightly circular: the only real evidence for the disfavored status is that the posited rule appears to be blocked; and the reason for the blocking is that the resultant structure would be disfavored. Halle and Idsardi point out that certain advantages derive from mixing rules with constraints in the analysis of individual languages. In general, the use of constraints allows us to formulate simpler rules. However, they note that a fully rule-based analysis is in principle always possible— Halle and Vergnaud (1987) is an example they cite. We propose that con- siderations of elegance for a theory of UG take precedence over elegance in the analysis of individual languages, and thus the Halle and Idsardi system, for example, should be adapted in a way that preserves its mathematical explicitness, while doing away with constraints on unattested structures. In general, a goal of future phonological research should be to take the idea of rule-based phonology seriously—by avoiding constraints altogether. Such an approach will offer a principled alternative to Optimality Theory and other constraint-based models. In other words, rather than stating simple but empirically inadequate rules, reinforced by an arsenal of language-particular or universal constraints, we should attempt to understand what kinds of rule we actually need if we are to do without constraints. This issue is explored in later chapters when we consider the question "What is a possible phonological rule?"

7.7 The mirage of enhancement

A particulary illustrative combination of what we consider to be the misuse of substantive considerations and functionalism can be found in the literature on phonetic enhancement and the maximization of contrast (e.g. Stevens et al. 1986). For example, the tendency of three-vowel systems to contain the maximally distinct set /i,u,a/ is taken as a reflection of a phonological principle demanding the "best" use of the available acoustic space. Like other claims concerning markedness and UG, this pattern is no more than a tendency. However, we can show that the view of markedness as an emergent property, outlined above, can give insight into this statistical pattern. Imagine a language $\mathcal{L}_1$ which had the four vowels /i,u,e,a/. Now we know that merger of acoustically similar vowels (like /i/ and /e/) is a common diachronic process. It would not be surprising if a learner constructing $\mathcal{L}_2$ on the basis of data from speakers of $\mathcal{L}_1$ were to fail to acquire a slight distinction and end up with a three-vowel system containing /i,u,a/. However, it is much less likely that the learner would fail to acquire an acoustically more robust distinction like /u/ *vs.* /a/ and end up with an inventory containing, say /i, u, e/.[13] So, vowels which are close together in the acoustic space are likely to merge diachronically. Vowels which are acoustically distant are not likely to merge diachronically. The observed pattern of maximal contrast is thus not built into the phonology, but is an emergent property of the set of observed phonological systems due to the nature of diachronic sound change.

---

[13] Note that "phonetic substance" may itself indicate how weak the reasoning is in this case: English [i], as well as the other front vowels, is significantly lower than Danish [i]. Why is the "maximization of contrast" not active at the phonetic level—precisely the level which provides the alleged "substance" (perceptual distinctness, in this case) for the functionalist claim?

7.8 Functionalism and dysfunctionalism

The rise of Optimality Theory has been accompanied by a revival of functionalism in phonology. In fact, there is no necessary connection between OT as a theory of computation and functionalist reasoning, and an OT proponent might invoke what we call the NRA defense ("Guns don't kill people; people kill people"): Computational theories aren't inherently functionalist, people are functionalist. However, the ease with which functionalist ideas can be implemented in OT has clearly invited this "functionalist" explosion, and may bear on the question of whether or not the theory is sufficiently constrained or even constrainable. Note also that the "logic" of functionalism (i.e. that *all* phenomena are explicable by reference to competition between universal, but violable, principles) is identical to the logic of OT. In this section we briefly show that the "substance" orientation of functionalism can be turned on its head to yield a theory which we will dub "dysfunctionalism".

Many functionalist theories of grammar can be summarized in almost Manichaean terms as consisting of a struggle between the "competing forces" of ease of articulation (what is presumed to be "good" for the speaker) and avoidance of ambiguity (what is presumed to be "good" for the hearer). As an example of the former, consider Kirchner's constraint "Lazy—Minimize articulatory effort" (1997: 104). For the avoidance of ambiguity, consider Flemming's (1995) Maintain Contrast constraints, which are violated by surface merger of underlying contrasts.

The interplay of what is "good for" the speaker and what is "good for" the hearer supposedly gives rise to the patterns we see in language: sometimes mergers occur and the speaker's output is "simplified"—potentially creating a difficulty for the hearer; sometimes the speaker maintains distinctions, perhaps producing a more "complex" output, thus avoiding ambiguity for the hearer.[14]

The problem with this theory is that functionalist principles can be replaced by their opposites, which we will call "dysfunctionalist" principles, with no significant change in the set of grammars predicted to exist. Consider the following principles, proposed by a linguist with a different view of human nature from that of the functionalists.

---

[14] Further evidence for the incoherence of the functionalist position is the fact that "careless" speech often can lead to supposedly complex outputs such as the stop cluster in [pt]*ato* for *potato*. Onset stop clusters are not found in careful speech, so it is surprising, from a functionalist perspective, that these "difficult to articulate" sequences should be found precisely when the speaker is *not* putting forth greater articulatory effort.

(69) Principles of dysfunctionalism

OBFUSCATE: merge contrasts, use a small inventory of distinctive sounds, etc.

NO PAIN–NO GAIN: maintain contrasts, use a large inventory, generate allomorphy, etc.

Merger, widely attested in the languages of the world, as well as the oft-proclaimed diachronic principle that "change is simplification", will be accounted for by the (dys)functional requirement that one should OBFUSCATE. The failure of merger, equally well attested, and the generally ignored diachronic process of "complexification", will be attributed to the effects of the NO PAIN–NO GAIN Principle. The competition of these two "dysfunctionalist" principles will thus lead to essentially the same results as the usually cited functionalist principles. While the ultimate question of whether human beings are fundamentally lazy, but helpful, or something seemingly more perverse is intriguing, it hardly seems that investigation into such matters should form the foundation of a theory of phonological computation.[15] We propose, therefore, that functionalism provides no insight into the nature of grammar. Again, we propose leaching all substance out of phonology in order to better observe the abstract computational system.

The alternative—which seems to be the focus of many current developments in phonological theory—seems clear. Given a sufficiently rich and explicit theory of the human personality (giving us principles such as "be lazy" and "be helpful to the listener"), the human articulatory and perceptual systems ("phonetic" substance), phonology itself will turn out to be epiphenomenal. While this seems considerably less promising to us, it has clear implications for the research strategy which phonologists should adopt. Phonologists, under such a view, should focus their energies in two domains: phonetics and the empirical explication of fundamental features of the human personality ("laziness", "helpfulness", etc.).

The anti-functionalist stance taken here is, of course, not new. For example, Halle (1975: 528), points out:

Since language is not, in its essence, a means for transmitting [cognitive] information—though no one denies that we constantly use language for this very purpose—then it is hardly surprising to find in languages much ambiguity and

---

[15] The authors would be happy to provide examples—drawn from the history of linguistic theory— of the evolutionary advantages of self-interested effort (NO PAIN–NO GAIN) and OBFUSCATE. We refrain for reasons of space, fully confident that the reader will have no difficulty generating ample evidence on his or her own.

redundancy, as well as other properties that are obviously undesirable in a good communication code.

Halle suggests that it is more fruitful to conceive of language as a kind of mathematical game than to concern ourselves with the "communicative functions" approach to studying language. The latter viewpoint led to such dead ends as the application of formal information theory to natural language.

Indeed, the history of the idea of "substance-free" phonology goes back quite far in linguistics, having had strong advocates in the so-called Copenhagen School, especially within the movement now generally known as "Glossematics", whose chief architects were Hjelmslev and Uldall. To quote from the excellent survey of the phonological work of these scholars presented in Fudge (2006), glossematicians held "that the scientific description of form must be entirely independent of substance, and, *a fortiori*, of purport". In response to critics asking how one might discover anything about form without making reference to substance, Fudge (2006: 88) notes that:

> The apparent paradox is resolved by noting that it is not on the level of discovery that substance must be excluded from consideration. The discovery phase of any scientific enterprise is inductive... in nature: the investigator must begin by examining observable data, which of course must involve physical properties of substance. He or she then proceeds to set up hypotheses about what must be the abstract formal system capable of accounting for the data. The workings of this formal system, on the other hand, are deductive...; here the starting point is the hypothesized basic entities, the relations between them being stated formally, i.e., in terms which are not related to substance...

While Hjelmslev and his students were not working under the kind of strong mentalist assumptions which have become the norm in modern linguistics, and which we ourselves clearly embrace, we share the glossematicians' belief that the computational system (which establishes the "relations" between "basic entites" mentioned in the quote) operates without regard to substance.

7.9 Conclusion on substance

We are advocating that phonologists, *qua* phonologists, attempt to explain less, but in a deeper way. As we hope to have indicated, empirical results provided by phoneticians and psycholinguists contribute to the development of a substance-free phonology, and we look forward to important cooperation with scholars in these fields. We recognize that only they can provide explanation for many (E-language) generalizations which are striking in their statistical regularity.[16] Since we believe that the focus of phonological theory should be on the cognitive architecture of the computational system, we also believe that the non-substantive aspects of Optimality Theory have been tremendously important for the development of the field. The best of the OT literature is far more explicit about the nature of the assumed computational system than its predecessors typically were. The mere existence of such a well-developed alternative to rule-based phonology is valuable, regardless of specific formal problems (e.g. synchronic "chainshifts") or the "substance abuse" found in any particular implementation. However, we have also raised the question of whether constraints are appropriate entities for scientific modeling, since they must always be accompanied by a somewhat redundant positive characterization of a universe of discourse.

The critique of markedness theory, and especially its role in determining segment inventories, is relevant to the Catalan problem in that we must dismiss any argument that rules out positing underlying /ɣ/ because it is a "marked" segment. Obviously, this provides no argument in favor of /ɣ/, but it may strengthen the case for /ɣ/ by weakening the case against it. We will pursue this further before we bring this book to a close.

---

[16] But see Engstrand (1997) for arguments that sometimes the statistics may be misleading. For example, the purported markedness of /p/, as evidenced by its relative rarity in voiceless stop inventories, vis-à-vis /t/ and /k/, is probably illusory. The overwhelming majority of the languages in a database like UPSID (Maddieson 1984; Maddieson and Precoda 1989) lacking a /p/ are found in Africa. Similarly, the languages of Africa do not "avoid" voiced velar stops, which are also commonly assumed to be marked (see the discussion of Boyle's Law in Section 7.3). "Thus, it cannot be concluded that velars and bilabials constitute underrepresented members of the respective voiced and voiceless stop series. Although this pattern is to be expected from proposed production and perception constraints, it is largely overridden by areal biases" (Engstrand 1997: 1).

Part III
Some aspects of Optimality Theory

8

Against constraints

That which is wanting cannot be numbered.

Ecclesiastes 1: 15

8.1 Introduction

Many linguists, especially phonologists, have assumed that both Universal Grammar and particular grammars contain constraints, *qua* prohibitions on grammatical structures.[1] However, such prohibitions *cannot* be learned by positive evidence (an infinite number of well-formed structures are absent from the PLD—we may find a supposed ill-formed structure in the next sentence we encounter). Therefore, these prohibitions could only be learned via negative evidence. However, it is generally accepted that negative evidence is neither supplied to the child with sufficient regularity, nor attended to sufficiently by the child when supplied, to play a significant role in language learning. Therefore, since the prohibitions cannot be learned via positive evidence (for reasons of logic), nor through negative evidence (according to the empirical data), they must be innate.

This conclusion follows from the premises, but we believe it to be false. The fault lies with the assumption that UG, and also particular grammars, consist of a set of constraints.

In this chapter we justify rejection of this premise, and demonstrate how the need for constraints can be circumvented, while still allowing a learner to converge on a grammar in a finite amount of time. In other words, we will outline a constrained learning path, but one which does not depend upon language-specific or universal constraints to achieve the relevant limitations on the acquirer's hypothesis space. We thus escape from the tendency to develop overly rich models of Universal Grammar that have culminated in recent theories such as Optimality Theory.

---

[1] We compare these approaches to recent developments in Minimalist syntax below.

The goal of this chapter is to argue that well-formedness constraints are inappropriate computational devices for modeling grammar. Thus the chapter attempts to do in phonology what recent work by scholars such as Samuel Epstein (Epstein 1999; Epstein et al. 1998; Epstein and Seely 2006) is attempting in syntax: to develop a purely derivational theory with minimal theroretical apparatus and no filters or well-formedness constraints. Similar ideas are discussed by Szabolcsi (1988). The conceptual arguments will be bolstered by reference to recent work which seeks to develop approaches to phonological computation which offer an alternative to constraint-based ones.

8.2 The universal NOBANANA constraint

Let's turn to a preposterous example. Suppose we are seeking a constrained theory of UG for syntax and we are trying to choose between a theory with the components in (70.a) and another with the components in (70.b):[2]

(70)   Which model of UG is better?

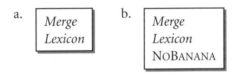

Model (a) contains the rule MERGE which operates on elements of the LEXI-CON. Model (b) contains both of these components as well as the constraint NOBANANA which marks as ungrammatical any representation of a sentence containing a banana—an actual banana, not the lexical item *banana*. At first blush, it may seem sensible to claim that (b) is a more constrained model than (a), since (a) has no way of ruling out sentences that contain bananas, whereas (b) quite explicitly does. However, imagine, we hope not too counterintuitively, that there are no bananas (actual bananas, remember) in the lexicon, and that no process of Merging elements drawn from the lexicon could ever give rise to an actual banana (because of the nature of lexical items and the properties of the MERGE operation). The more restric-tive theory would thus be (a), since it is characterized by a subset of the elements needed to characterize (b) in that it does not require the constraint NOBANANA to be part of the proper characterization of the grammar, and

---

[2] We are obviously making simplifying assumptions here. The point is just that one model has a set of entities and the second has all those plus an additional constraint.

the two models generate the same set of outputs (i.e. they have the same extension).

Consider another preposterous example in (71).

(71)   Which model of UG is better?

a.

Merge
Lexicon

b.

Merge
Lexicon
NoLexicalItemsSentToYpsilanti

In (70) we considered the effect of enriching a model of grammar by adding a constraint referring to entities not found in the set over which MERGE applies. In (71b), we have added a constraint referring to an operation that is not present in the model of the grammar in (71a). Let us assume, again in keeping with standard practice, that the proper formal characterization of the MERGE process will not give it the capacity to send lexical items to Ypsilanti. It should be clear that since *Merge* does not have such a capacity, and since the grammars characterized in (71) contain no other operations, it is not necessary to rule out representations for which lexical items have been sent to Ypsilanti.

What makes the preceding examples preposterous is that constraints are supposed to be formulated in terms of a (typically implicit) *universe of discourse*. Note that the claim intended by the constraint NoBanana, that no representation of a sentence contains bananas, is probably true for all human languages. However, there are an infinite number of true claims of this type. No language requires speakers to dance a jig to express iterativity; no language has pizza as an element of syntactic trees; etc. Bananas, pizza, dancing of jigs, sending, and Ypsilanti are not elements of grammatical models. In other words, we do not want our model of grammar to express every true statement about what structures do not occur, since there are an infinite number of such statements and the grammar must be statable in finite terms if it is to be instantiated in human brains.

The conclusion suggested by the preceding discussion is that the search for UG should be conceived of as the attempt to characterize the universe of discourse, the entities and operations that give rise to the representations computed by the language faculty. UG is thus to be characterized by a list of categories and formal operations that take these categories as arguments—and nothing else.

A coherent conception of the "perfection" of the language faculty, one that does not cave into the temptation of functionalism, is that the formal system that defines UG, as well as every particular grammar, is exhaustively definable: there is a finite list of categories and operations that uniquely determines all and only possible linguistic structures.[3] Again, UG should not be conceived of as a set of constraints defining directly what is *not* a possible human language, because this set has an infinite number of elements. The notion of what is not a possible language will follow from an appropriate characterization of the properties of possible languages, but this notion need not be independently formulated in the grammar.

This chapter not only develops this argument concerning what UG should not be, but also makes concrete suggestions concerning how the study of UG should be approached. In section 8.3 we define constraints in opposition to rules, then we return to the issues raised earlier in this chapter in order to point out two slightly different ways in which inviolable constraints have been used. We then turn to a discussion of violable constraints, as used in Optimality Theory. We conclude on philosophical grounds that linguistic theory should be rule-based (in a sense to be established) rather than constraint-based: grammars contain rules (as defined below), not constraints (as defined below).

In section 8.4 we briefly show that the ideas presented here converge with some recent work in syntax. We then discuss, in section 8.5, the use of constraints in conjunction with rule-based phonology, concentrating in section 8.6 on the Obligatory Contour Principle (OCP) for illustration. Following Odden (1988) we argue that there is no good theoretical or empirical motivation for positing the OCP. The argument extends readily to other constraints that have been posited in the literature.

Section 8.7 compares rule- and constraint-based approaches to phonology. We argue for a revival of rule-based phonology, but not a return to the mixing of rules and constraints, and offer a contribution to the understanding of *formal* aspects of Universal Grammar. The results presented here demonstrate that progress in our understanding of UG does not depend upon the characterization of substantive tendencies subsumed under the notion of markedness. The connection between these ideas and issues addressed earlier in the book concerning the acquisition of phonology, and how learning can be constrained without constraints, are presented, together with a conclusion, at the end of the chapter.

---

[3] In other words, the definition of UG, and of particular grammars, can be understood as including a final, exclusion clause of the type used in recursive definitions in logic. We address below the problem of overgeneration—the fact that the set of possible linguistics structures is a superset of attested structures.

8.3 On constraints

This section discusses in general terms various uses of the notion of constraint in linguistic theory. First we discuss the distinction between rules and constraints. We then discuss constraints on grammars, i.e. constraints on what is a possible language. We then turn to inviolable constraints within grammars. Next, we discuss violable constraints as the basis of grammatical computation, as in Optimality Theory. We argue that each of these approaches to defining UG suffers from a combination of a lack of elegance and a mistreatment of the problem of inductive uncertainty.

8.3.1 *What is a rule? What is a constraint?*

Mohanan (2000: 146) argues that, due to basic logical equivalences, the oft-drawn distinction between rules and constraints loses all significance once we recognize that both rules and constraints express propositions. However, in the following definitions we distinguish rules and constraints both in terms of their role in a computational system (a grammar) as a whole and in terms of their putative "grounding" in phonetics.

8.3.1.1 *A system-internal definition of rules vs. constraints*   Various practices in the literature may be at odds with the definitions developed here. This purely terminological issue does not bear on the validity of the dichotomy proposed. So, for example, we may find formal statements that are called "constraints" in the context of a given theoretical framework, but which are in fact examples of what is here called a "rule". In some work, e.g. Karttunen (1993), the terms "(declarative) rules" and "constraints" are used interchangeably.

A rule R can be viewed as a function that maps an input representation I defined in terms of a set of representational primitives (features and relations) to an output representation O which is defined in terms of the same set of primitives. The application of a rule depends upon a potential input representation matching the structural description of the rule. This representational matching procedure (RMP) outputs two possible results: YES, I satisfies the structural description of R; or NO, I does not satisfy the structural description of R. If the output of the RMP is YES, R applies and relevant parts of I are rewritten as O. If the output of the RMP is NO, I is not affected.

In a constraint-based theory, constraints also contain RMPs that serve to map an input I to one of the two possible results YES or NO, as above. However, for each constraint, one of the two values, YES or NO, maps to a further evaluation called VIOLATION and the other to NOVIOLATION. The use to which this evaluation is put rests with another part of the computational system. Violation of a constraint thus must be passed on to other parts of the computational system. In theories incorporating inviolable constraints, constraint violation prevents a representation from being evaluated as grammatical. In Optimality Theory the violations are used by EVAL, the evaluation procedure which interprets violation with respect to the relative ranking of the constraints.

To reiterate and summarize: a rule is defined as a function from representations to representations; a constraint is defined as a function from representations to the set {VIOLATION, NoVIOLATION}.

The role of constraints in a computational system, which inform another part of the system that a representation is somehow ill-formed, is related to the issue of NoBANANA, discussed above, as follows. There are an infinite number of ways in which a representation can be ill-formed. The NoBANANA discussion is intended to show that it is a bad move to try to constrain models of grammatical knowledge such that the grammar itself would have to be able to recognize them all.

8.3.1.2 *The system-external basis of well-formedness constraints*   In many constraint-based linguistic theories, a crucial aspect of constraint evaluation leading to the the equivalent of an output value VIOLATION is the notion of ill-formedness or markedness. This represents the second major problem with constraint-based formalisms, as defined here.

Depending on the formulation of a given constraint, either matching or failing to match the structural description of the constraint signals ill-formedness. For example, a constraint formulated as "Don't have a coda" leads to an evaluation of ill-formedness for a syllable which *has* a coda. A constraint formulated as "Have an onset" leads to an evaluation of ill-formedness for a syllable which *does not have* an onset.[4] The reasons for which linguists evaluate linguistic representation as marked, or as relatively or absolutely ill-formed often derive from factors external to the grammer. Marked or ill-formed structures typically are claimed to have at least one of the following properties:

(72)   Markedness criteria
  • Relative rarity in the languages of the world.
  • Late "acquisition" by children (typically referring to the absence in the bodily output of an acquiring child in the early stages).
  • Loss in aphasia (typically referring to the absence in the bodily output of the aphasic speaker).

---

[4] The distinction between such negatively stated and positively stated constraints will not be relevant to the remainder of this chapter.

- Relative difficulty of perception (not always experimentally validated).
- Relative difficulty of articulation (again, generally based on the advocate's impression of what is "hard to say").
- Tendency to be lost in language change and to not arise in language change.

All of these criteria have been criticized in some detail by us either earlier in this book or in other published work (Hale and Reiss 2000 and references therein). In Chapter 7 we argued that the best way to gain an understanding of the computational system of phonology is to assume that the phonetic substance (say, the spectral properties of sound-waves, or the physiology of articulation) that leads to the construction of phonological entities (say, feature matrices) *never* directly determines how the phonological entities are treated by the computational system. The computational system treats features as arbitrary symbols. Thus many of the so-called "phonological universals" (often discussed under the rubric of markedness) are in fact epiphenomena deriving from the interaction of extragrammatical factors like acoustic salience and the nature of language change. Phonology is not and should not be grounded in phonetics, since the facts which phonetic grounding is meant to explain can be derived without reference to phonology. We return to these issues in the critique of the Obligatory Contour Constraint later in the chapter.

Again, we can readily relate our discussion to the issues raised by the proposed NoBanana constraint. Why do bananas make representations bad? Because they are not part of the system under scrutiny. But why should a grammatical constraint refer to something that is not part of grammar at all? More commonplace constraints, such as NoFrontRoundVowel, are, to the extent they are conceived of as *substantive* constraints (without doubt the norm in OT and in earlier phonological literature), as poorly motivated as NoBanana once we recognize that phonetic substance *cannot* be encoded in the phonology. Neither the acoustic nor the articulatory properties of front, rounded vowels are directly accessible to the grammar.[5]

8.3.2 *Karttunen (1993)*

We will not review all the literature debating the status of intermediate levels of representation, distinct from both input and output forms, that has appeared in the history of phonology, especially that focusing on Optimality

---

[5] Note how irrelevant this makes the debates on whether it is better to characterize the feature set using acoustic or articulatory labels.

Theory and its immediate predecessors and contemporaries (particularly given the recent retreats from OT's original strong surface orientation as seen in McCarthy 2006). However, a few comments concerning the influential article of Karttunen (1993) are in order. We think that careful consideration will show that much of the debate concerning sequential vs. parallel derivation is empty.

Karttunen discusses the fact that phonological rewrite rules can be implemented by a finite state transducer. One advantage of expressing rules in this fashion is that transducers express relations between inputs and outputs bidirectionally, and thus can be more immediately useful in developing processing models for both production and parsing. A further advantage is that transducers corresponding to single rules can be composed into a single transducer that implements a "cascade" of ordered rules (1993: 180). Thus, the ordered rule format and the transducer format are alternate means of expressing phonological knowledge. The intermediate representations of traditional rule-based phonology need not have a real-time processing referent—they can be understood as corresponding to the contribution made by each component transducer of a complex transducer.

It is interesting to examine Karttunen's ultimate explanation for a turn to two-level models with neither complex transducers nor ordered rules: "the composition of large rule systems to a single transducer turned out to be unfeasible because of practical limitations. A single transducer encoding the complexities of a language like Finnish was too large for the computers available in the early 1980's" (1993: 180). Available computational resources have increased significantly over the last two decades, but in any event, such technological considerations are not obviously relevant to the evaluation of psychological theories, especially to the rejection of models that allow reference to intermediate levels of representation.

Whatever the status of the two-level models that arose from such considerations, there are a few points of interest in the context of this chapter. As Karttunen states, the "most fundamental aspect of the two-level rules is that they are deontic statements about correspondences that are possible, necessary, or prohibited in a certain environment": they are "modal statements about how a form can, must or must not be realized" (Karttunen 1993: 181). In other words, the rules/constraints of the two-level models that Karttunen discusses are purely formal statements, not grounded in phonetic substance. Thus, the arguments used to motivate such a model do not necessarily extend to Optimality Theoretic models which invoke substantive markedness as a computationally relevant aspect of the theory.

8.3.3 *Constraints on grammars*

It is a commonplace in the linguistic literature to find statements suggesting that a goal of linguistic research is to define UG by formulating the constraints on what is a possible language. This enterprise is typically seen as integral to explaining the paradox of language acquisition, in the following way. If the child is endowed with innate knowledge of the constraints delimiting the set of humanly attainable languages, then the child's hypothesis space is limited. Instead of choosing from the infinite set of (not even necessarily attainable) grammars, the learner need only select from a predetermined subset of those. Of course, we might make this idea more palatable to some by referring to constraints on the learner's ability to make hypotheses, rather than to knowledge of these constraints, but this is just a matter of terminology. We wish to argue that a characterization of UG in terms of such constraints can be at best merely a derivative notion.

It is necessary to stress that we are concerned in this subsection with constraints *on* grammars, not constraints *in* grammars. We are not concerned, for the moment, with evaluating the merits of constraint-based computational systems such as Optimality Theory vis-à-vis rule-based grammars, for example, although we turn to this topic below.

Instead of the preposterous examples in (70) and (71) above, consider the question of hierarchical structure in syntax. Let's return to an argument we mentioned earlier: imagine that we want to express the claim that all structure is hierachically organized as a trait of UG. How should this proposal be formulated? If one seeks to characterize UG by listing constraints on the set of possible languages, then one might say something like "Flat structure is not possible" or "All structure is hierarchical". Again, since UG is instantiated in real brains, it must consist of a finite set of characteristic properties. Note again that we would actually need an infinite set of constraining statements to characterize UG—those referring to bananas, jigs, etc. There are an infinite number of such constraints on the set of possible languages.

In order to avoid having an infinitely long list of constraints, constraint-based theories need a *list* of positive statements of entities (distinctive features, primitive operations like MERGE, etc.). This list will define the universe of discourse in which we interpret a constraint like "Flat structure is not possible". We see, then, that a theory which formulates linguistic universals in terms of constraints must *also* contain a vocabulary of elements and operations in which those constraints are expressed, or to which they refer. This vocabulary of items and processes is presumably based on empirical observations and inferences. Once again, we urge consideration of a simpler alternative.

If our current hypothesis concerning UG is stated only in *positive* terms, as statements of what grammars have access to or consist of, without prohibitions or constraints, we can achieve a more economical model. The positive terms are just those entities and operations (features, deletions, insertions, MERGE, MOVE, etc.) which have been observed empirically or inferred in the course of model construction. When faced with a phenomenon which is not immediately amenable to modeling using existing elements of the vocabulary, scientific methodology (basically Occam's Razor) guides us. We must first try to reduce the new phenomenon to an analysis in terms of the vocabulary we already have. If this can be shown to be impossible, only then can we justify expanding our apparatus.

Thus a "constraining approach" to UG, stated in terms of what is disallowed, requires a set of constraints, as well as a vocabulary which defines the universe of discourse in which the constraints are valid. The alternative proposed here requires only the vocabulary of possible entities and operations, along with the metatheoretic principle of Occam's Razor. This alternative is thus more elegant and should be preferred.

In more concrete terms this means that our theory of UG should consist of the minimum number of primitives that we need to describe the grammars we have seen.[6] Note that we should not be influenced in our search by preconceived notions of simplicity. For example, if we know that we need hierarchical structure for some phenomena, but there exist other phenomena which are ambiguous as to whether they require flat or hierarchical structure, then we should assume that the ambiguous cases also have hierarchical structure. If our current theory of UG contains an operation which obligatorily generates hierarchical structure from primitive elements, constraints against flat structure will be superfluous. In fact, positive statements like "Structures are organized hierarchically" and "All branching is binary" (assuming they are correct) are also superfluous within the grammar itself, even though they are descriptively accurate, since they are just a reflection of how structure-building operations work (see section 8.4).

8.3.4 *Inviolable constraints in grammars*

It was suggested above that the issues raised thus far are irrelevant to the choice between rule-based and constraint-based computational systems. In a sense this was an overstatement, and the discussion above is in fact clearly relevant to a certain class of constraints invoked in some versions of Optimality Theory, as

---

[6] According to Rennison (2000: 138) this principle has, in practice, been more vigorously upheld by proponents of Government Phonology (GP) than by members of other schools of phonology.

well as other models of phonology: constraints that are never violated, either universally or within individual grammars.

For the sake of concreteness let's adopt a version of Optimality Theory which assumes that it is never the case that the winning candidate in a derivation, in any language, has crossing association lines.[7] There are several ways to deal with this. One possibility is to claim that there exists a constraint, NoCross, that is part of the OT constraint hierarchy which incurs a mark when a candidate contains crossing association lines. This constraint can be posited to be universally undominated, or rather, universally undominated by a "competing" constraint, where a competing constraint which dominated NoCross would be defined as one whose satisfaction could "force" a violation of NoCross in the winning candidate. This can be construed as allowing simplicity in the theory—allow GEN to generate candidates freely, and leave it to universally undominated constraints like NoCross to rule out candidates with no chance of surfacing. However, the simplicity achieved is somewhat illusory.

This approach introduces a complication into the core idea of Optimality Theory, the idea that grammars are defined by constraint hierarchies. If one adopts the view that constraints are universal and innate, then certain constraints, the undominatable ones such as NoCross, will have to be kept in a separate stratum of the constraint hierarchy, one whose members are not subject to reranking. Equivalently, they can be marked as not susceptible to reranking.

Yet another approach is to claim that these constraints are high-ranked at the initial state of the grammar. According to the claim of Smolensky (1996) and most other scholars, they would therefore start out at the top of the block of initially high-ranked Well-formedness constraints. If one is willing to accept such a scenario,[8] then the undominatable constraints need not be marked as unrerankable, since by hypothesis no language ever has evidence that they are dominated. However, the significance of the generalization that OT grammars consist of freely rerankable constraints is greatly reduced if, in fact, some of the constraints are never reranked in any language.

We see then that each of the versions of undominatable constraints proposed here leads to complications in the theory of grammar. An obvious

---

[7] This is a particularly well-known and easily discussed constraint. However, Local and Coleman (1994) have demonstrated that it is basically contentless.

[8] But of course we have argued in some detail above that it is untenable. We claimed above that the (normal, rerankable) Well-formedness constraints must start out ranked below the Faithfulness constraints in order to allow the acquisition of a lexicon. If one adopts this assumption, then, the undominated Well-formedness constraints like NoCross would have to be initially ranked in a block separated from all the rerankable Well-formedness constraints, or somehow marked as not rerankable.

alternative is to state the constraints as limitations on GEN. In other words, assume that GEN freely generates—except that it does not generate forms that violate NoCross and other undominatable constraints. But this still fails to solve the need to define the universe of discourse for GEN. We would need constraints on GEN to keep it from generating representations that violate NoCross, but not ones that violate NoBanana, presumably. But GEN has certain properties, it does certain things with inputs, and we should try to characterize those properties. Therefore, it seems preferable to model GEN in such a way that it does not have the capacity to output forms with crossed association lines and other impossible traits (including bananas). In other words, the arguments against constraints *on* grammars and undominatable or inviolable constraints *in* grammars are the same—we always need a positive characterization of the formal system we are modeling.

8.3.5 *Free generation and constraints as filters*

The dominatable, or violable, constraints of both standard OT, which assumes universal, innate constraints, and other theories which allow language-specific constraints, do not immediately appear to pose the problems discussed thus far. Such constraints are formal devices for evaluating candidates, but they do not, each on its own, define what is a possible linguistic representation. However, we will argue in this subsection that even a constraint-based grammar which contains violable constraints is to be avoided. In section 8.6, we will see that the original motivation for such constraints may have been empirically and methodologically misguided.

Various theories of grammar, including Optimality Theory and some versions of Minimalism and its predecessors, posit a mechanism that allows unconstrained generation of linguistic representations. In OT this device is GEN, which, given an input, generates the universal candidate set of possible outputs. In various syntactic theories, an analog to GEN is the "free" concatenation of morphemes, or the "free" application of operations such as Move α. A derivation which is thus generated will either satisfy certain conditions at PF and LF, the grammar's interface levels, and thus *converge*; or it will not satisfy those conditions and it will *crash*. Both the OT approach and the free-generation-with-interface-conditions approach in syntax are, in our view, flawed in the following (related) ways.

First, it is easy to proclaim something like "GEN generates any possible linguistic representation" or "the syntactic component allows Move α to apply freely". However, it is not clear what such statements mean. One could argue that the theory of grammar need not be computationally tractable, since grammar models knowledge and does not necessarily map directly to an algorithm for generating grammatical output. However, it does not follow from this that we should immediately aim for a model that we cannot imagine being implemented in the mind. It seems that any implementation of GEN or the syntactic component that incorporates Move α will have to be very explicit about what it does, and how it is that it comes to do *that*. One way to achieve this is to be explicit about what the abstract grammar generates.

Second, the free generation-*cum*-filters model stinks somewhat of anti-mentalism. It basically says, "We don't care *how* the candidate forms are generated, as long as all of them *are* generated. One way is as good as the next, as long as the candidate sets are *extensionally* equivalent." This is parallel to the position taken by Quine (1972, discussed by Chomsky 1986) in arguing that it is incoherent to talk about the "correct" grammar among a class of extensionally equivalent ones (an argument we have dealt with earlier in this book). Recall that we noted than that in defining I-language, a matter of "individual psychology", as the domain of inquiry for linguistics, Chomsky (1986) argued convincingly that the fact that knowledge of language is instantiated in individual minds/brains means that there is necessarily a "correct" characterization of a speaker's grammar (or grammars). Unfortunately, Quinean anti-mentalism does continue to show up in current theorizing.

Once one accepts that modules/processes, like GEN and Move α, must have a certain set of properties, and that these properties ultimately must be described with a set of positive statements (a vocabulary), and that these properties can be incorporated into the structural descriptions of rules, it appears to be the case that a procedural or rule-based approach to grammar that generates a sequence of representations constituting a derivation is to be preferred to a constraint-based, non-derivational theory. Grammars can be understood as complex functions mapping inputs to outputs. A rule-based model just breaks the complex function into simpler components, in order to understand the whole. A theory that incorporates GEN or Move α avoids the problem of explicitly characterizing the function that is the grammar. Thus a rule-based derivational model of grammar has distinct methodological advantages, since it can be stated in purely positive terms, without prohibitions.

8.3.6 *The fallacy of imperfection*

> It ain't why, why, why. It just is.
>
> Van Morrison

In phonology at least, it appears that the obstacle to developing such a theory has been an a priori belief in the relative well-formedness of abstract representations based on the never explicitly (nor circularity-free) formalized notion of markedness. In other words, even the rule-based phonological literature is rife with constraints which are meant to "motivate" the application of rules that repair structure. In syntax, the tradition of appealing to markedness is more subtle, but it has basically been adapted in that the grammar, or perhaps the processor, is characterized with respect to derivations which "crash", as well as with respect to ones that "converge".

Consider for comparison the visual system. Given an input, the visual system is assumed to have certain biases, probably manipulable via the little-understood mechanism of *attention*; but no visual input leads to a failure to assign a representation. It is also not clear what it would mean to say that a given representation generated by the visual system was less well-formed, or more marked than another representation. Presumably the visual system generates representations based on the input it is given, and these representations are the best and the worst (or rather, neither the best nor the worst) that the system generates for that input. Outputs are generated which depend on the input and the state of the system processing the inputs—hardly a controversial view. The same holds true of phonological representations—they are not perfect or imperfect, better or worse, *they just are*.

Recall here that the violable OT constraints are posited on the basis of cross-linguistic typology, data from child speech, and the informal intuition of linguists. Defining markedness based on cross-linguistic *tendencies* of absolute and implicational patterns of attestation (e.g., if a language has voiced stops, it also has voiceless ones) raises many difficult issues, not least of which is "How do we count?" Do we count tokens? E-languages like "English" or "Chinese"? Grammars?[9] Without an explicit theory of what gets counted and *why* it is scientifically responsible to count these entities (as opposed to some others), generalizations based on intuitive "statistical" patterns are worthless. Furthermore, as mentioned above, at least some of the reported statistical tendencies, such as the more common absence of [p] from voiceless stop inventories, in comparison with [t] and [k], are highly reflective of areal biases in the sampling procedure (see Engstrand 1997).

---

[9] We are collapsing Chomsky's discussion of a sociopolitical conception of "language", common in everyday parlance, with the E-language conception which he includes among the scientific approaches to the study of language. The E-language approach treats a language as an external artifact, say a text or corpus of texts, rather than as a knowledge state. This collapse is, we believe, justified and consistent with Chomsky's views, since the decision to include various texts or utterances within a single E-language corpus is typically made on the basis of the everyday sociopolitical notion of language—how else can an E-linguist decide that a set of texts constitutes a single corpus, except by appealing to the pretheoretical notion that they are all French or English or Swahili?

We have argued in detail in Chapter 3 that the use of child speech data to determine markedness status is flawed, since this data is rendered opaque by the effects of children's performance systems. We need not repeat these arguments here. Linguists' intuitions concerning "better" (unmarked) and "worse" (marked) structures reflect a confusion of levels of analysis, as well as other conceptual problems. Discussion of the evaluation of "output" forms often fails to distinguish between the output of the grammar (a feature-based representation) and, say, the output of the speaker (an acoustic or articulatory event). As demonstrated most clearly by our ability to construct 3-D representations from the necessarily 2-D visual input data, there is a vast gap between physical stimuli and outputs and the representations that relate to them. Therefore, even if phonologists had a metric of the complexity or difficulty inherent in interpreting or creating certain physical stimuli or outputs (which they do not), it is apparent that there is no reason to believe that such a scale would translate straightforwardly to a markedness scale for representations. In short, we have found throughout our consideration of the relevant domains in this book no support for the alleged empirical foundations for substantive markedness.

8.3.7 OT constraints as fallible intuitions

> We should know that one intrinsic characteristic of a heuristic is that it is *fallible*, and that it may be unjustified.
>
> Piatelli-Palmarini (1994: 22)

The preceding discussion suggests an explanation of why the constraints of OT are violable. These constraints are for the most part derived from so-called "principles of well-formedness" or "markedness" found in other phonological theories. We believe that these "principles" are actually just the heuristic devices that constitute our intuitions as experienced linguists. To repeat our earlier example, we may assume that a sequence like [akra] will more likely have a syllable boundary before the stop-liquid cluster than between the two consonants. This is because we seem to believe, rightly or wrongly (it is hard to imagine how to collect the appropriate statistics under the I-language approach), that the majority of languages "maximize onsets" in such cases and leave the first syllable without a coda. However, as we pointed out in the last chapter, cross-linguistically both syllabifications are found. Lacking information to the contrary, it may be useful to assume that the more common syllabification is present in a new, unfamiliar language. Heuristics are used by the analyst to make useful guesses about data, and guesses can be wrong. This is why OT constraints need to be violable—they reflect the fallibility of our guesses.

It may be useful to refer to the error under discussion as a confusion of epistemological issues (concerning the nature of our knowledge) with onto-logical ones (concerning the nature of phonological systems). One explana-tion for the pervasiveness of such errors may lie with our terminology. A term like "physics" or "phonology" is used in a systematically ambiguous fashion. "Physics" means both "the study of the properties of the physical world, including gravitational attraction, etc." and "the properties of the physical world, including gravitational attraction, etc." When one falls down the stairs, one does so not because there is a field of study that concerns itself with gravity, but because of the nature of the physical world, because of gravity itself. One would fall down the stairs even if all the physicists and physics books disappeared—we assume people fell down the stairs before Newton. By failing to make this crucial distinction we can be misled into believing that the *tools* (intuitions) we use in phonology *qua* field of study of the nature of sound systems are constitutive of phonology *qua* the nature of sound systems.

We think the use of violable well-formedness or markedness constraints in OT that are based upon putative statistical tendencies has exactly the status of this kind of error.

8.3.8 *Overgeneration*

The computational possibility of forms not attested in any human language is not only plausible but highly likely, given the fact that the language faculty is embedded in a complex system of other cognitive and physiological modules with which it interfaces. Consider the following example. Suppose that the rule $\mathcal{R}$ of a formal system combines the primitive categories of the system $\{a, b, c, d, e\}$ into ordered pairs such as $< a, b >$, $< e, c >$, $< b, d >$. Sup-pose that after collecting a sample of data we notice that all ordered pairs have occurred except for $< a, d >$. If we then supplement our characterization of the formal system by adding a constraint $*<a, d >$, what have we gained? We have merely built the descriptive generalization into the grammar. Two preferable alternatives come to mind.

The alternative suggested by Pylyshyn's example of the "Morse code box" (discussed in the previous chapter) is to look outside the formal system itself. In phonology, for example, the shape of phoneme inventories reflects the nature of sound change and physiological constraints on articulation, not just the cognitive capacity of humans. Not only is it misleading and uninsightful to posit constraints on the formal system that do no more than recapitulate observation, but it also discourages us from looking for a real explanation in a domain other than the characterization of the formal system. The latter approach—that which seeks explanation outside the formal system itself—is adopted later in this chapter to provide an account for unattested patterns of quantification in phonological rules.

A second alternative to explore is to examine whether ℜ has been correctly formulated. Many constraint-based linguistic analyses are built by positing a spurious generalization (spurious not only because of the parade of empirical difficulties confronting the grounding of substantive markedness which we have presented above, but also in light of the attested output forms), then adding constraints to the model to account for the cases which do not match the generalization. It seems more elegant to posit our generalizations more carefully. This approach is taken below in our discussion of so-called OCP effects.

Does the preceding dismissal of concerns of overgeneration reduce to the following methodological lesson: "Posit a rule that generates all the attested data, and assume that unattested data is the result of accidental gaps in the corpus"? Fortunately, this is not the position we are advocating, and this is because of a simple claim that is in direct conflict with general practice, at least in the phonology literature—a claim we have sketched out in Chapter 4. The claim is that rules are formulated in the *least* general form that is compatible with the data.[10] Generality of application results from lack of specification in structural descriptions; lack of generality, i.e. restrictiveness of application, results from richly specified structural descriptions. Recall that in the view of acquisition developed here, it is claimed that representations that are more highly specified than necessary for the purposes of generating target output are a logical necessity in early grammars. Rules are only made more general, i.e., given less specified structural descriptions, upon exposure to positive evidence. Therefore, a rule of a particular grammar will generate all and only the data whose representations are subsumed by that encountered during the acquisition process. It follows, of course, that the well-established contrast between systematic and accidental gaps is preserved under our model (though the decision as to the empirical status of particular "gaps" will of course be different under our assumptions than under more traditional ones).

---

[10] For example, the reader will recall that we asserted that the Georgian lateral fronting rule that applies before the vowels [i,e], given that Georgian has only the vowels [i, e, a, u, o], should be formulated with the conditioning environment as "before [−back, −round, +tense, −low] vowels", and *not* as "before [−back] vowels".

8.4 A right-minded approach to syntax

The conclusion to be drawn from the discussion above is that it is in fact best to state our theory of UG in terms of a positive list of what can occur. This approach actually does delimit the set of possible languages as well as a theory that states constraints on possible linguistic structures, because the normal interpretation of a formal system defined by a set of properties (a vocabulary) is that the system is exhaustively defined by those properties. One can add or subtract one of Euclid's Postulates and explore the consequences of such a move, but any set of postulates is assumed to be exhaustive once stated. Similarly, in physics new elementary particles are posited only when a phenomenon cannot be accounted for by appeal to those currently identified, or when their existence is predicted on other grounds. Since linguistics posits formal models of (indirectly) observable systems, our current theory is open to revision when forced by new discoveries, but Occam's Razor serves as a check on the current version at any particular time. A model characterized by prohibitions in the form of constraints must implicitly be itself constrained by a vocabulary defining the universe of discourse in which the constraints hold. Therefore, such a model contains a certain amount of unnecessary redundancy.

The derivational approach to syntactic relations developed in Epstein et al. (1998) adopts a viewpoint consistent with the "rules only" approach to modeling grammar advocated here. These authors claim (1998: 13–14) that their theory has five innovative properties. The first and the last are most clearly relevant to the discussion in this chapter and can be summarized as follows:

(73)   Epstein et al. (1998)
   - The syntactic computational system consists only of syntactic rules. There are no relations (like *Government*) that are not derivable from the nature of the rules.
   - There are no filters or constraints (on nonexistent levels of representation such as DS and SS), but only lexical items and operations on these items.

These authors are able for the most part to do away with independently stipulated constraints on movement such as GREED and SHORTEST MOVE and instead build their effects into the nature of the rule/process MERGE itself. We understand the goal of this model to be to formulate a rule/process MERGE which applies in such a way that its outputs are well-formed, as long as it is possible to generate a well-formed output from the current input. Perhaps a better way to describe the model is to say that outputs are "formed", or "not formed", and that the notion 'well-formed" is undefined—and unnecessary.

In the rest of this chapter we explore a similar approach to phonological derivation. First, we recap some background on the use of constraints within primarily rule-based phonologies. Then we demonstrate the insight that can be gained by building the effects of constraints into the statements of the rules themselves.

8.5 Constraints in rule-based phonology

As we pointed out earlier, despite the fact that phonologists tend to character-ize current debate concerning OT as a question of "rules vs. constraints", this is misleading (see Archangeli 1997). Many rule-based analyses made (and, to the extent they are still practiced, continue to make) use of constraints (e.g. the Obligatory Contour Principle, or OCP). Constraints in otherwise rule-based phonologies serve two main purposes. Either they define certain structures as disfavored or ill-formed, and thus subject to modification by rule; or they are used to block the application of a rule just in case the rule's output would be disfavored or ill-formed. We mentioned in the last chapter that work by Paradis (1988) and Calabrese (1988; 2005) use constraints as diagnostics for repair of certain structures: if a string satisfies the structural description of a constraint, i.e., if it violates the constraint, it must be repaired by a rule. We also pointed out that the rule-based account of stress systems presented by Halle and Idsardi (1995) appeals to "Avoidance Constraints" (1995: 422ff.) which prevent the application of rules in cases where the rules' output would be a "disfavored" structure. Recall that the OCP has been invoked for both of these purposes in a number of papers, most notably McCarthy (1986) and Yip (1988).

Given the problems with markedness theory alluded to above, note that, in the absence of a theory of disfavoredness, this approach is circular: the only real evidence for the disfavored status is that the posited rule appears to be blocked; and the posited reason for the blocking is that the resultant structure would be disfavored. Halle and Idsardi (1995) point out that certain advan-tages derive from mixing rules with constraints in the analysis of individual languages. In general, the use of constraints allows us to formulate simpler rules. However, they note that a fully rule-based analysis is in principle always possible—Halle and Vergnaud (1987) is an example they cite:

In Halle & Vergnaud (1987), the full metrical constituency was constructed, and at the end disfavored configurations [like stress clash] were eliminated by the application of a rule.

We proposed above that considerations of elegance for a theory of UG take precedence over elegance in the analysis of individual languages, and thus the Halle and Idsardi system, for example, should be adapted in a way that preserves its mathematical explicitness, while doing away with constraints on unattested structures. A possibility which Halle and Idsardi (1995) do not consider[11] is to make the structural descriptions of their rules more complex. As they point out, some languages do tolerate stress clash, and thus their avoidance constraint is specific to those languages which do not tolerate clash. The rewards of allowing for more complex rules are considerable: constraints become unnecessary and the effects of earlier rules need not be undone.

In brief, Halle and Idsardi need the avoidance constraint AVOID(x(to prevent the generation of Line 0 metrical structures such as (x (x x (x x in a language like Garawa that (1) inserts the leftmost left parenthesis on the basis of an Edgemarking rule, and (2) inserts left parentheses iteratively from the right edge after every second syllable. In a word with an even number of syllables, steps (1) and (2) give e.g. *(watjim(paŋu*. However, in a word with an odd number of syllables the rules outlined above would generate a "disfavored" (x(structure like *(na(řiŋin(muku(njinam(iřa*, where the leftmost syllable has a left parenthesis on both its right and its left. The avoidance constraint blocks the insertion of a parenthesis to the left of the second syllable from the left, and the actually generated Line 0 form is *(nařiŋin(muku(njinam(iřa* with a trisyllabic leftmost constituent.

Instead of appealing to an avoidance constraint, the so-called Iterative Constituent Construction rule can be specified to insert a left parenthesis only in the environment x x _ x x. By the normal conventions of interpretation, the structural description is not satisfied by the following structure: x(x _ x x. Thus the stress clash configuration is not generated.[12] Again, we cannot rule out such complications to rules a priori, without considering that the use of the simpler rule requires adding an additional rule to the grammar (in the Halle and Vergnaud formulation) or else enriching grammatical theory by the use of avoidance constraints (in the Halle and Idsardi formulation).[13]

---

[11] Idsardi (1992), however, does have a useful discussion of rule-, constraint-, and rule-and-constraint-based approaches to stress.

[12] Because it is not relevant to the discussion, we ignore here the further steps in the derivation, those which follow the construction of the Line 0 structure.

[13] There are, in fact, other plausible rule-based analyses. Morris Halle (p.c.) points out that by first building a single binary foot from the *left* edge of the word, then building binary feet iteratively from the right, the third syllable from the left will remain unfooted in words with an odd number of syllables, but not in those with an even number.

Even number of syllables: x x) (x x (x x
Odd number of syllables: x x) x (x x (x x

We thus propose that a goal of future phonological research should be to take the idea of rule-based phonology seriously—by avoiding constraints altogether. Such an approach will offer a principled alternative to Optimality Theory and other constraint-based models. In other words, rather than stating simple but empirically inadequate rules, reinforced by an arsenal of language-particular or universal constraints, we should attempt to understand what kind of rule we actually need if we are to do without any constraints.

Part of the groundwork for this approach was done about two decades ago in a pair of underappreciated papers by David Odden (1986; 1988). Odden demonstrated that the OCP is demonstrably *not* a universal constraint on either underlying representations or on the workings of the phonological component. Odden also points out that work appealing to the OCP is unacceptably vague in defining how, for example, identity of representations is computed.

8.6 The Obligatory Contour Principle

McCarthy (1986) discusses data from several languages in which a vowel which is expected for independent reasons to be deleted is instead preserved if its deletion would cause identical consonants to be adjacent: Biblical Hebrew /ka:tab-u:/ → [ka:θvu:] but /sa:bab-u:/ → [sa:vavu:] because deletion would bring together the two underlying [b]s (both of which are spirantized by an unrelated process).[14] The "failure" of the deletion rule to apply is dubbed "antigemination" by McCarthy, since the rule is "blocked" if its application would produce a geminate. McCarthy invokes the Obligatory Contour Principle (OCP) as the constraint which blocks the rule from applying. This phenomenon involves the failure of deletion rules just in cases where the rule would result in a string of identical adjacent consonants.

Yip (1988) provides a very useful summary, elaboration, and discussion of McCarthy's treatment of the OCP as a blocker of rules. Consider the following argument:

If a language has a general phonological rule that is blocked just when the output would contain a sequence of identical feature matrices, we can conclude that the OCP is operating to constrain derivations . . . The alternative is an ad hoc condition on such rules, as in [(74)]:

By projecting the leftmost syllable of each foot, the correct Line 1 configuration is generated for all words.

---

[14] It has been brought to our attention that vowel length in the Hebrew is actually difficult to determine. However, this issue is irrelevant to the point under discussion—any example of "antigemination" will do. Additional examples from the phonological literature are provided in the discussion below.

(74) $A \rightarrow \emptyset / B\_\_C$
       Condition: $B \neq C$

Such a condition not only incurs an additional cost (whereas the OCP is taken to be universal) but also lacks explanatory power, particularly if contexts B and C are necessary only to state the ad hoc condition.

In other words, Yip argues that a theory with language-specific rules and a universal OCP is a better theory than one with language-specific rules that correctly encode where the rule applies, because adding the necessary conditions to the statement of such rules makes them more complex.

Note that the examples that Yip mentions conform to the first of the following three types of condition on rule application; but Odden (1988) points out that in fact vowel syncope rules are found with all three of the following types of conditioning:

(75)   Some conditions on vowel deletion rules (Odden 1988: 462)
       a.   Delete a vowel unless flanking Cs are identical.
       b.   Delete a vowel blindly (whatever the flanking Cs are).
       c.   Delete a vowel only if flanking Cs are identical.

Condition (a) can be restated as "Delete a vowel if flanking Cs are *not* identical". This is the condition described but rejected by Yip in (74) above: $B \neq C$. But note that Odden's type (c) condition would be written as follows:

(76)   Odden's Condition (c) in the notation Yip rejects: $B = C$

In other words (a) demands non-identity and (c) demands identity of segments in the structural description of a rule. A rule like (75c) *only* applies when it creates OCP violations—Odden refers to this phenomenon as "antiantigemination". So a theory of UG must allow for both types. There is thus no good reason to claim that a universal principle, the OCP, *blocks* deletion in the (a) cases, since deletion can also be *required* in cases that lead to apparent OCP violations when a rule with conditions (b) or (c) applies. Stated in McCarthy's terms (although he does not mention such cases), deletion can be blocked (in case (c)) if the rule will *not* generate an OCP violation. This point was clearly made by Odden, though it seems to have been ignored in most of the subsequent literature.[15]

Note that the logic of attributing cases that fit the profile of (a) to a universal principle, and ignoring cases that fit (c), is incoherent. Suppose we examine some data concerning a certain phenomenon and find that all cases fall into

---

[15] For example, Keer's (1999) recent OT thesis on the OCP lists Odden's papers in the bibliography, but makes no reference to them in the text, even in sections discussing antigemination.

two categories, *x* or *y*. If we present only cases of *x* and proclaim that we have found that *x* is always true, then our claim is not valid, *no matter how many positive examples of x we adduce*. The existence of (c) cases makes the existence of (a) cases uninteresting on their own. Odden's observations taken together *are* interesting, as we will see below. Simply put, case (c) is a counterexample to the claim that (a) is universal.[16]

8.6.1 *Treating phonological pathology: the OCP as a rule trigger*

The main point of Yip's paper is that the OCP not only *blocks* rule application as in McCarthy's antigemination cases, but also *triggers* it—it may be the case that a rule applies only to an input that violates the OCP. Instead of an argument based on formal simplicity in rule statements, as discussed above, Yip's discussion of the OCP as a rule trigger illustrates particularly well the assumption that the phonology repairs structures that are somehow pathological—ill-formed or "marked" or disfavored: "The main contribution of the OCP is that it allows us to separate out condition and cure. The OCP is a trigger, a pressure for change" (1988: 74).

In Yip's model the "cure" is effected by language specific rules. In OT models that make use of similar constraints, the "cure" emerges from the constraint ranking. Because of the violability of OT constraints, the winning candidate in an OT derivation is typically not fully "cured"—certain marked structures may be present in the output form.[17] One goal of this chapter is to work towards removing the notion of ill-formedness from the generative component of the phonology. There are representations that are generated, or formed, by grammars; there are representations that are not generated, i.e. not formed; but there is no reason to believe that anything a grammar actually generates has any special status along the ill-formed/well-formed dimension—all such representations are simply "formed".

Yip provides a range of examples that show how different solutions can be applied to OCP violations. They include deletion, dissimilation and assimilation rules (where assimilation represents multiple linking of a single node, and not identical adjacent nodes). One example of repair by deletion comes from Seri (Marlett and Stemberger 1983). This language has a rule that deletes a coda glottal stop in a syllable with a glottal stop in the onset:

---

[16] Providing a principled response to the reader who finds this discussion to constitute an argument for the violable constraints of Optimality Theory is beyond the scope of this chapter, or perhaps even impossible, reducing to a question of faith.

[17] We might refer to this idea as OT's Fallacy of Imperfection. Imperfection, or markedness, seems to be as irrelevant to linguistic theory as is the notion of perfection.

(77)   Seri glottal stops
    a.   Ɂa-a:Ɂ-sanx → Ɂ-a:-sanx "who was carried"
    b.   Ɂi-Ɂ-a:Ɂ-kašni → Ɂi-Ɂ-a:-kašni "my being bitten"
    c.   koɁpanšx "run like him!"

The rule only applies to tautosyllabic glottal stops, so the second glottal stop in (77b) is not affected. In general, coda glottal stops can surface, as shown by (77c).

    Yip's account of this process is the following:

[We can] assume that the Laryngeal node is absent except for /Ɂ/, and the entries for glottalization in [78ab] are thus adjacent and identical and violate the OCP. This violation triggers a rule that operates in the domain of the syllable, and the language chooses [one of the possibilities for repairing OCP violations,] deletion of one matrix (either [+constricted] or [Laryngeal]). The actual rule has four parts, as shown in [(78)]:

(78)   Glottal Degemination
    Domain: Syllable
    Tier: Laryngeal
    Trigger:
    Change: Delete second

The environment is not stated, so the rule is unable to operate unless triggered "from the outside". The outside trigger is, of course, the OCP, a universal principle and thus free of charge.

    In another example, Yip proposes that English uses epenthesis to "cure" OCP violations of adjacent coronal stridents, thus accounting e.g. for the form of the plural morpheme after coronal stridents: *judges, couches, bushes, cases,* etc. In other words, if epenthesis did not apply, the adjacent coronal stridents would constitute an OCP violation. As Odden (1988) points out, the OCP is invoked rather opportunistically—note that it appears to be irrelevant to identity of adjacent [+voice] specifications in words like *bins, rugs, hills, cars.* More seriously, Odden points out that there are rules that insert vowels only when doing so will specifically *not* repair an OCP violation. This is case (d) below. There are also rules that insert vowels regardless of the nature of the flanking consonants—case (e). And of course there are rules that, like English epenthesis, depend on the total or partial identity of flanking segments—case (f).

(79)   More conditions on vowel insertion rules (Odden 1988: 462)
    d.   Insert a vowel unless flanking Cs are identical.
    e.   Insert a vowel blindly [whatever the flanking Cs are].
    f.   Insert a vowel only if flanking Cs are identical.

Parallel to (a), condition (d) can be restated as "Insert a vowel if flanking Cs are *not* identical." Thus there is no reason to see (f) as reflecting the OCP as a trigger when (d) shows that rules may be triggered if and only if they *fail* to fix OCP violations. The existence of rules with conditions (c) and (d) make it unlikely that appealing to the OCP as either a trigger or blocker of rules is a fruitful endeavor.

8.6.2 *The Identity and Nonidentity Conditions*

More of Odden's data will be presented below. For now, note that it is just as possible for a rule to generate OCP violations (c) as it is to repair them (f). And it is just as possible for a rule to be "blocked" from generating OCP violations (a) as to be blocked from fixing them (d).[18] Since the goal of phonological theory should be to define the set of computationally possible human languages, Odden's observations provide an excellent opportunity to study the purely formal nature of linguistic rules. In the following discussion, we will concentrate on syncope rules as a matter of expository convenience. Again, for expository convenience, we will refer to a schematic representation C_1VC_2. Odden's conditions (a) and (c) can be restated the following:

(80) The NONIDENTITY CONDITION on syncope rules (Version 1)
      Delete a vowel if flanking Cs are *not* identical ($C_1 \neq C_2$).
(81) The IDENTITY CONDITION on syncope rules (Version 1)
      Delete a vowel if flanking Cs are identical ($C_1 = C_2$).

The apparatus of phonological representation must be at least powerful enough to express the Nonidentity Condition and the Identity Condition. This issue has implications for Feature Geometry as a model of phonological representation.

There is an insightful discussion of the need for Identity Conditions in Archangeli and Pulleyblank (1994: 368–73). These authors point out that "linked structures themselves are simply one type of configuration involving identity" (p. 369). Archangeli and Pulleyblank present the "Identity Predicate", a relation holding between two arguments, which "is important in a wide variety of phonological contexts" (p. 369). In addition to the OCP cases, they cite the case of Tiv, where [+round] spreads between vowels if and only if they agree in height. A linked-structure analysis of Identity Conditions will not work for many cases discussed in the literature, since the cases invoked

---

[18] Of course, (b) also potentially generates OCP violations, and (e) potentially repairs OCP violations.

include those in which where identity holds across a morpheme boundary: since the identical features in such a case belong to different lexical items, they cannot be stored as linked.

Reiss (2003a) formalizes the Identity and Nonidentity Conditions, and offers further arguments for the inadequacy of a "linked structure" analysis of these conditions. He also argues that autosegmental feature geometry cannot express such conditions, and that a sufficiently powerful formalism makes feature geometry unnecessary, and thus not part of phonological theory.

The crux of the argument against autosegmental representation is that nonidentity conditions require that two segments be distinct. This cannot be expressed using just feature-geometric association lines. For example, imagine a requirement that C_1 and C_2 be different with respect to some arbitrary feature, i.e. any feature, or any feature out of a predefined subset of all the features. In other words, the two segments must *not be identical*, but it doesn't matter how they differ. In order to express such a Nonidentity Condition we can make use of something like the existential quantifier: there exists at least one feature for which C_1 and C_2 have different values. We cannot depend on feature geometric association lines.

8.7 Constraints alone vs. Rules & Constraints vs. Rules alone

A reader may have been convinced by this brief sketch to accept the necessity for the additional power granted to the representational component argued for here—the necessity of quantification—without accepting our proposed rejection on methodological grounds of constraints. The formulation of constraints that can evaluate identity and nonidentity would also require the use of quantification. Therefore, constraints on their own, or constraints in conjunction with rules, do not vitiate the need for quantificational statements in grammars.

Consider, however, what we gain by adopting a minimalist approach to characterizing the phonological component in terms of rules: we have a rule component which allows the use of quantificational statements; we have no notion of well-formedness or ill-formedness—the phonology maps inputs to outputs. In the following table we compare three approaches to building a phonology, under the assumption that they are all empirically non-distinct, i.e. that they can generate the same sets of output. The Just Rules (JR) approach outlined in this chapter is compared to "standard" OT and a generic Rules & Constraints (RC) model.

(82)   Comparison of various approaches to phonology

	OT	RC	JR
a. List of primitive entities	yes	yes	yes
b. List of possible operations/functions	yes	yes	yes
c. List of constraints	yes	yes	no
d. Notion of ill-formedness	yes	yes	no
e. Notion of repair	no	yes	no
f. Quantifiers in SDs	yes	yes	yes
g. Representational matching procedure	yes	yes	yes

A complete formal theory of phonology must specify what it can generate, so it is necessary to define the universe of discourse by listing the entities (a) and operations (b) that the computations have access to. In OT there are no rules; but as discussed above, a fully explicit version of OT will have to provide a finite characterization of what GEN actually does—a list of ways in which the entities of the theory may be combined to form licit representations is in fact a necessary part of the model. In addition, OT contains other functions, such as EVAL, so all three theories contain functions. The three models cannot be distinguished on these grounds.

Obviously, there are constraints (c) in OT and RC models, and there are none in JR. As Yip explains, the use of constraints presupposes a notion of ill-formedness (d), which we have argued is circular at best and incoherent at worst, as an explanation of phonological alternation. The constraints are posited on the basis of this intuited sense of well-formedness vs. ill-formedness or markedness. This notion does not exist in the JR model, in which a set of rules map phonological inputs to outputs.

OT does not prescribe a specific repair (e) for individual markedness violations, but conceives of the grammar as finding an optimal solution across all outputs, which emerges from the ranking. In RC, rules are applied to repair ill-formed structures or to block rule application, thus also appealing to markedness theory. Repair is not part of JR theory.

In all three theories, quantifiers (f) are necessary to evaluate the SDs of rules or constraints which refer to identity and nonidentity. Similarly, all three theories need some kind of Representational Mapping Procedure to determine which representations satisfy the structural description of its rules or constraints.

Recall that we are assuming that we can compare extensionally equivalent grammars. While straightforward theory comparison is difficult, the "rules only" approach appears to be the most elegant. The list of possible operations is stated in positive terms and thus characterizes the universe of discourse with no additional apparatus. There is no notion of markedness, and thus no reason to conceive of rules as repairing representations. The theory requires rules with a sufficiently rich representational apparatus to define their condition of application. However, as exemplified by the discussion of quantification, this apparatus may be needed by any empirically adequate theory.

8.7.1 *Violability and universality in Optimality Theory*

Optimality Theory is a model of grammar which posits universal, violable constraints that are ranked on a language-particular basis. The universality and the violability of OT constraints are not independent. Obviously, different constraints appear to hold in different languages, so if constraints are universal, they must be violable.

One might maintain an OT-type computational system of ranked constraints while denying the universality of constraints. However, if constraints are not universal, then they must be learned for each language. If they are learned, then they could be learned with appropriate structural descriptions that make them surface true (putting to one side for now the possibly insurmountable problem of opacity for two-level theories like classic OT). If they are surface true, then they need not be violable. In other words, if we weaken the claim of OT constraints to universality, the rest of the theoretical edifice of OT becomes considerably less attractive.

8.7.2 *Structural descriptions are "constraints" on application*

Let's look back to the type of rule discussed by McCarthy to motivate the restriction of rule application by the OCP. Notice that blocking of a rule R can be achieved in one of two ways—either by applying R and undoing its effects if they are "undesirable", or by "looking ahead" to see what the output would be before applying R, and not applying R if the projected output is undesirable. There is, however, a simpler way of avoiding rule outputs that result in ungrammatical surface forms: reformulate the rule as R', so as to apply only when it should. We have said this much already; however, it is important to realize that the structural description of a rule, the representation that determines whether the rule applies via the representational matching procedure discussed in section 8.3.1, is nothing other than a constraint on application. McCarthy's rule of vowel syncope in Hebrew applies to vowels between consonants, not to any segment that is between any other two segments. The rule applies only under certain metrical conditions, not under others. The condition that the flanking consonants be nonidentical is thus of the same type as the other constraints on application, the other components of the rule's structural description. In other words, there is no motivation in a rule-based grammar that uses a Representational Matching Procedure to also have constraints that are not just part of the structural description of rules.

Analogies may again be useful. There is no reason to assume that a law of Newtonian physics, $f = ma$, that refers to entities like force, mass, and acceleration, is actually better seen as a relation between variables $x = yz$, which is constrained by a constraint system that rules out any possible instantiation of $x = yz$ other than $f = ma$. Similarly, a rule or law includes a specification of when it is applicable. Writing highly general rules that lack appropriate structural descriptions to sufficiently restrict when the rules actually apply, and then positing constraints that limit the applicability of a rule, seems unproductive. Why mis-state rules then posit constraints to correct the error? Why not just state rules correctly?

8.7.3 *What is a possible rule?*

Recall that Yip claims that the fact that OCP "effects" are quite common in the languages of the world should motivate us to remove identity and nonidentity conditions from structural descriptions. We suggest that this is exactly the wrong conclusion. These types of condition are among the most crucial things we need to understand if we want to understand how to characterize the class of possible phonological rules. Ironically, such work by Yip and McCarthy led to the rejection of rule-based phonology in favor of OT, when it should instead have led to a deepening of our understanding of the nature of phonological rules. By appealing to constraints we complicate the theory of grammar unnecessarily, since the RMP used in the structural description of rules already provides the computational power that additional constraints were meant to supply. In addition to this complication, we also make considerably more obscure the important question "what is a possible rule?".

8.7.4 *What is Universal Grammar?*

A common characterization of the content of a theory of universal grammar presents the goal of UG theorizing to be a search for properties found in all languages. OT in some sense has solved the problem of UG, thus formulated. All constraints are assumed to be present in all languages; however, because some constraints are outranked by conflicting ones, the effects of the former may not be visible in a particular grammar. For example, all grammars have a constraint FAITHSUC demanding input–output faithfulness for the suction feature associated wth clicks. However, in English, it is assumed, the markedness constraint NoSuc outranks the faithfulness constraint, so that clicks would not surface even if they appeared in an English input representation. Thus we see no evidence for FaithSuc by examining English.

Unfortunately, this approach to universalism seriously misconstrues the nature of theorizing about UG since Chomsky's earliest work. The issue is explicitly discussed even as early as Lyons (1970):

(83)   Lyons (1970) on Chomskyan UG
- Languages make use of the same formal operations (p. 115).
- Chomsky believes that there are certain ... units that are *universal*, not in the sense that they are necessarily present in all languages, but in the somewhat different and perhaps less usual, sense of the term "universal," that they can be defined independently of their occurrence in any particular language and can be identified, when they do occur in particular languages, on the basis of their definition within the general theory (p. 111).
- Chomsky accepts that any one of his allegedly universal features might be absent, not only "from the very next language that becomes accessible" but also from very many quite familiar languages (pp. 114–15)

Another angle on the Chomskyan view recognizes UG, not as a hypothesis, but as a topic of study, the study of the initial state of the language faculty: "In any computational theory, 'learning' can consist only of creating novel combinations of primitives already innately available" (Jackendoff 1990: 40; see our discussion in Chapter 2, as well as Fodor 1975 and Pylyshyn 1973). Therefore, the OT approach to universalism, which attempts to reduce all language variation to constraint ranking, follows from an overly simplistic conception of what UG is. By ascribing all constraints to all languages, OT has solved a problem that derives from a misunderstanding of the nature of the enterprise of UG: "How can we define the 'units' that are present in all languages?" As the quotations above from Lyons indicate, this is a very different problem from that of determining the nature of the human language faculty.

9

Against Output–Output Correspondence

9.1 The Rotuman phases

Output–Output Correspondence (OOC) constraints, which demand correspondence between independently occurring surface forms, have made their way into the working arsenal of constraint types in use with Optimality Theory. In this chapter[1] we examine some of the better-known arguments which have been advanced in support of OOC constraints, and argue that adoption of such a powerful mechanism within OT is not justified in the cases discussed. In particular, we will discuss the following analyses: the incomplete/complete phase distinction of Rotuman, as analyzed by McCarthy (1995)[2] and McCarthy (2000), and English truncated hypocoristics, as discussed by Benua (1995). Together with Kenstowicz's (1996) work on Base Identity and Uniform Exponence, discussed in detail later in the chapter, these were the earliest studies in the OOC literature, and have proven very influential.

We present three major criticisms of this OOC-based work. First, we find cases of "opportunism". For example, there is an unprincipled culling of the data and an unprincipled choice of bases in correspondence relations. Second, there is misanalysis, in that clearly significant generalizations are overlooked, technical aspects of the theory are improperly treated, and implausible generalizations are accepted. Third, we believe that the analyses based on OOC lead to problematic predictions, some of which are strongly contra-indicated by existing data, and others of which we consider highly suspect.

---

[1] This chapter builds directly upon Hale et al. (1998) and Hale (2000). The authors are indebted to Madelyn Kissock for allowing us to make use of her work so extensively in this book.

[2] McCarthy withdrew his 1995 paper from the Rutgers Optimality Archive and clearly intends his 2000 analysis to supersede this early attempt. We discuss both analyses, in part because we find it useful for understanding the history of the use of OOC within OT, and in part because it provides a terminologically up-to-date recharacterization of Churchward's earlier work (Churchward 1940). Since McCarthy (2000) freely cites his 1995 paper (e.g. 2000: 147, 162), we do not share the concerns of one of the manuscript reviewers of this book regarding our discussion of that work in this context.

We offer simple, principled solutions which we hope will contribute to a more constrained theory of phonology—one which is likely to have no place for as powerful a mechanism as OOC.

9.1.1 *McCarthy's 1995 analysis*

In discussing the distribution of the Rotuman phase distinctions, McCarthy (1995: 2) adopts the view of Churchward (1940), though no details as to why one might desire to do so are provided: "Rotuman has a contrast in major-category words between two phases, the complete and the incomplete, distributed according to syntactico-semantic principles." As we will show below, the phases are, instead, *phonologically* conditioned. To account for the phonological differences between the (in his view syntactico-semantically conditioned) phases, McCarthy proposed the following constraint:

(84) INC-PH Constraint (McCarthy 1995: 11)
      Every incomplete-phase stem ends in a monosyllabic foot (or heavy syllable).
      Align(Stem$_{Inc.Ph.}$, Right, $[\sigma]_{Ft}$, Right) (or Align(Stem$_{Inc.Ph.}$, Right, $\sigma_{\mu\mu}$, Right))

The ranking of this constraint within the larger OT constraint hierarchy, including the familiar types of OT Faithfulness and Well-formedness constraint, accounts for the descriptive observation that "the incomplete phase is identical to the complete phase, except for the fact that the *final foot* of the complete phase is realized as a *monosyllabic foot* in the incomplete phase" (McCarthy 1995: 11). This accounts for alternations of the type *tokiri*$_{comp}$/ *tokir*$_{inc}$ (deletion), *seseva*$_{comp}$/*seseav*$_{inc}$ (metathesis), etc.[3] McCarthy claims that the underlying representations of complete and incomplete phase forms in (85) differ in that the latter contains an additional morpheme which is sensitive to the constraint given in (84).

(85) Complete phase input: *tokiri*
      Incomplete phase input: *tokiri*+INCPH

First, we believe that the assumption that there is a "syntactico-semantic" basis for the phase distinctions must be rejected (a suggestion later adopted by McCarthy in his 2000 paper). According to Churchward (1940), the incomplete phase is associated with an "indefinite" interpretation when applied to nouns; in the case of verbs, Churchward proposes an imperfective or non-completive reading for the incomplete phase. In contrast,

---

[3] See Hale and Kissock (1998) for a discussion of a fuller range of data. The limited number of examples in this chapter should suffice to illustrate our points.

the complete phase is to be correlated with "definite" interpretation, "positiveness, finality, or emphasis", or a perfective or completive interpretation for verbs. We are dubious of Churchward's equation of noun definiteness and verbal aspect, since it is apparently without parallel in the precise form he advocates; but there are more basic reasons to discard his analysis.

We note in passing (though briefly, to avoid being side-tracked from our central concerns) that den Dikken (2003) presents an attempt to justify Churchward's essentially semantic analysis in Minimalist terms. Den Dikken is oddly negative regarding Hale and Kissock's (1998) criticisms of Churchward, and seems to imply at several points in his discussion that he is presenting an alternative, perhaps better morphosyntactic account of the phases. For example, he writes (2003: 73), regarding some particular facts of syntactic distribution of the phases, that "[a]pproaches (like Hale & Kissock's 1998, and McCarthy's 2000) which seek to harbour the account of the phase alternation entirely within the phonology will be hard pressed accommodating effects of the type" which he is citing. He notes on the same page that the data he is citing "is directly compatible with, and lends support to, our syntactic approach to Com[plete Phase]-marking". There appears to be some confusion in this passage regarding the architecture of the grammar. Phase marking is a postlexical phonological phenomenon triggered, like all such phenomena, by computation over objects which have been created in the course of the syntactic derivation of the string in question. The syntactic derivation itself is the result of computation over morphosyntactic features. Hale and Kissock (1998), as well as McCarthy (2000), present an analysis regarding the nature of the phonological computation in question; they do not present a comprehensive syntactic analysis of the distribution of each and every one of the morphemes which play a role in the syntactic derivation (though of course it is the *phonological* properties of these morphemes that serves as the input to the phonological computation). If this counts as "harbour[ing] the account of the phase alternation entirely within the phonology", then such "harbouring" has been the normal working method of phonologists at least since the early part of the twentieth century.

In other places in his monograph, den Dikken displays similar confusion regarding the overall architecture of the grammar. For example, he writes (2003: 10):

The marking of the complete phase is the province of the phonological component; but it is the syntax which, by tying Com[plete Phase] to members of the checking domain of D[+def], both narrows down the pool of candidates for phonological Com-marking and explains the transparent semantic effect of morphosyntactic

Com-marking (i.e. definiteness, the reflex of checking against D[+def]). This "divide and rule" approach to the distribution of Com-marking in Rotuman thus gives us the desired result that Com, while ultimately a phonological phenomenon, may have well-defined semantic repercussions.

The basic nature of the Minimalist conception of grammar, as near as we can tell, is that a set of lexical items (bundles of morphosyntactic and phonological features) enter into a syntactic derivation, being manipulated by operations such as Merge and Move. The representations thus constructed are sent to a logico-conceptual interface for semantic interpretation and to an articulatory-perceptual interface for phonological interpretation. There can, under such a conception of things, be no question of a "phonological phenomenon" such as phase formation having "semantic repercussions". The phonological interpretation of the representation built up in the course of the syntactic derivation (and sent, ultimately, to Spell-Out) takes place independently of and without reference to the semantic interpretation of the syntactic representation eventually passed off to the logico-conceptual interface.

It is the nature of the phonological interpretation which Hale and Kissock (1998) and McCarthy (2000) present theories of. And in spite of several chiding remarks along the way, den Dikken seems to fully endorse the phonological analysis of Hale and Kissock (1998). He writes (2003: 9) that he is restricting his discussion of Com[plete Phase] marking to its morphosyntactic properties, particularly those regarding definiteness. His proposed analysis "arguably has nothing to say about the instances of Com triggered by phonological properties of affixes . . . See Hale and Kissock (1998) for discussion of this—arguably not a syntactic issue." Hale and Kissock (1998) presents a unified analysis of all aspects of phase marking in Rotuman. What den Dikken seems not to understand is that phonological computation has access *only* to phonological structures and processes; so if, as he seems to recognize, phase formation is "the province of the phonological component" and "ultimately a phonological phenomenon", there can be no such thing as the "*morphosyntactic* Com-marking" he claims to be working on. Instead, he seems to be working on the distribution of some morphosyntactic object which may, because of its *phonological* properties, of course, trigger some phase-related effect. For a suggestion as to what that morpheme (or those morphemes) might be, we refer the reader to Hale and Kissock (1998) and Hale et al. (1998).

Let us return to some of our concerns with Churchward's claim, followed by McCarthy (1995), that definiteness is what is being marked by the phase distinctions.[4] A sentence like (86)[5] shows that even a personal pronoun like *gou* "I",[6] which corresponds to complete phase *goua*, can show phase distinctions. It seems highly unlikely that the first person pronoun could ever be interepreted as indefinite—it is certainly *not* to be so interpreted in (86).[7]

(86) *gou la tük iris*
I_{inc} FUT $stop_{inc}$ $them_{inc}$
'I will stop them'

Sentences (87) and (88) further demonstrate the problem of attributing phase alternations to syntactico-semantic principles. The verb *noh(o)* 'live' shows precisely the same aspectual form and interpretation in the two sentences, yet it is in the incomplete phase in (87) and in the complete phase in (88). In fact, *all verbs* are in the complete phase before the anaphoric clitic *e*, regardless of their aspectual interpretation. Note also that an "indefinite" interpretation of personal names such as *Titof* and *Rah* is semantically excluded—in spite of their being in the incomplete phase. The corresponding complete phase forms are *Titofo* and *Raho*.[8]

(87) *ma Titof noh ma tupue' te'is 'e Faufano* (II.9)
and $Titofo_{inc}$ $lived_{inc}$ with $tupu'a_{inc}$ $this_{inc}$ at Faufano
'and Titofo lived with this *tupu'a* at Faufano'
(88) *ia tä puer se hanue=t ne Rah noho e* (I.3)
he TNS $rule_{inc}$ over $land=the_{inc}$ where $Raho_{inc}$ $lived_{comp}$ there(in)
'he ruled over the land in which Raho lived'

In (89) and (90) we provide a partial list[9] of suffixes and clitics which invariably trigger the complete phase and incomplete phase, respectively.

[4] We note that Churchward (1940), unlike den Dikken (2003), does not recognize two distinct types of Complete Phase marking; one, morphosyntactic in nature, indicating definiteness, another, more purely phonological (whatever that might mean), triggered by certain types of affixes. Instead, he struggles to provide a unified semantic account of all instances of Complete Phase realization, believing that "completeness of form" correlates in some way with "completeness of sense". It is this view of his which Hale and Kissock label the "romanticism of terminological aesthetics", for which den Dikken (2003: 73) mocks them, setting himself up as a defender of Churchward's insightfulness, although den Dikken's own analysis simply disregards as "syntactically irrelevant" most of the data Churchward was trying to squeeze into his "definite" and "indefinite" semantic categories.

[5] All examples are from Churchward (1940), unless otherwise indicated.

[6] We will use traditional Rotuman orthography when it does not introduce confusion—here, for example, <g> represents the voiced velar nasal.

[7] The form *iris* is also an incomplete phase pronoun, corresponding (irregularly) to *irisa*.

[8] The references in parentheses after the Rotuman provide an indication as to the text from which the sentence was taken. The texts all come from Titifanua and Churchward (1938).

[9] The lists in (89) and (90) represent only a selection of the relevant clitics and suffixes; for a more complete survey see Hale and Kissock (1998).

(89)   Suffixes and clitics which invariably trigger the complete phase:
       -*ga* nominalizer: *puʻa* 'to be greedy', *puʻaga* 'greed'
       -*me* 'hither': *hoʻa* 'to take', *hoʻame* 'to bring'
       -*a* transitive suffix: *hili* 'to choose (intr.)', *hilia* 'to choose s.t. (tr.)'
       e locative anaphor: *noho* 'to dwell, live', *noho e* 'to dwell there'

(90)   Suffixes and clitics which invariably trigger the incomplete phase
       -*ʻia* ingressive: *sunu* 'to be hot', *sunʻia* 'to become hot'
       -*ʻāki* causative: *tole* 'to carry', *tolʻāki* 'to cause to be carried'
       -*kia* transitive: *hoʻa* 'to take (intr.)', *hoaʻkia* 'to take (tr.)'
       taʻa 'that': *vaka* 'canoe', *vak taʻa* 'that canoe'

Note that there is no sense in which the *hoʻa* of *hoʻame* 'to bring' is a "definite" version of *hoʻa* 'to take', nor is *sun* of *sunʻia* 'to become hot' an "indefinite" version of *sunu* 'to be hot'. Equally clearly, the incomplete phase *vak* (from *vaka* 'canoe') in *vak taʻa* 'that canoe' refers to a "definite" canoe. A coherent pattern does emerge, however, in that the suffixes and clitics in (89) are all *monosyllabic*, whereas those in (90) are *disyllabic*. It is not our goal in this context to present a complete OT analysis of the complete/incomplete alternations (deletion, metathesis, etc.). Some details of our analysis can be found in Hale and Kissock (1998). Many aspects of McCarthy's 1995 analysis can be preserved in the purely phonologically based account which we propose. We restrict ourselves here to stating the algorithm which describes where incomplete phase formation occurs within the prosodic domain of the clitic group:

(91a)   Phonological conditions for clitic group incomplete phase
       Build RL binary feet within each clitic group. If a vowel is both at the right edge of a foot and a morpheme, that vowel will undergo the effects of incomplete phase formation.

An example of the application of this algorithm to the sentence in (88) is given in (91b). The arrows indicate directions of enclisis (rightward arrows showing proclisis, leftward arrows enclisis). Proclitics do not show phase distinctions.[10]

(91b)   [ia→tä→pure]$_\omega$ [se→hanua←ta]$_\omega$ [ne→Raho]$_\omega$ [noho←e]$_\omega$
       : [ia-tä-puer]$_\omega$ [se-hanue-t]$_\omega$ [ne-Rah]$_\omega$ [noho-e]$_\omega$

Since the last vowel of *pure*, for example, occurs at the right edge of a morpheme *and* the right edge of a foot, it undergoes incomplete phase effects,

---

[10]   Note that the incomplete phase of *noho e* is simply *noho e*. This is its expected form, given the rules for incomplete phase formation. The change of *a* to *e* in *hanue=t* is due to the "narrow version" formation rule, to be discussed below.

as (91a) predicts. In this particular case, incomplete phase formation involves metathesis. The next three clitic groups, involving deletion, deletion, and no change respectively, are completely regular phonological reflexes of the strings in question in an incomplete phase environment.

McCarthy's description of the correspondence relations among underlying (lexical) form, complete phase surface form, and incomplete phase surface form is described in (92) and sketched in (93):

(92) "With respect to its vocalism and its foot structure, the incomplete phase is faithful to the complete phase, rather than the lexical form, strongly supporting the correspondence-based model in (54)." (McCarthy 1995: 47)

(93) McCarthy's (54) specifies the following correspondence relations:
Lexical Specification

Complete Phase Surface =========⟶ Incomplete Phase Surface

There exists, however, another set of phonologically conditioned alternations affecting Rotuman stems which interacts crucially with phase distinctions and which McCarthy (1995) apparently did not consider. This is the so-called "broad/narrow" alternation which involves shifting the vowel *a* to *e* in well-defined phonological environments (see Hale and Kissock 1998 for details). In (94) we see that a morpheme like *i'a* actually has four surface variants, depending on phase context and broad/narrow context. The morpheme *puga*, however, has only three variants, due to the phonological makeup of the stem (note the identical *a* vowel in the incomplete phase contexts):

(94) The broad/narrow alternation and its relationship to phase

	Complete phase contexts	Incomplete phase contexts
Broad version contexts	*i'a*	*ia'*
	puga	*puag*
Narrow version contexts	*i'e-*	*ie'-*
	puge-	*puag-*

The relevance of the broad/narrow alternation to an output–output analysis becomes apparent when we try to decide which complete phase form should serve as the basis for comparison in correspondence relations for narrow-version incomplete phase forms. If we choose the narrow-version complete phase form, we get the correct result in the case of *i'e-* and *ie'* since "[w]ith respect to its vocalism and its foot structure, the incomplete phase is faithful to the corresponding complete phase"; but we get the wrong result in the case of *puge-* and *puag*, since the latter has an *e* but the former has an *a*. If instead we choose the broad-version complete phase form as the basis of correspondence, then we get the correct result for *puga/puag*, but not for *i'a/ie'*. This is sketched in (95):

(95)   Which "Output" is the base for Narrow Incomplete Phase forms?

	Broad Complete		Narrow Incomplete
☹	*i'a*	≯	*ie'-*
☺	*puga*	>	*puag-*

	Narrow Complete		Narrow Incomplete
☺	*i'e-*	>	*ie'-*
☹	*puge-*	≯	*puag-*

We can summarize the discussion so far as follows. The syntactico-semantic basis for the phase distinctions which McCarthy (1995) adopts from Churchward is implausible, since no known language expresses the range of meanings which Churchward associates with the incomplete phase by means of a single morpheme. Furthermore, the existence of a definiteness distinction on personal pronouns is semantically incoherent. In addition, we have demonstrated the phonological conditioning of the phases, making it clear that there is no incomplete phase morpheme, contra McCarthy's analysis presented in (85) above. We note that a phonological account always trumps a semantic one (especially a semantic one that does not work). Therefore, there can be no OOC between the phases, since the two phases are *identical* in their underlying representation. Finally, even if we wanted to invoke OOC to capture the phase relations, we have no principled method for selecting a base that will also account for the productive broad/narrow alternation. It is the post-lexical prosodic environment which triggers the contrast between surface forms like *tokiri/tokir*, both of which have the UR /tokiri/.

9.1.2 *McCarthy's 2000 analysis*

McCarthy revises his 1995 analysis, in part in light of many of the arguments offered above, in his 2000 paper. The basic prosodic structure of the complete and incomplete phases are represented by McCarthy (2000) as in Figure 9.1.

The central task of McCarthy's (2000) treatment of Rotuman is, in some sense, to deal with the following problem. The incomplete phase *rak* is difficult to derive within OT from the underlying form /rako/, because the competitor *ra.ók* satisfies the INC-PH Constraint (given in example (84) above) *and* is more faithful to the input (/rako/) than is *rak* since it does not incur a

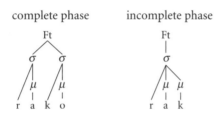

complete phase   incomplete phase

FIGURE 9.1 Phase contrast (after McCarthy 2000: 151)

gratuitous DEP violation (the failure to reflect underlying /o/ in the output). McCarthy (2000: 183) seeks to resolve this difficulty via OOC by positing the HEAD-MATCH constraint.

(96)   HEAD-MATCH
       If α is in H′(PrWd) and $\alpha \Re \beta$, then β is in H′(PrWd).

This constraint favors a form which keeps constant, in a related set of forms, the head of the Prosodic Word. McCarthy explains how HEAD-MATCH does the necessary work in this case as follows:

The idea is that HEAD-MATCH selects *(rák)* over **ra.(ók)* by comparing them to the complete-phase form *(ráko)*. Since the vowel *a* occupies the stressed nucleus in complete-phase *(ráko)*, only the actual output form *(rák)* satisfies HEAD-MATCH. (McCarthy 2000: 183)

It is the invocation of these paradigmatic relations between output forms in the process of the synchronic computational derivation of individual forms that we are somewhat anxious about. Here we explore whether it works, merely procedurally, *prima facie*, in the Rotuman case.

9.1.3 *Problem: the reification of the complete phase*

It seems clear that, if HEAD-MATCH is to provide the explanation for the favoring of incomplete phase *rák* over its (losing, and thus ungrammatical) competitor *ra.ók*, we must first be able to give an account of how the complete phase, *ráko*, gets *its* prosodic structure. In this regard, it is important to point out that McCarthy (2000: 161 *et passim*) accepts the conclusions of Hale and Kissock (1998) that the complete phase is found *only* before monomoraic suffixes.

   McCarthy derives the general conditions on the phase distinction by positing that underlying forms undergo incomplete phase formation when they are prosodically independent, remaining in complete phase when prosodically dependent. The foot structure of a root (e.g. *rako* 'study') suffixed by a bimoraic suffix (e.g. -ʿ*ạki*) is thus (*rako*)(ʿ*ạki*), with the convergence of foot and root boundary leading to prosodic independence, thus incomplete phase formation (the form surfaces, if not further suffixed, as *rakʻâk*). By contrast, when suffixed by a monomoraic suffix (such as the nominalizer *-ga*), the foot structure is *ra(koga)*, and the root is now prosodically dependent—this dependence-blocking incomplete phase formation (the resulting output form is *rakoag*).[11] Note that in both cases the final syllable meets the conditions for incomplete phase formation and thus shows up in that phase.

As we work our way through McCarthy's (2000) analysis it is important for the reader to realize that, because of the restrictions on complete phases just outlined, the complete phase representation in Figure 9.1 is not, in fact, a possible Rotuman representation. It cannot be an underlying representation, because those are not footed, and it is. On the other hand, it cannot be an output representation, because as noted above the complete phase only surfaces before monomoraic suffixes, and the form given in Figure 9.1 is not suffixed.

As McCarthy (2000: 167) notes, following Churchward (1940), there are in fact two types of monomoraic suffix in Rotuman: "stress-neutral" and "stress-determining".[12] "Stress-neutral" monomoraic suffixes, as one might infer from their name, do not give rise to a stress shift in the root to which they attach. "Stress-determining" monomoraic suffixes, by contrast, do. An example of the former, "stress-neutral" class would be the directional suffix *-me* "hither". The result of suffixing *-me* onto the root *seke-* 'to walk' is thus *sékem* 'to walk hither'. The suffix *-me* in this form shows up, as expected, in its incomplete phase form *-m*, since it is not itself followed by a monomoraic suffix.

By contrast, we can examine the case of the stress-determining suffix *-ga*, which is a nominalizer. If we affix this nominalizer to the root *puʻa-* 'to be greedy' the result is *puʻág* 'greed', rather than the unattested **púʻag*.[13] The default prosodic structure of *sékem* 'to walk hither' and *puʻág* 'greed' should be, given the constraints proposed by McCarthy (2000) without considering OOCs, as in Figure 9.2.

Like other analysts before him, McCarthy (2000: 151) posits a trochaic stress pattern for Rotuman. Without further analysis, then, McCarthy predicts that all monomoraic suffixes should trigger a stress shift, as can clearly be seen from

---

[11] This solution is strongly parallel to that of Hale et al. (1998).

[12] McCarthy (2000) thus represents a more comprehensive account of the facts of Rotuman prosody than Hale et al. (1998), which considered phase in isolation. This consideration of a broader set of forms represents a distinct improvement on our earlier analysis—or would, if McCarthy's (2000) analysis actually worked.

[13] Again, *-ga* shows up in its incomplete phase form since it is not itself followed by a monomoraic suffix.

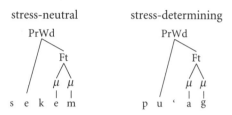

FIGURE 9.2 The two prosodic types of complete phase

the identical foot structure built on top of *sékem* and *puʻág* in Figure 9.2. It is important to point out that the prosodic structure posited in this figure for the stress-neutral suffixed form *sékem* is *required* to be as given, if we are to ensure the prosodic dependence of *seke-*, and thus avoid incomplete phase formation from affecting the root-final syllable. McCarthy is, of course, well aware of the problem. He says (2000: 167): "Stress-neutral behavior can then be analyzed as an output-output faithfulness effect, as in Benua's (1997) analysis of English."

When we ask what form words such as *sékem*, which have stress-neutral suffixation, show Output–Output faithfulness to, only one answer is possible. They cannot owe their stress placement to any *complete phase* form—the two types of complete phase form are given in Figure 9.2. One of them represents the forms we are trying to reshape by positing an Output–Output Constraint, the other (*puʻág*) has the wrong stress. The relevant Output–Output faithfulness must therefore be to the *incomplete phase* form, whose structure we present in Figure 9.3.

But, as you will recall from our discussion above, McCarthy (2000) attributes the prosodic structure of the incomplete phase is itself to the workings of the HEAD-MATCH constraint (cited above as (96))—an OOC which forces the incomplete-phase prosodic head to match that of the complete phase! Thus to derive the prosodic structure of the incomplete phase we must first derive that of the complete phase, which is itself dependent on examining

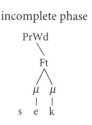

FIGURE 9.3 The incomplete phase of *seke* 'to walk'

the output of the derivation of the incomplete phase. We are in an infinite loop. Moreover, given that the stress-neutral suffixed complete phase forms *must* have the prosodic structure in Figure 9.2, HEAD-MATCH will give exactly the wrong result for the incomplete phase, in any event.

9.1.4 *The importance of morphological structure*

It is well worth our while examining some additional properties of phase formation in Rotuman, since our earlier work (including Hale and Kissock 1998 and Hale et al. 1998) did not give all of the evidence which the language provides to support our analysis. Our claim in that work was that one finds incomplete phase in Rotuman when foot and morpheme boundaries coincide. Valuable support for this contention comes from the treatment of quadrisyllables in Rotuman. We find two treatments of the "phase" of the first foot of such forms: in some forms, such as those in (97), the first foot shows up in the incomplete phase.

(97) Quadrisyllabic words whose first foot undergoes incomplete phase formation (selected)
- *faka* (causative) + *laga* ('raise/lift') → *faklag*
- *rima* ('to flash') + reduplication → *riamriam*
- *tuku* ('to go away') + *faʻu* ('back') → *tukfàʻ* 'backwards'

Other quadrisyllabic words show the complete phase in their first foot. Some examples of this type can be seen in (98).

(98) Quadrisyllabic words whose first foot does *not* undergo incomplete phase formation (selected)
- *potaʻa* ('to aim') + *ga* (nominalizer) → *potaʻag*
- *gagaja* ('story') + *t* (indef. art.) → *gagajat*
- *loloʻi* ('to increase') + *a* (transitive) → *loloʻia*

Clearly, the relevant factor here is the coming together, in the examples in (97), of the morpheme and foot boundaries, contrasting clearly with their mismatch in the examples in (98). Further support for this analysis can be seen from the treatment of monomorphemic quadrisyllables, such as those in (99).

(99) Monomorphemic quadrisyllables (selected)
ʻatakoa 'all', *ʻuʻapea* tree sp., *nanumea* 'round basket used for food', *papalàg* [< *papalagi*] 'bread (of foreign manufacture)', *pikalös* [< *pikalosi*] 'cockle', *tamamuaʻ* [< *tamamuʻa*] 'to take liberties', *ʻaparam* [< *ʻaparama*] 'a kind of taro'

The generalization seems clear (as claimed in Hale et al. 1998): when the morpheme and foot boundaries coincide (as they do in the "2 mora + 2 mora" cases in (97), but *not* in the "3 mora + 1 mora" cases of (98) or the "4 mora + Ø mora" cases in (99)), "prosodic independence" is maintained and incomplete phase formation may take place. Otherwise, it may not. Note that this is a purely phonological solution—semantics plays no role.

9.1.5 *Another problem: Richness of the Base*

McCarthy (2000: 171) notes that "the ranking of ALIGN-HEAD above SYLL= μ gives Rotuman its non-uniform prosodic structure, with heavy syllables required finally in incomplete phase words and *prohibited* everywhere else". As the evidence in (97) indicates, this claim is too strong,[14] since the incomplete phase formation process licenses word-internal heavy syllables (under appropriate circumstances) as well as word-final ones. However, there is still a clear phonological generalization at work in Rotuman: morphemes which display only open syllables when in complete phase contexts will show up in the incomplete phase, and thus surface with a closed morpheme- (not word-) final syllable, when phonologically appropriate. If some version of McCarthy's 2000 analysis which avoided the "infinite loop" problem introduced by his use of OOC could be developed, it would also need to be sensitive to morpheme, rather than word edges. But we believe that an analysis along these lines, which attempted to maintain the spirit of McCarthy's analysis, would still run afoul of another Optimality Theory principle: Richness of the Base.

A corollary of "Richness of the Base" is the observation that, given any input, the OT grammar will generate well-formed (for the phonological system in question) output. It is generally asserted that loanwords provide the linguist with an opportunity to test whether or not the proper constraints have been posited, since they provide "new" inputs for the grammar, which may not match in canonical shape the indigenous lexical material. We are highly skeptical of the use of loanword data to justify phonological analyses, there being too many extragrammatical factors involved in determining the shape

---

[14] McCarthy (2000: 163) notes that "[a] stem is prosodically independent when it is followed by a long suffix..., or when it is part of a compound, or when it has no suffixes at all". Prosodic independence entails incomplete phase realization. He thus recognizes the significance of the compounding data presented in (97). However, it is worth pointing out that "prosodic independence" is a *derived* property, generated by the constraints giving rise to Foot and Prosodic Word structure, in the case of stems followed by "long suffixes" and in the case of stems which are followed by "no suffix at all". The fact that first compound members undergo incomplete phase formation is not, however, derivable from McCarthy's posited constraints—it is merely stipulated in passing in the passage just cited. That is, although McCarthy recognizes the existence of the incomplete phases in first compound members, his analysis provides no account for their presence in that context.

taken by loanwords,[15] but since this is a technique broadly applied in OT (as well as in more traditional generative) phonology, we will take a moment to show how it plays out in the Rotuman context.

English loanwords into Rotuman turn out to be quite problematic for Richness of the Base. They appear to allow closed syllables (in spite of McCarthy's claim of high-ranking SYLL = μ in Rotuman), as can be seen from the examples in (100).

(100)   Some English loanwords in Rotuman
         novempa 'November', *pensini* 'benzine', *pulagkete* 'blanket', *pulsai*
         'bullseye', *seksepạni* 'sixpence', *sepitemba* 'September', *sistā* '(religious)
         sister', *tagkē*[16] 'donkey'

One could in principle argue that some of these coda consonants have arisen via incomplete phase formation (as is at least plausibly the case in *sospạni* 'saucepan' next to *soso* 'sauce'), but note that this requires (given 91a) that morpheme boundaries be posited in these words (even where there are none in the source language).

The plausibility of such an assumption, however, does not seem high, given the lack of morphological parse (as indicated by the use of the complete phase in the first foot) of more blatantly polymorphemic forms such as those in (101).

(101)   English loanwords with no internal morpheme boundary after the first
         foot
         motokā 'motor car' (next to *motolori* 'motor lorry' and *motopäeke*
         'motorbike'), *firipene* 'three penny', etc.

It appears, then, that underlying forms with closed syllables, such as the English loanwords in (100), whose first foot does not meet the conditions for incomplete phase formation (since no morpheme boundary coincides with its foot boundary), surface not with open second syllables, as the OT analysis would predict, but with heavy final syllables. If these loanwords are taken as evidence for the workings of Richness of the Base, then the relatively high ranking of SYLL = μ in McCarthy's (2000) analysis must also be on the wrong track. Of course, we have given reasons at several points in this book for our belief that Richness of the Base has no interesting role to play in phonological theory construction.

---

[15] The reader need only consider the well-known case of the borrowing of, e.g., English *h* as Russian *g*.

[16] The reader will recall that Rotuman <g> represents the velar nasal [ŋ].

Rotuman represents an interesting case for Optimality Theory, as noted by McCarthy. As we hope to have shown in some detail above, its interest does not lie, however, in supporting the addition to the computational machinery already provided by OT of constraint types which require FAITH across sets of output forms. We think that McCarthy has not considered carefully enough what may be the most interesting feature of Rotuman for OT. If we consider only native vocabulary (i.e. ignore the problematic English loans mentioned in 100), it seems clear that the underlying forms of Rotuman do indeed consist entirely of strings which would be syllabified with only open syllables, with the closed syllables of the incomplete phase arising from less faithful phonological computation. OT is generally held to contain two types of constraint: Well-formedness constraints (sometimes called "markedness" constraints), which aim to reduce the markedness of the output forms, and Faithfulness constraints, which license the maintenance of markedness in the output by requiring faith to features of the input representations. In the Rotuman case, starting with input representations which would surface as highly unmarked structures, the interaction of constraints which seek to reduce markedness and constraints which seek to preserve the (in this case already unmarked) features of the input gives rise to more highly marked output. It would be fascinating if Optimality Theory could achieve this result, though it would presumably represent yet another reason for discarding "markedness" as relevant to the enterprise.

9.1.6 *Summary*

Because of the shortcomings confronting McCarthy's analyses of Rotuman, that language cannot be cited in support of the expansion of the set of operations available to Optimality Theory so as to include Output–Output Correspondence. Other oft-mentioned OT concepts such as "Richness of the Base" and "Well-formedness constraints" do not fare particularly well, in our view, in light of the Rotuman data. While it is not possible for us to consider *all* the ways in which OOCs have been invoked in the OT literature, in the next section we will turn to some additional uses, and argue that the claimed empirical support is also lacking in these cases.

9.2 Other uses of output–output correspondence

A guiding principle of all scientific inquiry is that the power of a theory should be extended only if such an extension leads to greater insight than a more constrained theory. This principle, which goes by the name of Occam's Razor, should be taken into consideration when approaching the problem of imposing limits on the types of universal constraint to be exploited in constructing an OT model of grammar. Recent work in OT has seen a burgeoning of proposals for new kinds of constraint, including the family of constraints we are considering in this chapter, known as Output–Output Correspondence constraints. "Normal" OT Correspondence constraints value similarity between underlying form and surface form, but OOC constraints are posited to value similarity between morphologically related surface forms.

OOC constraints have been proposed to capture a variety of phenomena, including those known as "cyclic effects" in earlier generative literature. However, given the evidence that the prominent example presented by the Rotuman Phase analysis, which provided an impetus to much later work on OOC, is flawed, it is important to remember Occam's Razor and re-evaluate all other uses of OOC. If we find that we can account for the same range of data without OOC, then we have a better, more constrained theory of phonology. We recognize, of course, that Occam's Razor is not the *only* principle guiding scientific research; it is, however, one which must be respected.

The purpose of this section is to argue that the use of OOC to account for what is described in the traditional historical linguistics literature as "analogy" is neither necessary nor desirable. The use of OOC to account for "cyclic" effects has been an issue of hot debate, but there have been many well-developed alternatives, even within an OT framework. One of the most complete is that of Orgun (1997). The examples considered in this paper show no clear evidence of requiring anything like a "cyclic" account, and in general a very straightforward account is available. The arguments for rejecting OOC in these cases can be sketched as follows:

(102)   Four arguments against invoking OOC for "analogy"

    i. OOC has been proposed to account for a subset of what is known as "analogy" in the historical linguistics literature; there is a different explanation that covers basically *all* cases of analogy; therefore OOC is not needed for the subset of cases.

    ii. We will offer an alternative to the OOC account which involves only lexical restructuring. It turns out, however, that the OOC account also relies on lexical restructuring. Therefore, the OOC account is overly powerful.

    iii. The OOC analyses we will examine are incompatible with widely accepted assumptions concerning acquisition in OT, particularly the process of Lexicon Optimization and the notion of Richness of the Base.

iv. The data under examination are drawn from distinct diachronic stages. Since "analogy" is a diachronic event, it should not be explained by OT, which is a theory of synchronic phonological computation (see Hale 2007 for detailed consideration of such matters).

Before analyzing particular cases of analogy in detail, it will be useful to provide some familiar examples in purely descriptive terms. One type of analogy (paradigm leveling) can be illustrated by the change from Early Modern English *reach / raught* to *reach / reached*. This change decreases allomorphy for a given verb, but is by no means regular, since *teach / taught* survives. The other relevant types of analogy (four-part proportional analogy) can be illustrated by the pronunciation *my*[θ] / *my*[ðz] (as against historically prior *my*[θ] / *my*[θs]) by some speakers of English. Note that this innovation parallels paradigms such as *ba*[θ] / *ba*[ðz]. This type of analogy may *increase* allomorphy.

(103)   Two major types of analogy
- Paradigm leveling: *reach / raught* → *reach / reached*
- Four-part proportional analogy: *my*[θs] → *my*[ðz]
  ba[θ] : *my*[θ] :: *ba*[ðz] : X, X= *my*[ðz]

Many examples of both kinds of analogy can be found in a standard historical text such as Hock (1991).

We will next provide an explanation for why analogy is expected to occur, given some simple assumptions about grammars, language acquisition and processing. If we accept the constancy of functional principles and the constancy of UG, it is clear that neither of these can be the cause of change. This fundamental principle is discussed most thoroughly by Hale (2007), but it was clearly recognized already by Bloomfield (1933: 386): "No permanent factor ... can account for specific changes which occur at one time and place and not at another." Change must therefore be due to varying factors such as the the order of presentation of the PLD. The diffusion of changes is affected by varying factors like intensity and types of sociolinguistic contact. Neither of these can be modeled in a deterministic fashion at present, so the goal of historical linguistics should be to characterize possible/impossible and more/less likely changes and diffusion events, not to model precise paths of change and diffusion.

9.2.1 *The nature of parsing*

When one considers the phonology of a language as a formal computational device in isolation from the rest of the grammar, there is an obvious difference between the generative processes of producing surface forms from underlying representations and that of parsing surface forms to converge on a given underlying representation. We have seen in Chapter 3 how this fact impacted Smolensky's attempt to resolve the so-called "comprehension–production dilemma" in child language. This difference, you will doubtless recall, is that the former procedure is a one-to-one mapping (a given underlying representation (UR) is mapped to a single surface form) or many-to-one, since different URs can all map to the same phonetic representation (PR);[17] whereas the latter can clearly be a one-to-many mapping (a single surface form can be mapped to a set of URs which are neutralized by the grammar). In other words, production is deterministic, whereas parsing is not.[18] This can be illustrated by any number of well-known examples, such as the following data from German:

(104)   Production is one/many-to-one, parsing is one-to-many

Production	Parsing
/bunt/ AND /bund/ > [bunt]	[bunt] > /bunt/ OR /bund/

Surface merger of underlyingly distinct forms is a well-known phenomenon, with examples available from a tremendous variety of human languages.

9.2.2 *Two kinds of analogy*

We believe that the partial indeterminacy of parsing provides a straightforward explanation for the diachronic process commonly referred to as analogy, both within and across paradigms. Analogy can be defined as diachronic replacement of a form which is regular in terms of historical phonological development by one which is irregular.[19]

Locating language change in the acquisition process, and referring to the nature of parsing as sketched above, we can offer the following explanation for why analogy is expected to occur in the course of learning:

---

[17] This can be due to lexical or structural ambiguity, as we pointed out in Ch. 3 (see especially n. 4).

[18] We follow standard generative practice in assuming an ideal speaker-hearer and abstract away from register and dialect variation. We assume that these effects are best modeled as resulting from different grammars.

[19] Typically (e.g. in Hock 1991) the replacement is assumed to be morphologically motivated. This assumption will prove to be unnecessary in the discussion below.

(105)   Parsing basis of analogical change: ambiguity → *restructuring*
Given a grammar G_1, URs /a,b/ and a surface form ϕ s.t. $G_1(a) =$
$G_1(b) = \phi$, ϕ is ambiguous for a learner constructing G_2 using the
output of G_1 as PLD.

One result of the existence of parsing ambiguity is analogy. Note that this
explanation of analogy is independent of the notion of the paradigm.[20] This
is a strength of the proposal, since analogical effects are attested both within
and across paradigms, as mentioned above.

Any of the well-known cases of analogy would suffice to illustrate the
proposal in (105), but for the sake of concreteness, consider two examples
from the history of Old Icelandic, shown in (106). Based on comparative evidence, we know that there was a paradigm at stage 1 which included nom. sg.
*mann-r / gen.pl. *mann-a* 'man'. These forms are attested at stage 2 as *maðr* /
manna. The change of **mannr* to *maðr* is not a phonological one, as shown
in Reiss (1997), but rather parallels the inherited paradigm of nom. sg. *guðr* /
gen. pl. *gunna* 'battle', which has an etymological dental fricative.[21]

(106)   Two kinds of analogy in the history of Old Icelandic (Reiss 1997)

	1.Pre-OI	2.Oldest manuscripts	3.Later OI
'man'	**mannr* / *manna*	*maðr* / *manna*	*maðr* / *manna*
'battle'	**guðr* / *gunna*	*guðr* / *gunna*	*gunnr* / *gunna*
URs	/mann/, /gunð/	/manð/, /gunð/	/manð/, /gunn/

The transition from stage 1 to stage 2 shows interparadigm, four-part analogy
for the "man" word.

The transition from stage 2 to stage 3 shows paradigm leveling for the
'battle' word. The paradigm *guðr* / *gunna* was leveled to *gunnr* /*gunna* in
later Old Icelandic (stage 3). The 'man' word was not leveled, however, and
survives with *ð* in the nom. sg. into Modern Icelandic. This type of change
reduces allomorphy within paradigms, and will typically also have the effect
of reducing opacity through the reduction of allomorphy.

It is worth noting that these changes in the history of Old Icelandic can be
best explained without positing any change in the phonology of the successive

[20] We use the term "paradigm" in its traditional (and vague) sense of a group of words which can
be viewed as inflected forms of a given base. We attribute no theoretical status to the paradigm, since
we believe it to be an epiphenomenon resulting from the generativity of the grammar.

[21] The reconstructions in Pre-Old Icelandic are clear, given Old English *mann* and *gūð*. Parallel
changes are also attested in adjectival and verbal paradigms, which demonstrates that four-part or
proportional analogy need not be based on a morphologically parallel relationship among participants
forms, as Hock (1991: 172) suggests is normally the case. For fuller discussion of the Old Icelandic data
see Reiss (1995; 1997).

stages. We need only posit changes in underlying representations. At each stage, both before and after the analogy, the relevant alternations can be generated by assuming, for example, a rule of cluster simplification which deletes *n* before *ðr* and a rule of cluster assimilation which assimilates *ð* to *n* between vowels:

(107)   Two rules present at all stages of Old Icelandic

$\mathscr{R}$1   n → Ø/ __ ð C   ex. /gunð-r/ > *guðr*

$\mathscr{R}$2   ð → n / n __ V   ex. /gunð-a/ > *gunna*

At each stage, the surface sequence *-nn-* is derivable either from underlying /nn/ or from underlying /nð/, when occurring between vowels. Therefore, a learner who is depending on output such as *manna* could "mistakenly" posit /manð-/ as the UR of the word meaning 'man'. Note that the posited underlying *-nð-* cluster never surfaces in either form, since the *n* gets deleted by $\mathscr{R}$1 or the *ð* assimilates by $\mathscr{R}$2.

This illustration of two kinds of analogy has three features relevant to our present concerns. First, analogy is not necessarily based upon any existing surface form within the paradigm, but rather on the neutralizing effect of the grammar which must be constructed once a learner acquires the *-nn-*/-*ð*- alternation for some morphemes. In fact, the change of etymological *nn* sequences to underlying /nð/ sequences which alternate is attested in adjectival and verbal paradigms, as well as nominal paradigms. Second, the effect of the analogy from stage 1 to stage 2 is to increase surface allomorphy within paradigms. Third, as already mentioned, analogy refers to a diachronic change and is thus not directly relevant to the study of grammars as static knowledge states, the object of inquiry recognized by the generative program.

9.2.3 *A unified account of analogy*

In this section we propose a single account for the two kinds of analogy illustrated above, starting with paradigm leveling. The reduction of opacity through paradigm leveling occurs, not because of the learner's desire to simplify the grammar, as a functionalist might suggest,[22] but rather merely because, as Kiparsky and Menn (1977: 73) point out, "Opacity is a property of the relation between the grammar and the data[; a]n opaque rule is not more complex, merely harder to discover." While it is intuitively obvious that it is

---

[22] Note that the view that learners simplify the grammar they are exposed to requires them to correctly acquire the target grammar, and then replace the acquired grammar with a simpler one. Besides justifying the obvious complexity of such a learning path, proponents of such a view will also have to explicitly formalize and empirically verify the exploitation by the acquirer of some kind of simplicity metric.

hard to discover, for example, that surface [nn] is derived from underlying /nð/, this intuition can be explained on the basis of a theory of phonological learnability. As we have argued earlier in this book, a child can acquire a lexicon only if the initial state of the grammar is such that surface forms and underlying representations are (a) identical to each other and (b) identical to the child's parse of the PLD, the output of speakers of the target language. In OT terms this means that Faithfulness constraints must be ranked above Well-formedness constraints initially.[23] In rule-based phonology, it means that the child's grammar initially contains no phonological rules (*contra* Natural Phonology theories of acquisition). Given that UG provides for maximally faithful mapping between UR and surface form as a default assumption, it is not surprising that earlier /gunða/> [gunna] can be parsed by a learner as /gunna/. More precisely, given our assumptions, it is not only possible but necessary that the direct parse be the child's initial hypothesis. If s/he fails to discover that which is 'hard to discover" the learner would continue to parse [gunna] as derived from /gunna/, and thus provide evidence for the attested analogical change. The change is to be located in the new underlying representation which lacks an ð.

Four-part proportional analogy, such as the diachronic restructuring of URs like /mann-/ > /manð-/ in inter-paradigm analogy, is a change which increases allomorphy. It is best understood by appeal to the non-unique solution to the parse of surface -*VnnV* sequences by learners exposed to the output of grammars that neutralize underlying -*nn*- and -*nð*- under some conditions. (All three stages of Old Icelandic in (106) have this property.) Given this indeterminacy of the grammar, we propose that the child may be influenced by language-specific (i.e. specific to language, not a *particular* language)— but extragrammatical—factors such as processing strategies, priming, and "neighborhood" or list effects in constructing URs. Both neighborhood and priming effects reflect "spreading of activation" that may be best accounted for by connectionist-type models of implementation strategies. As is generally assumed in the cognitive science literature, such phenomena are to be modeled in a manner which is separate from, though related to, the level of analysis with which linguistic theory is concerned—the level of representation and

---

[23] To briefly recapitulate, the argument is the following. In order to store a form, the learner must parse it. Parsing consists of finding a lexical entry that would surface as the observed form, given the current state of the grammar. If a child has all faithfulness constraints ranked low, as many OT phonologists propose, then there is *no* possible underlying representation that could surface as the observed form (except perhaps for the maximally unmarked utterance, say [ta]). The child cannot, therefore, converge on a lexicon. When we play the OT game, Faithfulness is initially high-ranked, so the child assumes that surface forms and underlying forms should be identical.

algorithm.[24] For an example of a list effect, consider the final *m* of Latin *novem* 'nine'. This segment is unexpected historically, since the reconstructed consonant is *n*; however, the form is assumed to be due to the "influence" of the numbers *septem* 'seven' and *decem* 'ten', which do have etymological *m* (Buck 1933).[25] These factors will sometimes have the effect of overriding the default grammatical analysis which assumes identity between UR and surface form.

By "priming effects" we refer to the influence of context on the top-down processes that the speech processor employs to construct a parse of linguistic input. Having recently heard a sequence [x], which is known to be derived from underlying /y/ (in both the learner's grammar and that of speakers of the target language), the learner might be led to assign the UR /y/ to a subsequent token of [x]. This processing preference lessens the probability of the parser taking the new token of [x] as merely derived from underlying /x/ for speakers of the target language. The resulting misanalysis by the learner is exactly the process we can assume occurred in Old Icelandic.

As we see, analogy occurs independently of the existence of words which are morphologically related to the one which changes diachronically. It is now apparent that a simple account of analogy, both (a) interparadigm (four-part) analogy and (b) paradigm leveling, within the context of the development of a generative theory of grammar, is provided by the restructuring of the lexicon in the process of lexical acquisition. The shifts discussed above involved (a) the acquisition of the morpheme meaning "man" with an underlying *nð* instead of underlying *nn* and (b) the acquisition of "battle" with underlying *nn* instead of *nð*.

As was already understood by the Neogrammarians, analogy is neither regular nor predictable. There have been various attempts to explain certain presumed "tendencies" of analogical change, but the Neogrammarian position that analogy, as opposed to sound change, is not regular has prevailed, and is illustrated by the data in (106). In fact, one of the motivations for the formulation of "analogy" as a recognizable process was to provide an explanation of apparent exceptions to sound change. So, we need not be concerned with explaining individual cases of analogical change, since these will depend upon such factors as the order of presentation of the PLD. We

---

[24] See the contributions of Osherson, Pinker, and Dell in Gleitman and Liberman (1995) for references and discussion of these issues.

[25] This looks dangerously close to claiming that general problem-solving skills are invoked in language acquisition. As Morris Halle (p.c.) points out, these skills may not be part of the grammar, but they must be specific to language, since they operate on linguistic representations. Perhaps they can be compared to the task of providing pairs of rhyming words. No language contains rules demanding e.g. that a subject rhyme with its verb, so it is not clear that *grammars* need to be able to compute rhyme. Yet *speakers* can compute rhyme for the purposes of poetry or language games.

can be satisfied with the insight that analogy is predicted to happen in the acquisition process, given the fact that grammars generate ambiguous output in the course of derivations.[26] For convenience we summarize below the main points we have established thus far:

(108) Summary to this point:
- Analogy is not necessarily based upon existing surface forms within a "paradigm", just on the *neutralizing effect of the grammar*.
- The effect of the analogy from stage 1 to stage 2 in (106) is to *increase surface allomorphy* within "paradigms".
- Analogy is a *diachronic* change and is thus not directly relevant to the study of grammars as static knowledge states, the object of inquiry recognized by the generative program.
- Both paradigm leveling and proportional analogy can be attributed to the operation of a single mechanism—Lexical Restructuring.
- No new theoretical apparatus is necessary—"analogy" follows as a natural consequence of the nature of parsing and acquisition.

9.2.4 *Base Identity in Kenstowicz (1996)*

We can turn now to an evaluation of the claim made by Kenstowicz (1996) that Optimality Theory, enriched by two forms of Output–Output Correspondence, namely Base Identity (BI) and Uniform Exponence (UE), provides an account of apparent cases of analogy or leveling. While Kenstowicz only uses the terms "analogy", "analogical", and "leveling" in passing, it will become clear that the data he discusses is of the type included in traditional discussions of analogical change. However, we must note that Kenstowicz does not discuss any cases that would correspond to proportional analogy, the type of change which may increase allomorphy within a paradigm (such as that which gave rise to Old Icelandic *maðr* or Modern English *my*[ðz]). This already provides support for argument (102i) concerning the empirical coverage of the competing proposals, since the discussion of analogy provided above covers both paradigm leveling and proportional analogy. We will see that Kenstowicz's discussion covers only the former. Below, we summarize two of Kenstowicz's examples, one for BI and one for UE, then evaluate the analyses.

The notion of Base Identity, which motivates a set of OOC constraints, is defined by Kenstowicz as in (109).

---

[26] A reviewer suggests that Kiparsky's Alternation Condition may be relevant to this account of analogy. Whatever its status, the Alternation Condition was proposed as a constraint on grammars, and thus a constant part of UG. As discussed above, a constant cannot be the cause of change. A diachronic event cannot be caused by a principle of UG (cf. Hale 2007). However, our discussion of opacity and neutralization does of course echo many of Kiparsky's insights.

(109)   Base Identity
        Given an input structure [X Y], output candidates are evaluated for
        how well they match [X] and [Y], if the latter occur as independent
        words.

Kenstowicz goes on to propose that BI can explain some asymmetries
between nouns and verbs in Korean. According to Kenstowicz, Korean allows
no clusters in onsets or in codas, so stem-final /ps/, for example, must
simplify to [p] when a consonant-initial suffix (or no suffix) follows. The
stem /kaps-/ 'price' loses its /s/ before the conjunctive suffix /-kwa/, but not
before the vowel-initial nominative suffix /-i/. In the citation form there is
no suffix, so the final cluster is again reduced, and the surface form is [kap].
The verbal stem /ēps/ 'not have' also loses its /s/ before a consonant-initial
suffix, but retains it before a vowel-initial suffix. Korean verbs are bound
morphemes, however, and so never appear without some kind of suffix.
There is, therefore, no simple citation form for verb stems as there is for
nouns. Kenstowicz derives the correct Korean output by ranking constraints
against complex codas and onsets (*Complex) above a constraint requiring
input consonants to appear in the output (Parse-C), as reproduced in (110)
and (111).

(110)   Forms in Standard Korean (from Kenstowicz 1996)
        /kaps/ 'price'   /ēps/ 'not have'
        kap   citation form   –   no citation form
        kaps-i   nominative   ēps-essē   past-informal
        kap-k'wa   "price and ..."   ēp-t'a   nonpast-formal

(111)   Constraint ranking to generate cluster simplification

/kaps/	*Complex	Parse-C
☞ kap		*
kaps	*!	

/kaps+i/	*Complex	Parse-C
☞ kapsi		
kapi		*!

Kenstowicz continues his discussion by noting that the above analysis does
not generate the correct output for the "younger generation of Seoul speakers" who never have stem-final consonant clusters in nouns, yet do have
clusters (like their elders) in verb forms. Kenstowicz provides the following
data:

(112) Paradigms for "younger" Korean speakers

/kaps/ 'price'		/ēps/ 'not have'	
kap	citation form	—	no citation form
kap-i	nominative	ēps-ēssē	past-informal
kap-k'wa	"price and ..."	ēp-t'a	nonpast-formal

Kenstowicz's analysis of this dialectal difference is the following:

Thus, while /kaps+i/ surfaces as [kapi] with deletion of the /s/, /ēps-ēssē/ can never be realized as *[ēp-ēssē]. We can account for this asymmetry straightforwardly if the younger generation ranks Base-Identity above Parse-C. In other words, it is more important for the output of /kaps+i/ to resemble the output form of /kaps/ than to resemble the underlying input form.

The relevant tableau is reproduced in (113). The independent word which serves as the Base is given at the bottom of the left-hand column, following Kenstowicz.

(113) Constraint ranking for younger speakers

/kaps+i/	*Complex	Base-Identity	Parse-C
kapsi		*!	
☞ kapi			*

Base:[kap]

Kenstowicz further explains (1996: 13):

Since Korean verbs always require an inflection there is no independently occurring output form of the stem to which the verb stem in /ēps+ēss+ē/ can be compared and so the identity constraint is vacuously satisfied. The Parse-C constraint demanding faithfulness to the underlying form will then choose the candidate that preserves the cluster.

In a footnote, Kenstowicz mentions, but rejects, what is clearly the correct analysis: "While it is possible that younger speakers have restructured the input representation the Base-Identity constraint explains why verb stems may terminate in a CC cluster while noun stems systematically fail to do so."

In fact, it turns out that Kenstowicz's proposal requires *both* OOC *and* lexical restructuring. OT grammars can only vary in two ways: through constraint ranking and through the lexicon. In order for a *universal* constraint of BI to affect only a restricted class of morphemes (nouns) with respect to a given phonological structure (consonant clusters), it is necessary to mark the relevant morphemes in some way. The only way to achieve this is by adding some kind of diacritic to their lexical representations. This diacritic will have to specify, first, which form serves as a base for Base Identity, since the citation form, however defined, will not be the same cross-linguistically; and, second, which markedness constraints (e.g. *Complex) are to be overapplied from the base. The lexical entries of nouns in the grammar of Standard Korean does not contain these diacritics, so lexical restructuring has occurred. This is the argument alluded to in (102ii).

The proposed correspondence relations are strictly speaking outside the domain of theoretical synchronic linguistics. In the Korean example, the grammar of younger speakers is analyzed with respect to the grammar of older speakers. The two grammars differ in output, and Kenstowicz assumes that this difference is located in the ranking of relevant constraints and not in the form of lexical entries. Since younger speakers never exhibit consonant clusters in any forms of the word for price, the null hypothesis should be that there is no cluster underlyingly (see below). The grammars of their parents are irrelevant to an analysis of the new generation's grammars. This point is the basis of argument (102iv).

It is worth recalling at this point that, as Kenstowicz's title indicates, his aim is to utilize OOC to account for what have been called "cyclic" effects. Note that the total absence of forms without diachronic cluster simplification removes any motivation for a cyclic analysis. If a linguist were unaware of earlier stages of Korean, s/he would never posit a cyclic analysis of a morpheme that never alternates. A child learner is in a situation similar to such a linguist—there is no motivation to posit anything but the constant surface form.[27]

A similar point has been made by Alan Prince in electronic discussion:

A correspondent to this list wonders why, in a grammar G such that G(a)=G(b) for potential input elements /a/,/b/, a nonalternating observed element [a] is not (sometimes, always, freely) lexically /b/. The correct answer is surely "why bother?"— i.e. to set up /b/ for [a] when /a/ will do [...] The basic idea reappears as "lexicon optimization" in recent discussions.

So, the OOC approach posited by Kenstowicz is completely incompatible with the standard OT theory of acquisition, which is based on Lexicon Optimization. This is part of argument (102iii).

---

[27] A reviewer comments: "suppose the morpheme /kaps/ 'price' also functioned as a verb root. The O–O analysis claims that it would still keep its cluster in the verb inflection while the restructuring analysis claims that the simplified form should be generalized here." This is a good point, but it assumes that the data were different than it is—it assumes that there might be some *synchronic* evidence for the underlying cluster. There is none according to Kenstowicz's account.

9.2.5 *Regular analogy in lexical categories*

We turn now to the question of how analogy could possibly occur regularly within a definable subcomponent of the lexicon: as Kenstowicz states, the historical cluster simplification in Korean nouns is regular, whereas verbs are unaffected.[28] An explanation for this again can be sought in the acquisition process. We assume that the only goal children have—if, indeed, goal is an appropriate term for the unconscious pattern recognition process of language acquisition[29]—is to acquire the ambient language.

Given the non-uniqueness of the solutions provided by the parser (discussed above), and given the fact that fact that lexical restructuring can lead to both an increase and a decrease in allomorphy, we must assume that non-grammatical factors can come into play in the construction of URs.

A possible solution relies on a form of staged, diachronic lexical diffusion and hypercorrection. Given any number of misacquired URs, even a single one, the dialectal discrepancy between such forms and forms with the historically correct clusters can be extended in sociolinguistic dialect borrowing. Besides the cases which Kenstowicz discusses, it is also true that Korean has nouns which never contain stem-final clusters, for either older or younger speakers: /cip/ 'house' (Martin 1954). Therefore, a child may mistakenly adopt the hypothesis that the citation form of a noun and the UR are identical, since there are stems like *cip-*, for which such a hypothesis is valid. In the appropriate sociolinguistic context, this child's missing cluster in a form like [kapi] can serve as a model of imitation and overgeneralization for others. This will even cause other speakers to replace in usage forms with clusters by forms without clusters. To be precise, such speakers will have two different forms of a single etymological root, and the selection between the two will depend on sociolinguistic factors.[30]

We are safe in assuming that such sociolinguistic diffusion took place, since it is implausible that a whole generation of Seoul Koreans spontaneously misacquired their parents' language in exactly the same way, viz. by failing to produce exactly the same set of consonant clusters in nouns.

---

[28] First note, however, that even if the explanation given here for regular analogical change within a lexical category is incomplete, it does not follow that an account which is flawed for the reasons discussed above is any better.

[29] "Language acquisition is something that happens to a child placed in a certain environment, not something that the child does" (Chomsky 1993: 29).

[30] There are two noteworthy aspects of this discussion: (1) it is not necessarily the case that the hypercorrected or borrowed form of the root replace one which was acquired earlier; (2) this account does not rely on indeterminacy in the functioning of the grammar, since the choice of root form is sociolinguistically conditioned. See Hale (2007) for fuller discussion.

(It is equally implausible, of course, that they all spontaneously acquired grammars with exactly the same ranking difference from that of the older generation, namely one with high-ranked Base Identity with respect to final consonant clusters for nouns. So, neither theory can do without the assumption of sociolinguistic diffusion.) This sociolinguistic phenomenon is a necessary aspect of an explanation of the diffusion of change, but irrelevant to the analysis of synchronic grammatical states. The lexical nature of such diffusion processes (i.e. the lexeme-by-lexeme spread) is well attested in the sociolinguistic and historical literature (see e.g. Labov 1994: ch. 15).

Furthermore, it is worth pointing out that the *kaps/kap* alternation is not merely triggered by the presence/absence of a following vowel. As Martin (1954: 20) explains, Standard Korean presents many cases in which final stem-final clusters are simplified before a vowel:

Before a vowel which does not begin a particle, the copula, or an inflectional ending, the usual treatment is to reduce the excess: *kap olumyen* 'when the price rises', *kap ālki elyewe* 'it's hard to find out the price'.

Martin is describing the deletion of stem-final material which cannot be syllabified in the coda or in a following onset when the syntactic juncture with the following word is not "strong enough" to allow resyllabification. The existence of such surface forms with simplified clusters, despite the existence of a following vowel, is surely relevant to the opacity of underlying forms. Nouns in Standard Korean thus show two variants with a very complex distribution: clusters surface before vowel-initial morphemes within some phonological domain in which resyllabification occurs, say the phonological word or the clitic group. Cluster simplification occurs before consonant initial morphemes within such domains, or before vowels which lie outside such domains. Since, as Kenstowicz points out, verbs are always inflected, the conditions on cluster simplification in verb stems are less opaque (and thus "easier to discover"): the following morpheme is always within the domain of potential resyllabification, so clusters survive before a vowel and are simplified before a consonant. Such differences of opacity between the conditioning of cluster simplification in verbs and nouns may have contributed to a consistent reanalysis of underlying representations in only one of these categories. Also, since noun stems can occur in uninflected form, whereas verb stems cannot, the former can occur prepausally, whereas the latter never do (Martin 1954: 20). In citation form, noun stems are clearly prepausal, and thus subject to cluster simplification in Standard Korean.

9.2.6 *Uniform Exponence in Kenstowicz (1996)*

Kenstowicz adopts a second type of OOC which can be invoked in cases where there is no isolation form of a morpheme to which other forms can be compared. The effect of such a constraint, which is dubbed Uniform Exponence (UE), is to "minimize allomorphic differences":

(114) Uniform Exponence
       Minimize the differences in the realization of a lexical item (morpheme, stem, affix, word).

Kenstowicz proposes using this constraint to account for the behavior in some Spanish dialects of the morpheme written *des-*. This morpheme is realized as [deh]- invariantly, whereas other tokens of [h] are clearly synchronically derivable from /s/. In diachronic terms, the aspiration of coda /s/ has been generalized to prevocalic (onset) contexts for this morpheme:

(115) Spanish aspiration

/mes/		/des-/	
meh	'month'	*deh-calzar*	'unshoe'
mes-eh	plural	*de.h-e.cho*	'refuse'

Rather than assuming that there is a difference in underlying form, i.e. that the relevant URs are /mes-/ and /deh-/, Kenstowicz assumes that both types of morpheme have underlying /s/. In order to assure that *des-* is realized invariantly as [deh-], Kenstowicz posits a Uniform Exponence constraint which is apparently specific to this one morpheme (since he gives no other examples): "the Uniform Exponence Constraint must be specific to the prefix /des/" (1996: 22). This is instead of assuming that the language has both underlying and derived [h]. To get the correct result, the UE constraint must be ranked above the constraint demanding faithfulness to underlying /s/. What we must ask ourselves is this: given a non-alternating morpheme of the shape [deh-], what is a learner most likely to posit as the underlying form? Kenstowicz states that, in general, underlying /s/ is the only source for [h]; but we must ask whether the more salient, synchronically relevant generalization is this historical fact, or the fact that the morpheme in question has one, and only one, realization. Since this morpheme must be lexically marked to ensure that it is always realized with [h], we can consider two ways of achieving this. Kenstowicz's solution is to posit an abstract diacritic which applies to a single morpheme and causes it to surface with [h] in onsets. An alternative is to differentiate this morpheme by assigning it a UR which contains /h/. Again, Lexicon Optimization demands the UR with /h/.

Kenstowicz's solution raises another problem. Obviously, all theories must come to grips with exceptions, but invoking UE "opportunistically" is a blatant example of the arbitrary appeal to co-phonologies discussed by Inkelas et al. (1997). These authors argue convincingly against unprincipled appeals to co-phonologies to account for apparent exceptional behavior. In general, they license appeal to a co-phonology only in cases where the exceptional morphemes constitute a well-defined morphological or syntactic category. Otherwise, apparent exceptions should be handled by positing distinct URs for morphemes which display different alternation patterns.

> It is clear that co-phonologies are required to handle cases of competing sets of alternations triggered in disjoint sets of morphological constructions . . . However, *morpheme-specific* co-phonologies are an entirely different analytic device engendering a number of serious problems. . .
>
> In sum, prespecification is the most constrained while simultaneously the only descriptively adequate way of handling lexical exceptionality to static patterns and alternations. (Inkelas et al. 1997: 398, 410)

Of course, we might consider that a class of morphemes containing just one member, *des-*, would constitute a coherent, well-defined class. However, it turns out that in at least some of the Spanish dialects which have invariant [deh] there are other morphemes with invariant [h], regardless of whether a vowel or consonant follows. These include the plural forms of the article, orthographic *las*, *los*, which are pronounced [lah], [loh], not only in *La*[h] *Palmas*, but even in a form like *Lo*[h] *Angeles*, as well as uninflected forms like *ma*[h] 'more'. This set of morphemes clearly does not form a coherent class. Therefore, we are forced to adopt a prespecification analysis (to adopt the terminology of Inkelas et al.), namely that surface [h] is derived from /s/ only in morphemes which alternate.[31]

It has been pointed out that such an analysis fails to capture the fact that very many Spanish [h]s are derived from /s/. In response, consider that the situation in Spanish is formally identical to German devoicing, mentioned above in (104). Consider how one might apply the use of BI or UE to an analysis of the German coda devoicing facts. Rather than positing a difference in UR between what is traditionally assumed to be the two roots, /bunt/ and

---

[31] This analysis finds anecdotal support from Kenneth Hill (p.c.), who reports the following facts from San Salvador Spanish, an aspirating dialect. When trying to speak in a more formal register, speakers may "undo" the effects of what we have analyzed as synchronic aspiration, producing e.g. [mes] for their normal outcome [meh] 'month'. However, they never undo the effects of what we have analyzed as diachronic aspiration, i.e. they do not produce [s] for morphemes with non-alternating [h], like *mas*. This suggests that the alternating and non-alternating sounds have different underlying sources, thus providing support for the prespecification analysis.

/bund/, we might assume that the two roots are both /bund/ underlyingly. The well-known alternations exhibited by these roots ([bunt]/[buntəs] *vs.* [bunt]/[bundəs]) could then be accounted for in the following fashion: the alternating paradigm is due to standard phonological processes—coda devoicing or its OT equivalent; the non-alternating paradigm is subject to the same phonology, but a (set of) morpheme-specific UE constraint(s) guarantees that alternations are suppressed for some morphemes. If one sought to be truly perverse, it could be claimed that such an account allows for the expression of a newly discovered generalization: no German roots end with a voiceless obstruent.

This argument leads to one more objection to Kenstowicz's account of the Spanish facts. The decision to posit underlying /des/ for a morpheme which surfaces uniformly as [deh] is apparently motivated by some kind of economy considerations, such as the goal of minimizing the inventory of underlying segments. In other words, Kenstowicz is attempting to constrain underlying representations. This goal is in direct conflict with the OT principle of Richness of the Base (Prince and Smolensky 1993), which precludes constraints on underlying forms, deriving distributional effects instead from constraint interaction. This is part of argument (102iii).

9.2.7 *Summary*

We can now reiterate the arguments against invoking Output–Output Correspondence constraints to account for cases of "analogy". We have seen that analyzing the Korean and Spanish data by means of OOC is unmotivated—there is no evidence of cyclic effects. The OOC accounts are also in violation of Lexicon Optimization and Richness of the Base.

Furthermore, Kenstowicz is really analyzing correspondences that hold between *different grammars*. We would not expect OOC to provide an account of analogy, since OT is a theory of grammar, and analogy is a diachronic process, a relationship between grammars. Alternative accounts for widespread analogy shown by different dialects require lexical restructuring and sociolinguistic diffusion. The OOC proposal requires both of these factors as well as a powerful new constraint type.

In addition, the OOC account is only relevant to a subset of analogical changes, namely those that reduce allomorphy in a given paradigm. By contrast, the account of analogy we propose here does not even require reference to a paradigm or a base form, since lexical restructuring in acquisition arises as a result of the nature of parsing. Note that both forms of OOC considered here demand Correspondence between related forms, forms that at least share certain morphological material. The discussion of Base Identity in Korean made reference to paradigms which are leveled in the direction of a base form which, crucially, occurs as an independent word. The discussion of Uniform Exponence in Spanish relied crucially on a single morpheme being assigned a unique phonetic realization at the cost of violating (by hypothesis) some otherwise general patterns in the distribution of sounds. If we refer back to the extension of ð into the 'man' word in Old Icelandic, or indeed to any of the well-attested cases of interparadigm analogy, we find that OOC cannot even begin to provide a motivation for such diachronic processes. The diachronic restructuring of URs like /mann-/ > /manð-/ actually *decreases* the uniformity of exponence (i.e. increases allomorphy).

The theory proposed here, one which posits lexical restructuring, accounts for both inter- and intra-paradigm analogy in a unified fashion: both result from restructuring of underlying representations by an acquirer vis-à-vis the target language. The theory provides a diachronic solution to a diachronic phenomenon. It does not confuse the generative notion of language as mental grammar with the sociopolitical notion of language as speech community, in which context, for example, one might describe relationships between the speech of younger and older speakers. The theory proposed here thus better explains the diachronic nature of what is traditionally called analogical change by maintaining an explicit generative theory of grammar. By removing the burden of explanation for analogy from the theory of grammar (in the generative tradition), and locating the source of analogy in acquisition and sociolinguistic borrowing, we end up with a more constrained theory of grammar.

Once the data discussed by Kenstowicz are seen in this light, it becomes clear that at least some of the puzzles for which OOC was proposed disappear. The empirical basis for such powerful constraint types is thus significantly weakened. Recalling that the application of OOC to Rotuman was also flawed should only strengthen our skepticism.

Finally, recall that Kenstowicz's account of Spanish and Korean itself requires *both* OOC *and* lexical restructuring. In an OT grammar, the only sources of cross-linguistic variation are in the constraint ranking and in the lexicon. Since Kenstowicz proposes that UE and BI affect only certain morphemes, the grammar will have to specify which ones they are. Since the universal constraint set does not contain constraints which refer to specific morphemes of Spanish or Korean, the sensitivity to these OOC constraints will have to be somehow encoded in the morphemes themselves. This represents a change in underlying representation from the grammars which do not show UE or BI. Reranking alone cannot selectively affect an arbitrary set of morphemes. Again, Occam's Razor is relevant to the evaluation of competing theories—the theory that needs lexical restructuring alone is to be preferred over that which needs lexical restructuring *and* OOC.[32]

For convenience we restate in point form the six main arguments made against Kenstowicz's analysis:

- The synchrony/diachrony distinction is not maintained in the OOC account.
- Our alternative account requires only lexical restructuring, but the OOC account *also* requires lexical restructuring.
- OOC is relevant to only one kind of analogy; our alternative account works for both kinds.
- The OOC account is incompatible with Lexicon Optimization.
- The OOC account is incompatible with Richness of the Base.
- The OOC account represents arbitrary appeal to morpheme-specific co-phonologies.

Of course it is impossible to critique and provide alternatives for every single use of OOC in the literature, but the issues raised here are not atypical. Further examples are discussed in Hale et al. (1998*b*; 1998*a*).

9.3 Conclusions

The appeal to OOC is part of a general resurgence of functionalist thinking in linguistics: it is intuitively satisfying to imagine that a principle like Uniform Exponence, which would minimize allomorphy, is relevant to grammar. However, as we have seen, there are serious problems with this view. First, lexical restructuring can account for all the cases of analogy in which OOC has been invoked, as well as for cases where OOC is not only irrelevant but is also violated outright. Basic scientific methodology (Occam's Razor) forces us to reject the OOC explanation. Second, even if one were willing to accept functionalist arguments for why leveling of paradigms occurs (to reduce allomorphy), it would still be misguided to build OOC into the grammar: analogy occurs in the course of transmission/acquisition of language. Since aspects of acquisition are responsible for analogy, it would be redundant to posit that OOC (grammar) was responsible for analogy as well. Again, basic scientific methodology forces us to reject the OOC explanation. Finally, the view of opacity expounded by Kiparsky and Menn (1977), referred to above, has

---

[32] Skeptics may argue that OOC is needed anyway to account for cyclic effects, so its use in accounting for "analogy" is not costly. Even if we were to grant that OOC *may* be necessary for cyclic effects, formal elegance would still favor the avoidance of diacritics for sensitivity to OOC constraints, especially in the absence of any proposals about how such a formalism could be implemented.

leveling as a natural consequence. No new grammatical machinery is posited under such a view. Once again, we must reject the OOC analysis. Functional considerations may or may not be relevant to a full understanding of language, including the nature of change and acquisition; but strictly speaking, these notions are neither useful for understanding analogy, nor are they part of grammar *per se*.

This chapter has argued against the inclusion of Output–Output Correspondence constraints within the synchronic grammar. This discussion allows us to reject a class of solutions to the Catalan problem that we did not include in the original list in Chapter 1 (feeling it would be too cumbersome to explain its workings in detail without a full treatment of OOC). If we allow the existence of morpheme-specific paradigm uniformity constraints, we could just say that the 'dry' word and the 'blind' word have *same* underlying consonants. The computational system (rules or constraints) would generate an alternation for both lexical items, but the 'blind' word could be subject to a paradigm uniformity constraint that overrode the alternation. Given the challenges confronting such a solution—challenges we have attempted to outline in detail in this chapter—we will consider it no further here.

Part IV
Conclusions

10

A principled solution to Catalan

10.1 Further observations on the computational machinery of phonology

Some readers of the manuscript version of this book have taken it to be an extended critique of Optimality Theory, at least in some of its manifestations. While we have presented what we feel are methodological shortcomings of certain aspects of OT, including fairly fundamental aspects, the real purpose of our work here is much broader. Our reading of the generative literature on phonology finds therein a strong tendency for a knee-jerk reaction to recalcitrant data: expansion of the computational power of the phonology, often in formally ill-defined or even incoherent ways. The best science, in our view, results when, rather than bloat theories with machinery which makes possible highly accurate data-matching, we adopt a critical attitude towards the alleged data itself. Does it truly fall within the purview of a theory of phonology as computation? Surrendering overly readily (and sometimes without explicit acknowledgement of the surrender) fundamental assumptions which underlie the pursuit of scientific phonology is a last-resort move, and we are far from having a sufficiently rich understanding of the nature of phonology for such drastic moves to be necessary. Optimality Theory has certainly expanded the *explicitness* with which certain fundamental aspects of building a theory of phonological computation are being treated (e.g. learning-theoretic issues, as well the nature of phonological UG). Our target is thus not a particular theory of phonology, but a particular *practice*.

Before presenting our final discussion of the Catalan problem in light of all that has come before, there is one more critical issue which must be treated in some detail. The problem existed in traditional rule-based approaches to phonology (and continues to plague such approaches, to the extent they are still practiced); and if such approaches are to be resuscitated in some form in the post-OT phonological world, it would be best if it could be dealt with from the outset. We outline our solution to it here as a first step in this direction.

In practice, as inspection of any introductory phonology book will show, it has been implicitly assumed in generative phonology that a rule will apply to any representation that contains a superset of the information contained in the rule's structural description (SD). In other words, if the SD of a rule R subsumes a representation Q, then Q is an input to R. Rules apply to natural classes of segments, and natural classes are symbolized as a representation that subsumes the representation of each of its members.

It turns out, however, that this is *not* the interpretive procedure developed in *SPE* (Chomsky and Halle 1968), the foundational work in the field:

(116)   Interpretive procedure from *SPE* (ch. 8, p. 337)
A rule of the form $A \rightarrow B/X\_\_\_Y$ applies to any string $Z = \ldots X'A'Y'\ldots$, where X', A', Y' are not distinct from X, A, Y, respectively; and it converts Z to $Z' = \ldots X'B'Y' \ldots$, where B' contains all specified features of B in addition to all features of A' not specified in B.

Distinctness is defined as follows:[1]

(117)   Distinctness in *SPE* (p. 336)
Two units U1 and U2 are distinct if and only if there is at least one feature F such that U1 is specified $[\alpha F]$ and U2 is specified $[\beta F]$ where α is plus and β is minus...

The (typically implicit) appeal to subsumption in general phonological practice derives from the assumption of a logical equivalence between subsumption and non-distinctness, the idea that if x is non-distinct from y, then either x subsumes y or y subsumes x. This equivalence does not hold, however, except under the working assumption of the *SPE* era that representations are fully specified for all features. It *is* true that if either x subsumes y or y subsumes x, then x and y are non-distinct; but a simple example can illustrate that the converse is not valid if we allow for partially specified feature matrices in lexical entries.

Let $x = [+round, -back]$ and let $y = [+round, +hi]$. The representations x and y do not disagree with respect to any features, and are thus non-distinct, but one clearly does not subsume the other. And we clearly do not expect, say, that x would satisfy a structural description specified as y.

As a further example, consider that by strict application of the *SPE* interpretive procedure, an underspecified vowel that had only the feature

---

[1] We have abridged the cited passage to reflect our assumption of binary features—the original allows for various feature systems. We adopt without argument binary-valued feature but the points made here are compatible with theories that allow various kinds of underspecification.

[−round] would satisfy the SD of a rule like (118), since the representation [−round] is not distinct from the representation [−nasal]:

(118)   [−nasal] → [−voice]

This is surely an undesirable result.

Non-distinct representations are, in the general case, what is called "consistent" in unification-based frameworks—that is, they have no incompatible feature values. But non-distinctness, or consistency, does not reduce to subsumption.[2] The preceding discussion should make it clear that the interpretation of structural descriptions is yet another topic in generative phonology that warrants re-examination.

10.2 Feature-counting evaluation metrics

Perhaps all that is needed is to reject the *SPE* interpretive procedure in favor of one appealing to subsumption, since this is what the practice has been for the last several decades. Under this view, any representation subsumed by (containing a superset of the information contained in) a rule's Structural Description is taken to be a licit input to the rule. This interpretive procedure has the desirable effect of allowing rules to apply to more than just single representations—they can apply to a natural class of representations whose description is subsumed by the rule's SD.

This interpretive procedure entails that a rule that changed feature values, say from +F to −F for some feature F, would apply vacuously to representations that are already −F before the application of the rule. For example, a straightforward statement of Russian or Polish coda devoicing might be written as in (119):

(119)   [+cons, −son] → [−voice] in CODA

This rule applies non-vacuously to [+voice] inputs that are [+cons, −son]—in other words it makes them [−voice]. However, if one were to fully implement the convention of rule interpretation based on subsumption, the rule also applies, albeit vacuously, to [−voice] inputs that are [+cons, −son]. To reiterate, both [+voice] and [−voice] satisfy the SD to be inputs to the rule.

---

[2] We have found the same point made by Bayer and Johnson (1995: section 2) in a discussion of Lambek Categorial Grammar: "Interestingly, in cases where features are fully specified, these subsumption and consistency requirements are equivalent." However, it appears that the relevance of this observation to the application of phonological rules has not been noted before Reiss (2003b) from which this discussion is derived.

This interpretation of SDs is related to the *SPE* feature-counting evaluation metric, the overarching goal of which is to minimize redundancy in the grammar, as seen in the Conciseness Condition formulated by Kenstowicz and Kisseberth (1979).

(120)   The Conciseness Condition (one component of the *SPE* evaluation metric, from Kenstowicz and Kisseberth 1979: 336)

If there is more than one possible grammar that can be constructed for a given body of data, choose the grammar that is most concise in terms of the number of feature specifications.

With hindsight, it is now apparent that the Conciseness Condition is flawed by virtue of its parochialness—the model of grammar chosen by the analyst should take into account the models necessary to generate other languages as well as the one in question, and not just choose the most concise grammar that can generate a given corpus.[3] Thus we can see that the Conciseness Condition as stated here is in direct conflict with the search for Universal Grammar—the grammar of S_0, the initial state of the language faculty—as can be seen from this quote (cited earlier by us in another context) from Chomsky:[4]

(121)   Choosing among extensionally equivalent grammars (Chomsky 1986: 38)
         Because evidence from Japanese can evidently bear on the correctness of a theory of S_0, it can have indirect—but very powerful– bearing on the choice of the grammar that attempts to characterize the I-language attained by a speaker of English.

In other words, evidence from one language should bear on the best analysis of other languages. As the reader will recall from our earlier discussion, if two hypotheses, A and B, concerning UG are empirically adequate to provide an explanatory account of English, but only one of the two, say A, is adequate to provide an explanatory account of Japanese, then we should select A as the best available hypothesis for a theory of S_0 that can lead to acquisition of *both languages*.

---

[3] Actually, this point is already made in *Syntactic Structures*, where Chomsky says that the "ultimate outcome of linguistic analysis should be a theory in which the descriptive devices utilized in particular grammars are presented and studied abstractly with no specific reference to particular languages".

[4] An important question, discussed in Ch. 4, is whether the correct formulation of a rule is necessarily the most concise one that is consistent with the data and with the cross-linguistic (universal) demands discussed in this chapter. Recall that we argued in the discussion of Georgian that learnability considerations provide a reason to favor less concise rules than we traditionally posit. This chapter provides another argument for non-conciseness.

The traditional interpretation of SDs such as (119) is not the only logical possibility—it could have been argued that a rule like Polish devoicing should be formulated so as not to apply vacuously, as in (122):

(122)   [+cons, −son, +voice] → [−voice] in CODA

It seems that the decision to adopt the Conciseness Condition, and thus the rule format of (119), rather than (122), was motivated by the influence that engineering approaches to information theory had on the pioneers of generative phonology, an influence that has been described as leading to a dead end (Morris Halle 1975: 532 and p.c.). Formulation (119) was seen as the more efficient, and thus better, engineering solution since it was more concise than (122).[5]

In this chapter, we explore another logical possibility for the interpretation of SDs and show that it solves long-standing problems in phonological theory—the question of how to allow rules to target unmarked or unspecified feature values and the intimately related issue of the distinction between feature-filling and feature-changing rules.

10.3 Subsumption and structural descriptions—a problem

The SD in (119) subsumes various possible input representations. Crucially, all inputs which satisfy the SD must be specified for at least the features [+cons, −son]. For us to further understand the nature of the set of representations that can serve as inputs to the rule, we need to focus on features that are *absent* from the rule's SD. The traditional understanding of (119) depends on two distinct interpretations of the absence of a specification:

(123)   Interpreting the absence of a specification
a.   Absence of a feature value implies that the feature is *irrelevant* to the application of the rule.
b.   Absence of a feature value implies that the feature does not need to be mentioned in the rule, because the rule neutralizes different values for the feature.

---

[5] The belief that the mind organized language in a maximally efficient manner may have also motivated the Conciseness Condition. However, it could also have been argued that avoiding vacuous application would have constituted a more efficient solution. Anderson's (1985: 327) remarks on the topic are also telling: "Early concern for evaluation procedures...turned out to be something of a dead end...The appeal of feature counting went away...not with a bang, but with a whimper."

The absence of reference to features for place of articulation in the input of (119), for example, is interpreted as in (123a) to mean that the rule applies *regardless* of the place of articulation of the input consonant. In other words, features such as [cor] and [lab] do not appear in the rule because they are irrelevant to its application—Polish devoicing applies to obstruents at all places of articulation.

Assuming that Polish alternating stops are underlyingly [+voice],[6] under the subsumption interpretation of SDs the rule applies vacuously to underlying [−voice] stops and it changes underlyingly [+voice] stops to [−voice]. Thus the rule's Structural Description (SD) contains no reference to [voice] since the rule neutralizes the distinction between [+voice] and [−voice]. This is interpretation (123b).

So, some features are absent from the SD because the rule does not affect them or depend on them in any way (123a), and others are absent because the rule neutralizes their two possible values (123b). To reiterate, any representation that is subsumed by the SD of the rule satisfies that SD. Thus (120) can apply to the following inputs:

(124a)   representations in which the absent features are irrelevant to rule application; *and*

(124b)   representations in which the absent features are neutralized by the rule.

Consider, in contrast to the standard view of Polish-type patterns, a type of data which only became known much later in the history of generative phonology, a pattern which requires rules that fill in values on necessarily underspecified segments.

In Turkish, for example, Inkelas (1996; Inkelas and Orgun 1995) argues that there is necessarily a three-way contrast in voicing. Some stem-final stops show a t/d alternation (125a), with [t] appearing in codas and [d] appearing in onsets. Inkelas convincingly argues for an underlying segment that has all the features of a coronal stop, but is unspecified for [voice]. She denotes this feature bundle as /D/. She states that the segment is assigned the value [−voice] in codas, and [+voice] elsewhere. Other stem-final stops consistently surface as [t] and thus are posited to be /t/ underlyingly (125b), and others surface as [d] consistently and are thus posited to be underlying /d/ (125c).

---

[6] We will do so without argument here. The reader will notice that if Polish alternating stops are instead unmarked for voicing, the problem is to voice them in the appropriate contexts without targeting the non-alternating voiceless ones.

(125)   Turkish voicing alternations[7]
   a.   Alternating: [Øvoice] (unmarked for [voice]) /D/
        kanat 'wing' *kanatlar* 'wing-plural' *kanadım* 'wing-1sg.poss'
   b.   Non-alternating voiceless: [−voice] /t/
        sanat 'art' *sanatlar* 'art-plural' *sanatım* 'art-1sg.poss'
   c.   Non-alternating voiced: [+voice] /d/
        etüd 'etude' *etüdler* 'etude-plural' *etüdüm* 'etude-1sg.poss'

The rule responsible for making /D/ surface as [t] in codas would be identical to (119), but would have to be interpreted differently, since it crucially cannot apply to underlying /d/. In other words the representation of /D/ subsumes that of /d/ (and also that of /t/), but the rule that affects /D/ does not affect /d/. It is necessary to interpret the absence of [voice] in the SD as in (126c), which completes the list of interpretations of absent features under discussion:

(126)   Interpreting the absence of a specification (revised)
   a.   Absence of a feature value implies that the feature is *irrelevant* to the application of the rule (=124a).
   b.   Absence of a feature value implies that the feature does not need to be mentioned in the rule, because the rule neutralizes different values for the feature (=124b).
   c.   Absence of a feature value implies that the feature *must* be absent from a potential input representation for the rule to apply.

Without an intelligent homunculus, a mental grammar needs a solution to the problem of correctly selecting the relevant interpretation of an SD.

---

[7] This data has been challenged in discussion on the grounds that some Turkish speakers do not pronounce the (c) forms with voiced obstruent in coda position. The irrelevance of such an objection is apparent, as long as the data represents a possible language. Since Orgun is a native speaker, we accept the data as given. The presence of inflectional morphology suggests that the forms should be treated as Turkish and not as French (the language they were borrowed from). We refer the reader to the cited works for further data showing that this Turkish case is not isolated—Inkelas discusses several cases with the same logical structure. She further shows that these data cannot be handled by labeling certain morphemes as "exceptions". For example, she provides examples of a single morpheme with both an obstruent that alternates in voicing and one that is consistently voiced (even in coda position): *edʒdat* 'ancestor', *edʒdatlar* 'ancestor-plural', *edʒdadɯ* 'ancestor-acc'. This example shows that failure to devoice obstruents in coda position cannot be a property of individual morphemes, since the stem-medial /dʒ/ remains voiced although it is always in coda position, whereas the stem-final /d/ alternates. Instead the two segments must be representationally distinct: the former is [+voice] and the latter is underspecified for voicing.

10.4 Earlier approaches

One way out of this dilemma would be to allow the grammar to refer to [Øvoice] as a possible specification:

(127)   [+cons, −son, Øvoice] → [−voice] in CODA

We provide below a principled argument against allowing [Øvoice] as a possible specification. Traditionally, this move has been avoided by most researchers on the intuitive grounds that it represents an overly powerful enrichment of the representational apparatus of phonology.

Instead, however, the notational apparatus of rules has been enriched. Typically, a rule label, **Feature Filling** or, equivalently, **Structure Filling**, is used, as in (128), to ensure that such a rule is not (over-)applied to fully specified segments and can only apply to provide feature values to underspecified segments. In the absence of such a label, the correct interpretation is left to the intelligence of the reader.

(128)   **Feature Filling:**   [+cons, −son] → [−voice] in CODA

This is the solution proposed by Inkelas and Orgun (1995: 777). We reproduce their rules exactly in (129).

(129)   Feature-filling rules from Inkelas and Orgun (1995: 777)
        a.   DEVOICING: Coda plosive → [−voice]   (structure-filling)
        b.   VOICING: Onset plosive → [+voice]   (structure-filling)

Their rule (129a) is basically equivalent to (128), and they provide a second feature filling rule (129b) to provide the alternating stops with [+voice] in onsets.

Another example of the **Feature Filling** label can be found in McCarthy (1994: 210), which formulates a rule spreading [pharyngeal] from a consonant to a following vowel. In addition to an autosegmental representation of spreading, McCarthy includes the following in the rule statement: "Condition: Feature-filling." He notes that the "intent of the condition restricting [the spreading] to feature-filling is to block the rule from lowering any vowel other than the featureless vowel schwa". Because it is featureless, consisting just of enough of a representation to identify it as a vowel, the representation of schwa will subsume that of every other vowel—less specification entails greater generality.

Kiparsky's (1985) discussion of coronal underspecification briefly notes the problem treated here, stating that it is necessary "to work out some way of referring to unmarked segments" when representations are not fully specified.

However, his manner of distinguishing underspecified segments is not satisfactory, since he introduces a new diacritic into representations just in places where, for example, [+coronal] (or a CORONAL class node) would be specified. Kiparsky proposes that (130a) be the representation of a coronal fricative such as /s/, where the x on the line to the missing node means "there is no specification on the tier of place features". How do we know (or more importantly, how does the grammar "know") that the x doesn't denote underspecification for some other feature?

(130)   Representations of /s/ and /f/ (Kiparsky 1985)
        a.   /s/   b.   /f/

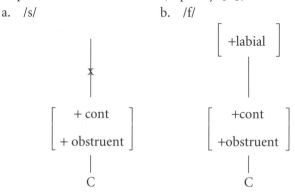

Kiparsky represents a non-coronal voiceless fricative, such as /f/ as in (130b), where the root node is associated to a labial place node. The natural class including both these voiceless fricatives would presumably be represented by Kiparsky as in (131), unspecified for features on the place tier:

(131)   Representation of all fricatives in Kiparsky's (1985) system

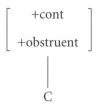

Obviously, Kiparsky's system of representing /s/ in (130a) is the equivalent of specifying [+coronal], since the representation of /s/ contains information not present in (131), and thus it can hardly be called underspecified.[8]

    Similar use of a diacritic denoting the absence of an association to a given node can be found in Archangeli (1988): where a "melody unit or anchor" Z

---

[8] Kiparsky's suggestion leads to other problems as well—does the line in (130a) block spreading?

can be linked to a feature F via normal association lines between Z and F; obligatorily unlinked to F if Z is enclosed in a circle; or ambiguously linked or unlinked to F in the absence of an association line or circle.

(132)   Linkage notation (adapted from Archangeli 1988): Z is a "melody unit or anchor"

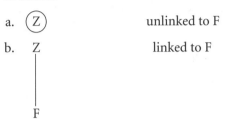

a.   (Z)   unlinked to F

b.   Z   linked to F

        |

        F

c.   Z   ambiguously linked or unlinked to F

This notation presents a problem similar to that in Kiparsky's (1985) system, since the meaning of the circle around the Z in a given rule is "unlinked to the feature F which the rule will provide". Thus this notation of "underspecification" requires reference to the very feature whose mention it is meant to avoid.

In the next section, we develop a Unified Interpretive Procedure (UIP) for Structural Descriptions that vitiates the need for explicit **Feature Filling** or **Feature Changing** diacritics, as well as the need to refer to features that are absent from a representation—we do not use [ØF] as a possible specification. This strikes us as the most restrictive approach to the problem of the interpretation of SDs.

10.5 The Unified Interpretive Procedure

For a given rule $\mathcal{R}_a$, we can refer to its Structural Description as SD_a, its Structural Change as SC_a, and its Environment as Env_a, giving us the simple rule schema in (133):

(133)   Rule schema[9]
         $\mathcal{R}_a\colon SD_a \to SC_a$ in Env_a

We will employ Greek letter variables in the usual way: $\alpha \in \{+, -\}$.

---

[9] More discussion is required for deletion, insertion, and metathesis rules. These problems are addressed in work in progress by Charles Reiss. Also, the environment *Env* is, strictly speaking, part of the SD, but we will treat them separately for the sake of clarity.

We also assume that something like Principle 6 of Chomsky (1967) is valid: "Two successive lines of a derivation can differ by at most one feature specification."[10] One of the advantages that classical Optimality Theory phonology can claim over traditional rule-based approaches is the greater restrictiveness of the (assumed to be universal) constraint set vis-à-vis the highly unrestricted set of possible phonological rules. Chomsky's Principle 6 helps restrict the notion of "possible phonological rule", and thus its adoption gives rise to a more restrictive theory of phonology, with all the advantages that that confers on the acquirer in the learning context. For our purposes, this principle means that SC_a will always contain a single feature specification, $+F$, $-F$ or αF. We can now formulate the interpretive procedure for structural descriptions, replacing αF for SC_a.

(134)   Unified Interpretive Procedure for structural descriptions
A representation Q is an input to a rule $\mathcal{R}_a$:
$SD_a \rightarrow \alpha F$ in Env_a
if and only if SD_a subsumes Q and one of the following holds:
a. $-\alpha F \in SD_a$ (SD_a and thus each Q that satisfies SD_a is specified $-\alpha F$) OR
b. $-\alpha F \notin Q$ (no Q that satisfies SD_a is specified $-\alpha F$, and thus neither is SD_a specified $-\alpha F$)

First consider (134a): since (135a) requires that SD_a be specified $-\alpha F$, it follows that every representation Q subsumed by SD_a be thus specified. Since SD_a must subsume every input to the rule, each input must also be specified $-\alpha F$. A representation Q that satisfies this condition will undergo feature changing to αF.

Now consider (134b): the requirement of (134b) is that Q not be specified $-\alpha F$, so it can be either specified αF or *not specified at all* for feature F. Since Q is required not to be specified $-\alpha F$, any Q that satisfies this condition will not be subsumed by a SD_a which is $-\alpha F$. In other words, if Q is not $-\alpha F$, and Q is an input to $\mathcal{R}_a$, then SD_a is also not $-\alpha F$. (We thus see that (134a) and (134b) are mutually exclusive—they cannot be satisfied simultaneously.) If condition (134b) is fulfilled, the rule will either fill in the value αF or vacuously "change" αF to αF.

The two conditions thus require either (a) Q is $-\alpha F$ or (b) Q is not $-\alpha F$. (Further conditions are imposed by SD_a, of course.) The existence of

---

[10]   This notion can be adapted for more recent theories of representation. We do not make use of, for example, feature geometry, and we have argued elsewhere that feature geometry is not a necessary or desirable part of phonological theory (Reiss 2003a and chapter 8 of this book).

underspecification means that "not $-\alpha$F" does not mean "αF", but rather "either αF or unspecified for F".

Thus, if SC_a is $-$F, and SD_a is specified $+$F, then an input to $\mathcal{R}_a$ must contain $+$F in order to satisfy SD_a by condition a. However, if SC_a is $-$F but SD_a is not specified $+$F, then an input to $\mathcal{R}_a$ may not contain $+$F. It may be specified $-$F ($\mathcal{R}_a$ will apply vacuously in this case) or it may be unspecified for F ($\mathcal{R}_a$ will fill in $-$F in this case) and thus satisfy SD_a by condition b.

Similarly, we can switch all the signs. If SC_a is $+$F, and SD_a is specified $-$F, then an input to $\mathcal{R}_a$ must contain $-$F in order to satisfy SD_a by condition a. However, if SC_a is $+$F but SD_a is not specified $-$F, then an input to $\mathcal{R}_a$ may not contain $-$F, but it may be specified $+$F ($\mathcal{R}_a$ will apply vacuously in this case) or it may be unspecified for F ($\mathcal{R}_a$ will fill-in $+$F in this case) and thus satisfy SD_a by condition b.

So, (134a) corresponds to traditional **Feature Changing** rules and (134b) to traditional **Feature Filling** rules. However, the UIP precludes both the necessity of labeling rules as to what type they are and of referring to unmarked values such as [Ø voice]. The crucial advance we have made is this: instead of having "to work out some way of referring to unmarked segments", we have a way to ensure that they are treated as a class with representations that are vacuously affected by rules.

In a language like Polish, where we have a two-way voiced/voiceless contrast in obstruents, we might be tempted to retain the traditional formulation of the devoicing rule and the traditional interpretation of structural descriptions. We would still generate Polish-type output. However, a truly explanatory approach to phonology allows us to see that Turkish can tell us something about Polish—the correct formulation of the rule must be something closer to (122) than to (119). Since we are interested in Universal Grammar, we are interested in a single interpretive procedure for all grammars. This was the point of the quotation from Chomsky above.

In this particular case of the representation of Polish devoicing, UG should be assumed to use the same interpretive procedure as is used in Turkish. More concise rules can be written for just the Polish data, but they would not be rules of human phonology, if the UIP is correct. We do not want a rule to be interpreted differently depending on what language it is a rule of. Since the interpretive procedure for all languages is assumed to be identical, but the patterns to be accounted for are different, the rules themselves must differ as well. Polish uses (122), whereas Turkish uses (119).

In other words, the traditional account of Polish devoicing using the subsumption-based interpretive procedure would be extensionally equivalent to the account proposed here (using (122) and the UIP), but we now can choose between them in a principled fashion. Again, this is the type of argumentation suggested by Chomsky's statement regarding Japanese.

A further implication of the UIP is that we now derive the intuitively valid result that rules do not treat representations that are +F and representations that are −F as a natural class to the exclusion of representations that are unmarked for F. With respect to the Turkish data discussed above this means that, for example, /t/ and /D/ constitute a natural class (they are *not* [+voice]), and /d/ and /D/ do so as well (they are *not* [−voice]), but that /t/ and /d/ do not, to the exclusion of /D/.

For the sake of explicitness, let us reiterate the difference between the simple subsumption-based interpretation of *SDs* and that given by the UIP. A rule like (119) should apply to [+voice] stops according to the traditional interpretive procedure. The *SD* of (119) is given as [+cons, −son], and since the representation of, say, /t/, /D/ and /d/ are subsumed by [+cons, −son], the rule should apply to all three. But this would not let us distinguish /d/ from /D/, which we need to do for Turkish.

However, using the UIP, a rule like (119), where the *SC* is [−voice], cannot apply to [+voice] representations like /d/:

- (134a) is not satisfied since [+voice] is not in the *SD* of the rule as stated.
- By (134b) any Q which is an input to the rule cannot be specified as [+voice].

Since neither condition is satisfied, the rule cannot apply to [+voice] representations. However, both /t/ and /D/ satisfy condition (134a), since /t/ is [−voice] and the rule applies vacuously; and /D/ satisfies condition (134b), since /D/ is *not* [−voice] and thus the rule fills in this value. This would work perfectly for our model of Turkish.

Consider now the rule in (122), repeated here:

(122)   [+cons, −son, +voice] → [−voice] in CODA

Since the *SD* of the rule contains [+voice], the rule can obviously apply to [+voice] representations. It cannot apply to representations that are either specified [−voice] or are unspecified for [voice]—the *SD* does not subsume such representations. This would work perfectly for our model of Polish.

A reviewer once objected to the UIP on the grounds that it is an extremely powerful device, since it is meant to be relevant to all rules in all languages. This objection reflects a misunderstanding of the notion of power in theory construction. In fact, a single interpretive procedure that holds for all rules in all languages provides a *less* powerful (and thus better) model than one that allows various devices on an ad hoc rule-by-rule and language-by-language basis. The objection can thus be dismissed.

Note that the result of the UIP in (134) can also be derived by allowing the use of logical negation in phonological representations. For example, if Turkish /t/ and /D/ were both specified [NOT+voice], then the rule that fills in [−voice] on /D/ in codas could refer to this specification:

(135)   [+cons, −son, NOT+voice] → [−voice] in CODA

Allowing negation in representations to have scope over a single valued feature such as [+voice] will not obviously create problems. However, allowing negation to have scope over sets of valued features would wreak havoc with the notion of natural class. It would allow us to treat the complement set of each natural class as a natural class. For example, the segments described by the set NOT[+voiced, +labial] would include both [d] and [p], but not [b].

What the UIP does is introduce logical negation into the interpretation of rules without enriching the set of primitives that can appear in lexical representations. The UIP does redefine the notion of natural class, in fact, but in a very restricted fashion: "[αF]" and "unspecified for F" constitute a natural class to the exclusion of "[$-\alpha$F]" in the sense that the difference between otherwise identical members of a natural class "NOT[$-\alpha$F]" is neutralized by a rule. Under this view, natural classes are not defined by a feature matrix that subsumes a set of phonological representations, but instead by a set of phonological representations that are accepted as inputs to a rule, given the UIP. In other words, natural classes are derived from the nature of rule application, rather than constituting a primitive notion of phonological theory. This appears to be a desirable result.

We can now return to the rejection of the use of Ø as a coefficient value for features. Obviously, we could introduce this value, allowing the set of values to range over {+, −, Ø}. However, this move would have implications for the behavior of natural classes that appear to be undesirable. If phonological rules could refer to [ØF] in structural descriptions, then it would be possible to apply rules to segments so specified without affecting other segments. For example, it should be possible to affect Turkish /D/ to the exclusion of both /d/ and /t/, say by rounding it before round vowels:

(136)   A hypothetical rule
        [Ø voice] → [+round] before [+round]

We suspect that we won't find such processes, but introducing Ø as a feature value allows such possibilities since [Øvoice] describes a natural class to the exclusion of /d/ and /t/. In contrast, such a process cannot be modeled using the UIP approach. Underspecified segments can never be referred to without referring to the segments with which they neutralize on the surface.

Either the introduction of negation into the set of lexical representational primitives ([NOT+voice]) or the use of Ø as a possible feature coefficient ([Øvoice]) can be used to correctly model data with the logical structure of the Turkish stop alternations. However, we have provided arguments that introducing logical negation into the *interpretive procedure for rules* is empirically preferable to both of these alternatives.

In Reiss (2003b) the UIP is further discussed to show that it applies to rules containing variables. It is then utilized to develop a partial analysis of Hungarian vowel harmony. For our purposes—justifying some solution to the Catalan problem—we have gone far enough. We now have the apparatus we need to distinguish feature-filling and feature-changing rules in a principled fashion. We are finally ready to turn back to this simple data set and provide a solution which, if not more correct than that advocated by others, is, we hope, at least better justified.

10.6 Catalan, finally

At this point we are ready to consider where our discussion has led us in formulating a principled solution to the Catalan problem we set forth in the introduction.

We repeat here the seven solutions we considered:

(137)   Approaches to the Catalan data
  1. *sek* and *seɣə* are "related" in a grammar in the same way that *go* and *went* are related in the grammar of an English speaker. They share some part of their meaning, but each is memorized as an idiosyncratic entity. The same holds for *sɛk* and *sɛkə*.
  2. The members of each pair of words are related morphologically by the presence vs. absence of a suffix, and the alternants of the root (and the distribution of those alternants) are memorized: the root for 'blind' is *sek* in the masculine and *seɣ* in the feminine; the root for 'dry' is *sɛk* in the masculine and the feminine.
  3. The invariant [k] of *sɛk* 'dry' in various environments conforms to a recurring pattern in the language, as does the alternating [k]/[ɣ] of *sek* / *seɣə* 'blind'. However, both alternants of the *sek* and *seɣə* pattern are stored in memory, and declarative rules determine which is used in particular environments.

4. A single form /sek/ is stored for the 'blind' word, and a single form /sɛk/ is stored for the 'dry' word, but the former also is stored with a stipulation that the /k/ changes to [ɣ] under certain circumstances (say, between vowels).

5. A single form /seɣ/ is stored for 'blind' and general phonological rules convert this, and all cases of /ɣ/ to [k] when it is at the end of a syllable. For this morpheme, the rules yield [sek]. A single form /sɛk/ is stored for 'dry'.

6. A single form /seg/ is stored for 'blind' and general phonological rules convert this, and all cases of /g/ to [k] when it is at the end of a syllable. Other general rules convert the /g/ to [ɣ] between vowels.[11] For this morpheme, the rules yield [sek]. As above, a single form /sɛk/ is stored for 'dry'.

7. A single form /seG/ is stored for 'blind', where /G/ denotes an abstract velar obstruent with no specification for voicing or continuancy, and general phonological rules convert this, and all cases of /G/ to [k] when it is at the end of a syllable. Other general rules convert the /G/ to [ɣ] between vowels. As above, a single form /sɛk/ is stored for 'dry'.

We decided not to pursue solutions 1–3 on the grounds that to accept them is to deny the generative nature of the grammar. Recall that the patterns of alternations seen in the very limited data we are considering here is not limited to these forms. What can we now say about solutions 4–7?

Solution 4 is most easily rejected by comparing it to solutions 5–7. Solution 4 requires, like solutions 5–7, phonological representations for the two morphemes and phonological rules that derive underlying forms. However, solution 4 also requires morpheme-specific stipulations concerning which representations are subject to which rules, while 5–7 do not. Solution 4 is therefore unparsimonious. It also fails to account for various distributional facts—for example the non-occurrence of [ɣ] in final position. Of course, there is no reason a priori to expect every segment to occur in every position, but the remaining solutions, 5–7, do capture this fact as an automatic consequence—it follows from these solutions without any additional theoretical apparatus.

We consider now solution 6, which posits underlying /g/ in the 'blind' morpheme. Since we ourselves have taught this as the correct solution in the past, our Socratic quest to reveal our own ignorance obliges us to examine it particularly closely—what reasons can be offered for accepting that the *k*/ɣ

---

[11] Or rather between continuants, as we will see. We will not continue to point this out in the discussion in this chapter.

alternation is generated from context-sensitive rules applied to underlying /g/? Here are some possibilities, along with reasons why we think they should not be accepted:

- */g/ is historically the source of the alternating sounds.* We have already discussed the fact that language learners have no access to the history of their language, in any sense relevant to their acquisition of a mental grammar. The fact that speakers in the past had an underlying /g/ has no direct bearing on what speakers now have. The irrelevance of the past was discussed in passing in Chapter 6.

- *We should choose /g/ since the writing system uses the letter <g>.* We won't bother responding to this, though, unfortunately, we cannot say that the field has reached the point where such suggestions are not occasionally encountered in the linguistics literature.

- */g/ is a less marked phoneme than /ɣ/.* At numerous points in this book we have argued that markedness is an incoherent notion, and that typological arguments, as well as putative generalizations concerning order of recognizable production by children and the like, should play no role in a theory of grammar.

- *There are non-alternating /g/s in the language, in initial position, so we should minimize the size of the segment inventory by treating these k/ɣ alternations as reflecting the same underlying segment in the inventory.* In the approach we have developed, there is no need for the notion segment, as distinct from the bundles of features associated with timing slots, so no appeal can be made to such entities in deciding on underlying representations. Furthermore, since we see no role for the segment, we see no role for the inventory. Inventories may be useful descriptive tools for linguists, but there is no evidence that they are part of the grammar *qua* speaker's knowledge of language.

- *[ɣ] is in complementary distribution with [g].* The stop [g] occurs in word initial position, and after a non-continuant, whereas [ɣ] appears only between continuants (including vowels). Two issues must be separated:

  i. If there are no morphemes which manifest an alternation between [ɣ] and [g], should the two necessarily be derived from a single underlying source solely by virtue of the complementarity of their distribution?

  ii. If the two do derive from the same underlying source, i.e. if there exists a representation *x* occurring in lexical items that sometimes surfaces as [ɣ] and sometimes as [g], is it necessarily the case that *x* is identical to [g]?

Consideration of these two questions should make it apparent that the the choice of [g] as the underlying source of both [g] and [ɣ] would be arbitrary, even if we accepted the notion that the two should be derived from the same source: [ɣ] would be just as good a choice—in other words, it is no less arbitrary.

We thus find no compelling reason to select [g] as underlying and we move on to consider solutions 5 and 7.

Solution 5 posits underlying /ɣ/ for the alternation in question. In the history of phonology it has been suggested that the underlying representation of a segment and or a morpheme must appear in at least some surface forms. In other words, it should be a point in favor of underlying /ɣ/ that it appears in some surface forms. However, we find no reason to accept this kind of arbitrary appeal to "concreteness". Lexical representations are stored in memory based on a process of construction. There is no a priori reason to require that this construction be identical to one of the inputs that it is meant to map to. So we reject the fact that /ɣ/ occurs in surface forms as an argument in favor of positing it in underlying forms.

Of course, rejecting a bad argument in favor of underlying /ɣ/ does not, in itself, constitute an argument to reject that underlying representation. There may be some good arguments for underlying /ɣ/. At this point we have merely rejected bad arguments for both underlying /ɣ/ and /g/. Thus we still are in the situation of being able to posit extensionally equivalent grammars with underlying /g/, /ɣ/, or /G/, the last option (7), a feature bundle unspecified for the features [voice] and [continuant], but otherwise specified as a velar obstruent.

Theory comparison sometimes takes the form of arguments over which of several competitor theories can account for some empirical facts. However, an equally important issue in the evaluation of a theory is the problem of being so vague as to allow several analyses for a data set. We propose that the only way to choose among competing extensionally equivalent grammars is appeal to the nature of phonological acquisition, the manner in which underlying representations are formed. Of course, the "correct" learning theory is not presented to us as such, and so we have to develop our model of grammar and our model of learning in tandem. The two enterprises must be mutually constraining.

Recall that in solving the Georgian problem we also appealed to a simple model of the learning path. In the Georgian case we focused on the correct formulation of the rule's triggering environment. In Catalan, we are focusing on the correct formulation of the underlying input representation that shows up in various context-sensitive alternants. We find that we can basically propose the same simple set-theroretic model for the Catalan as for the Georgian:

let the acquired rule be the intersection of the statements of the individual instances, as long as the general representation arrived at in this manner subsumes all and only the relevant forms.

Now, the most highly specified representation that subsumes or is consistent with /k/ and /ɣ/ is exactly the underspecified /G/ proposed in solution 7. By positing /G/ in the relevant lexical items, however, we are in danger of generating the wrong output in words with underlying /k/. After all, it appears that any rule that applies to /G/, a a velar obstruent unspecified for the features [voice] and [continuant], should apply to /k/, since /G/ subsumes /k/. Or does it? In fact, given the Universal Interpretive Procedure outlined and justified earlier in this chapter, it does not. In other words, in constructing underlying /G/ in the lexicon, given Catalan-type input, the learner also has to posit a feature-filling rule to account for the occurring alternations. Of course, the feature-filling nature of the rule will follow, via the UIP, from its formulation.

We conclude that apparent arguments for solutions 4–6 do not withstand scrutiny, and that solution 7 appears to follow from the (admittedly still somewhat sketchy) acquisition model we have developed. We thus accept solution 7 as representing our best hypothesis concerning the nature of a Catalan-type grammar. Fleshing out the details of the acquistion process, the construction of underlying forms, awaits a comprehensive theory of "lexicon optimization".

We left open the question of whether the complementary distribution of [ɣ] and [g] should be dealt with by the phonology. After all, there is no reason to not store non-alternating [g] as /g/, with full specification, i.e. different from the /G/ that surfaces as either a voiceless stop or a voiced fricative. From an acquisition perspective, there are no alternations driving the unification of the *k/ɣ* forms and the *g* forms. However, given the UIP, it is possible to also derive the surface forms with [g] from the same underlying underspecified source. We must acknowledge that at this point we have no convincing arguments as to whether we *should* adopt this course, but we now provide a set of ordered "feature-filling" rules that can generate all three surface forms from a single underspecified input.

(138) Catalan rules for deriving *g* and alternating *k/ɣ/g* from a single source
    a. [+velar, −sonorant]→[−voice] / ___#
    b. [+velar, −sonorant]→[+voice]
    c. [+velar, −sonorant]→[+continuant] / [+continuant] ___ [+continuant]
    d. [+velar, −sonorant]→[−continuant]

Rule (a) fills in the feature [−voice] word finally. This rule and rule (d), which applies word-finally (and elsewhere) to fill in [−continuant], combine to neutralize underlying underspecified /G/ with underlying /k/ word-finally. Rule (a) inserts [−voice] in word-final position, and since the segment surfaces as [+voice] everywhere else, no context is needed in rule (b) as long as it follows rule (a). Once again we see that evaluating economy is not so simple— what is more economical, starting with /g/ and changing it to /k/ or having two feature-filling rules?

The same strategy is adopted with rules (c) and (d)—the former fills in [+continuant] between [+continuant] segments, which with the effect of rule (b) leads to the generation of surface [ɣ]. In other environments, the underlying feature bundle surfaces as a [−continuant], either [k] or [g], depending on which of (a) and (b) is applicable.

The keys to the development of our solution to the Catalan and, earlier, Georgian problems are found in the various chapters of this book. Our solution arises from a rejection of markedness and of the significance of inventories, from our proposals regarding the formal machinery necessary for a procedure for referring to underspecified segments which is universal, rather than language-specific, and from our insistence upon taking acquisition issues, especially the competence-performance distinction, seriously. All of these issues are immensely complex, and we would be frankly astonished if any other phonologist, examining the issues to the depth that we have here, adopted all aspects of our resolutions of each of them. But we do believe our approach is logically consistent, and follows from our assumptions, many of which are widely held in the generative community, though not always observed in the scholarly literature produced by that community.

Final Remarks

We started this book by invoking the example of Socrates, who achieved recognition for wisdom by acknowledging his ignorance. At this point, we hope to have at least demonstrated that some of the most basic assumptions of practicing phonologists warrant scrutiny, that many ideas that we teach and implement in our own research cannot be taken for granted. Along the way we have made some positive suggestions as well, but mostly these have not been phonological proposals, strictly speaking. A recurring theme, in fact, has been to offload from phonological theory certain problems that recur in the phonological literature. For this reason, we have made use of the (interrelated) domains of language acquisition and learnability and diachronic linguistics as components for a full explanation of why the set of attested phonological systems is what it is.

It should be clear that it *not* our opinion that phonology itself can be explained away by reference to these other domains. We completely endorse a traditional cognitive science symbol-processing approach to phonology, and in some of the chapters in this book we hope to have contributed to an understanding of the computational mechanisms that constitute the phonological component of the human language faculty. The discussion of Rotuman phase alternations, in addition to providing arguments against Output–Output Correpondence constraints, provided a phonological analysis of the data that appears to be clearly superior to previous analyses which assumed that the phases appeared in distinct morphosyntactic environments. The Unified Interpretive Procedure is an obvious example of our formalistic approach to phonology. In other work, we explore topics like the nature of locality in phonology and the need for quantification in phonological rules.

There are interesting issues that arise from these studies—for example, the need for quantification appears to require an algebraic representational system that is more powerful than feature geometry, and thus it vitiates the need for feature geometry. Like the discovery of structure dependence in syntax, these proposals may not seem dramatic, but it is worthwhile to step back to realize that these proposed properties are not logically necessary aspects of natural languages, and that they cannot be explained on functional grounds. They just seem to be properties that the phonology has—in principle, things could have been different.

We hope to have demonstrated that a consideration of fundamental issues allows us to develop a coherent picture of the study of phonology and its relationship to other fields of study, as well as how evidence concerning the phonological component of the human language faculty is skewed by the mere fact that the phonology is embedded in a massively complex flesh-and-blood system, and thus not directly observable.

We have thus been forced to confront an array of epistemological and ontological questions. Our discussion of linguistic data has been restricted to some mundane examples, yet we hope to have convinced the reader that even such data leads us into difficult, fascinating problems. Even if all of our proposals are rejected, we will be satisfied if our discussion has at least aroused in phonologists a healthy dose of Socratic skepticism.

References

Abo, Takaji, Bender, Byron W., Capelle, Alfred and DeBrum, Tony (1976). *Marshallese–English Dictionary*. University of Hawaii Press, Honolulu.

Aissen, Judith and Bresnan, Joan (2002). Categoricity and variation in syntax: the Stochastic Generalization. Paper presented at the Potsdam Conference on Gradedness.

Anderson, Stephen R. (1985). *Phonology in the Twentieth Century*. University of Chicago Press.

Archangeli, Diana (1988). *Underspecification in Yawelmani Phonology and Morphology* (revision of 1984 MIT dissertation). Garland, New York.

Archangeli, Diana (1997). Optimality Theory: an introduction to linguistics in the 1990s. In *Optimality Theory: An Overview* (ed. D. Archangeli and D. T. Langendoen), pp. 1–32. Blackwell, Cambridge, MA.

Archangeli, Diana and Pulleyblank, Douglas (1994). *Grounded Phonology*. MIT Press, Cambridge, MA.

Bayer, Sam and Johnson, Mark (1995). *Features and Agreement: Proceedings of the 33rd Annual Meeting of the Association for Computational Linguistics*. Morgan Kaufmann, San Francisco, CA.

Beckman, Jill (1997). Positional faithfulness, positional neutralisation and Shona vowel harmony. *Phonology*, 14, 1–16.

Bender, Byron W. (1963). Marshallese phonemics: labialization or palatalization? *Word*, 19, 335–341.

Bender, Byron W. (1968). Marshallese phonology. *Oceanic Linguistics*, 7, 16–35.

Bender, Byron W. (1969). *Spoken Marshallese*. University Press of Hawaii, Honolulu.

Benua, Laura (1995). Identity effects in morphological truncation. In *University of Massachusetts Occasional Papers 18: Papers in Optimality Theory* (ed. J. Beckman, L. W. Dickey and S. Urbanczyk), pp. 77–136. GLSA, Amherst, MA.

Benua, Laura (1997). Phonological relations between words (ROA 259). Ph.D., University of Massachusetts at Amherst.

Berko, Jean (1958). The child's learning of English morphology. *Word*, 14, 150–77.

Berwick, R. (1986). *The Acquisition of Syntactic Knowledge*. MIT Press, Cambridge, MA.

Blevins, Juliette (1994). The bimoraic foot in Rotuman phonology and morphology. *Oceanic Linguistics*, 33, 491–516.

Blevins, Juliette (2003). *Evolutionary Phonology: The Emergence of Sound Patterns*. Cambridge University Press.

Blevins, Juliette and Garrett, Andrew (1998). The origins of consonant–vowel metathesis. *Language*, 74, 508–56.

Bloomfield, Leonard (1933). *Language*. Holt, Rinehart & Winston.

Bod, Rens, Hay, Jennifer and Jannedy, Stefanie (2003). *Probabilistic Linguistics*. MIT Press, Cambridge, MA.

Boersma, P. and Hayes, Bruce (2001). Empirical tests of the Gradual Learning Algorithm. *Linguistic Inquiry*, 32, 45–86.

Bregman, Albert S. (1990). *Auditory Scene Analysis: The Perceptual Organization of Sound*. MIT Press, Cambridge, MA.

Bresnan, Joan and Deo, Ashwini (2001). Grammatical constraints on variation: 'be' in the Survey of English Dialects and (stochastic) Optimality Theory. MS, Stanford University.

Buck, Carl Darling (1933). *Comparative Grammar of Greek and Latin*. University of Chicago Press.

Burton-Roberts, N. (2000). Where and what is phonology? A representational view. In *Phonological Knowledge: Its Nature and Status* (ed. N. Burton-Roberts, P. Carr and G. Docherty), pp. 39–66. Oxford University Press.

Calabrese, Andrea (1988). A Theory of Phonological Alphabets. Ph.D., MIT, Cambridge, MA.

Calabrese, Andrea (2005). *Markedness and Economy in a Derivational Model of Phonology*. De Gruyter, Berlin.

Choi, John D. (1992, December). *Phonetic Underspecification and Target Interpolation: An Acoustic Study of Marshallese Vowel Allophony*. Vol. 82, UCLA Working Papers in Phonetics.

Chomsky, Noam (1957). *Syntactic Structures*. Mouton, The Hague.

Chomsky, Noam (1964). Formal discussion in response to W. Miller and S. Ervin. In *The Acquisition of Language* (ed. U. Bellugi and R. Brown), pp. 35–9. University of Chicago Press.

Chomsky, Noam (1965). *Aspects of the Theory of Syntax*. MIT Press, Cambridge, MA.

Chomsky, Noam (1967). Some general properties of phonological rules. *Language*, 43, 102–28.

Chomsky, Noam (1971). Deep structure, surface structure and semantic interpretation. In *Semantics: An Interdisciplinary Reader in Linguistics, Philosophy and Psychology* (ed. D. Steinberg and L. Jakobovits), pp. 183–216. Cambridge University Press.

Chomsky, Noam (1986). *Knowledge of Language*. Praeger, Westport, CT.

Chomsky, Noam (1993). *Language and Thought*. Moyer Bell, London.

Chomsky, Noam (2002). *On Nature and Language*. Cambridge University Press.

Chomsky, Noam (2005). Three factors in language design. *Linguistic Inquiry*, 36, 1–22.

Chomsky, Noam and Halle, Morris (1968). *The Sound Pattern of English*. Harper & Row, New York.

Churchward, C. M. (1940). *Rotuman Grammar and Dictionary*. Methodist Church of Australia, Sydney.

Clark, H., Robin, D., McCullagh, G. and Schmidt, R. (2001). Motor control in children and adults during a non-speech oral task. *Journal of Speech, Language, and Hearing Research*, 4, 1015–25.

Crystal, David A. (2003). *A Dictionary of Linguistics and Phonetics*, 5th edn. Blackwell, Malden, MA.

Culicover, Peter W. (1999). *Syntactic Nuts: Hard Cases, Syntactic Theory, and Language Acquisition*. Oxford University Press.

Dell, F. (1981). On the learnability of optional phonological rules. *Linguistic Inquiry*, 12, 31–7.

den Dikken, Marcel (2003). *The Structure of the Noun Phrase in Rotuman*. Lincom Europa, Munich.

Derrow, Avram (2000). The Empirical Content of Differentiating Redundancy. BA dissertation, University of Michigan.

Dodd, Barbara (1975). Children's understanding of their own phonological forms. *Quarterly Journal of Experimental Psychology*, 27, 165–72.

Drachman, Gabarell (1978). Child language and language change: a conjecture and some refutations. In *Recent Developments in Historical Phonology* (ed. J. Fisiak), pp. 123–44. Mouton, The Hague.

Engstrand, O. (1997). Areal biases in stop paradigms. *PHONUM*, 4, 191–4.

Epstein, Samuel David (1999). Un-principled syntax and the derivation of syntactic relations. In *Working Minimalism* (ed. S. D. Epstein and N. Hornstein), pp. 317–45. MIT Press, Cambridge, MA.

Epstein, Samuel D., Flynn, Suzanne and Martohardjono, Gita (1996). Second language acquisition: theoretical and experimental issues in contemporary research. *Brain and Behavioral Sciences*, 19, 677–758.

Epstein, S. D., Groat, E., Kawashima, R. and Kitahara, H. (1998). *A Derivational Approach to Syntactic Relations*. Oxford University Press.

Epstein, Samuel D. and Seely, Daniel (2006). *Derivations in Minimalism*. Cambridge University Press.

Faber, Alice and Best, Catherine T. (1994). The perceptual infrastructure of early phonological development. In *Reality of Linguistic Rules* (ed. S. D. Lima, R. L. Corrigan and G. K. Iverson), pp. 261–80. Benjamins, Philadelphia.

Ferguson, Charles (1986). Discovering sound units and constructing sound systems: it's child's play. In *Invariance and Variability in Speech Processes* (ed. J. S. Perkell and D. H. Klatt), pp. 36–53. Erlbaum, Hillsdale, NJ.

Flemming, Edward (1995). Phonetic detail in phonology: toward a unified account of assimilation and coarticulation. *Coyote Papers: Proceedings of the Arizona Phonology Conference, Features in Optimality Theory*, 5. University of Arizona.

Fodor, Janet Dean and Sakas, William Gregory (2005). The subset principle in syntax: costs of compliance. *Journal of Linguistics*, 41, 513–69.

Fodor, Jerry (1975). *The Language of Thought*. Harvester, Brighton, Sussex.

Fudge, E. (2006). Glossematics. In *Encyclopedia of Language and Linguistics*, 2nd edn. (ed. K. Brown), pp. 1439–44. Elsevier, Oxford.

Gallistel, C. R. (1996). Insect navigation: brains as symbol-processing organ. In *Invitation to Cognitive Science*, vol. 4 (ed. D. Scarborough and S. Sternberg), pp. 1–51. MIT Press, Cambridge, MA.

Gibbon, F. (1990). Lingual activity in two speech-disordered children's attempts to produce velar and alveolar stop consonants: evidence from electropalatographic (EPG) data. *British Journal of Disorders of Communication*, **25**, 329–40.

Gleitman, Lila R. and Liberman, Mark (1995). *An Invitation to Cognitive Science*, vol. 1: *Language*, 2nd edn. MIT Press, Cambridge, MA.

Gnanadesikan, Amalia E. (1995). Markedness and faithfulness constraints in child phonology. MS. Rutgers Optimality Archive.

Goodman, Judith and Nussbaum, Howard (1994). *The Development of Speech Perception*. MIT Press, Cambridge, MA.

Hale, Mark (1995). Theory and method in historical linguistics. MS, Department of Classics, Modern Languages, and Linguistics, Concordia University, Montreal.

Hale, Mark (2000). Marshallese phonology, the phonetics–phonology interface, and historical linguistics. *Linguistic Review*, **17**, 241–57.

Hale, Mark (2007). *Historical Linguistics: Theory and Method*. Blackwell, Oxford.

Hale, Mark and Kissock, Madelyn (1998). The phonology–syntax interface in Rotuman. In *Proceedings of the Fourth Austronesian Formal Linguistics Association* (ed. M. Pearson), pp. 115–28. UCLA, Los Angeles.

Hale, Mark, Kissock, Madelyn and Reiss, Charles (1998*a*). Evaluating the empirical basis for output–output correspondence. In *Proceedings of the Annual Meeting of the Berkeley Linguistics Society 23* (ed. M. Juge and J. Moxley), pp. 137–47. University of California at Berkeley.

Hale, Mark, Kissock, Madelyn and Reiss, Charles (1998*b*). What is output? Output–output correspondence in OT phonology. In *Proceedings of the Sixteenth West Coast Conference on Formal Linguistics* (ed. E. Curtis, J. Lyle and G. Webster), pp. 223–36. CSLI, Stanford, CA.

Hale, Mark, Kissock, Madelyn and Reiss, Charles (2007). Microvariation, variation and the features of Universal Grammar. *Lingua*, **117**, 645–65.

Hale, Mark and Reiss, Charles (1997). Grammar optimization: the simultaneous acquisition of constraint ranking and a lexicon. MS, Concordia University, Montreal.

Hale, Mark and Reiss, Charles (1998). Formal and empirical arguments concerning phonological acquisition. *Linguistic Inquiry*, **29**, 656–83.

Hale, Mark and Reiss, Charles (2000). Substance abuse and dysfunctionalism: current trends in phonology. *Linguistic Inquiry*, **31**, 157–69.

Hale, Mark and Reiss, Charles (2000). Phonology as cognition. In *Phonological Knowledge: Conceptual and Empirical Issues* (ed. N. Burton-Roberts, P. Carr and G. Docherty), pp. 161–84. Oxford University Press.

Hale, Mark and Reiss, Charles (2003). The Subset Principle in phonology: why the *tabula* can't be *rasa*. *Journal of Linguistics*, **39**, 219–44.

Halle, Morris (1975). Confessio grammatici. *Language*, **51**, 525–35.

Halle, Morris and Idsardi, William (1995). Stress and metrical structure. In *Handbook of Phonological Theory* (ed. J. A. Goldsmith), pp. 403–43. Blackwell, Oxford.

Halle, Morris and Idsardi, William J. (1997). R, hypercorrection and the Elsewhere Condition. In *Derivations and Constraints in Phonology* (ed. I. Roca), pp. 331–48. Oxford University Press.

Halle, Morris and Vergnaud, J. R. (1987). *An Essay on Stress*. MIT Press, Cambridge, MA.

Hamburger, H. and Wexler, K. (1975). A mathematical theory of learning transformational grammar. *Journal of Mathematical Psychology*, 12, 137–77.

Hammarberg, R. (1976). The metaphysics of coarticulation. *Journal of Phonetics*, 4, 353–63.

Hawkins, Sarah (1999). Reevaluating assumptions about speech perception. In *The Acoustics of Speech Perception* (ed. J. Pickett), pp. 183–288. Allyn & Bacon, Boston.

Hay, Jennifer (2000). Causes and consequences of word structure. Ph.D., Northwestern University.

Hayes, Bruce (1999). Phonetically driven phonology: the role of Optimality Theory and inductive grounding. In *Functionalism and Formalism in Linguistics* (ed. M. Darnell, E. Moravcsik, F. Newmeyer, M. Noonan and K. Wheatley), pp. 243–85. Benjamins, Amsterdam.

Hellberg, S. (1980). Apparent naturalness in Faroese phonology. *Nordic Journal of Linguistics*, 3, 1–24.

Hock, Hans Henrich (1991). *Principles of Historical Linguistics*, 2nd edn. Mouton de Gruyter, Berlin.

Hoffman, Donald D. (1998). *Visual Intelligence*. Norton, New York.

Hyams, N. and Sigurjónsdóttir, S. (1990). The development of 'long distance anaphora'. *Language Acquisition*, 1, 57–93.

Hyman, Larry (2001). On the limits of phonetic determinism in phonology: *NC revisited. In *The Role of Speech Perception Phenomena in Phonology* (ed. Beth Hume and Keith Johnston). Academic Press, New York, pp. 141–85.

Idsardi, William (1992). The computation of prosody. Ph.D., MIT.

Ingram, David (1976). Phonological analysis of a child. *Glossa*, 10, 3–27.

Ingram, David (1989a). *First Language Acquisition: Method, Description, Explanation*. Cambridge University Press.

Ingram, David (1989b). *Phonological Disability in Children*, 2nd edn. Cole & Whurr, London.

Ingram, David (1995). The acquisition of negative constraints, the OCP, and underspecified representations. In *Phonological Acquisition and Phonological Theory* (ed. J. Archibald), pp. 63–79. Erlbaum, Hillsdale, NJ.

Inkelas, Sharon (1994). The consequences of optimization for underspecification. MS, Department of Linguistics, University of California at Berkeley (ROA 40-1294).

Inkelas, Sharon (1996). Archiphonemic underspecification. MS, University of California at Berkeley.

Inkelas, Sharon and Orgun, Orhan (1995). Level ordering and economy in the lexical phonology of Turkish. *Language*, 71, 763–93.

Inkelas, Sharon, Orgun, Orhan and Zoll, Cheryl (1997). The implications of lexical exceptions for the nature of grammar. In *Derivations and Constraints in Phonology* (ed. I. Roca), pp. 393–418. Oxford University Press.

Jackendoff, Ray (1987). *Consciousness and the Computational Mind*. MIT Press, Cambridge, MA.

Jackendoff, Ray (1990). *Semantic Structures*. MIT Press, Cambridge, MA.

Jackendoff, Ray (1994). *Patterns In The Mind: Language and Human Nature*. Basic Books, New York.

Jakobson, Roman (1941/1968). *Kindersprache, aphasie und allgemeine lautgesetze*. Trans. as *Child Language, Aphasia and Phonological Universals*. Mouton, 1968, The Hague.

Johnson, Keith, Pisoni, David and Bernacki, Robert (1990). Do voice recordings reveal whether a person is intoxicated? *Phonetica*, 47, 215–37.

Kager, René (1997). Rhythmic vowel deletion in Optimality Theory. In *Derivations and Constraints in Phonology* (ed. I. Roca), pp. 463–99. Oxford University Press.

Kager, René (1999). *Optimality Theory*. Cambridge University Press.

Karttunen, Lauri (1993). Finite state constraints. In *The Last Phonological Rule* (ed. J. Goldsmith), pp. 173–94. University of Chicago Press.

Keating, Patricia (1988). Underspecification in phonetics. *Phonology*, 5, 275–92.

Keer, Edward (1999). Geminates, the OCP and the nature of CON. Ph.D., Rutgers University.

Keller, Frank and Asudeh, Ash (2002). Probabilistic learning algorithms and Optimality Theory. *Linguistic Inquiry*, 33, 225–44.

Kenstowicz, Michael (1994). *Phonology in Generative Grammar*. Blackwell, Oxford.

Kenstowicz, Michael (1995). Cyclic vs. non-cyclic constraint evaluation. *Phonology*, 12, 397–436.

Kenstowicz, Michael (1996). Base-identity and uniform exponence: alternatives to cyclicity. In *Current Trends in Phonology: Models and Methods* (ed. J. Durand and B. Laks), pp. 363–93. CNRS, Paris X, and University of Salford.

Kenstowicz, Michael and Kisseberth, Charles (1979). *Generative Phonology: Description and Theory*. Academic Press, New York.

Kent, R. D. (1992). The biology of phonological development. In *Phonological Development: Models, Research, Implications* (ed. C. A. Ferguson, L. Menn and C. Stoel-Gammon), pp. 65–90. York Press, Timonium, MD.

Kiparsky, Paul (1973). Phonological representations. In *Three Dimensions of Linguistic Theory* (ed. O. Fujimura), pp. 1–135. TEC Corporation, Tokyo.

Kiparsky, Paul (1985). Some consequences of lexical phonology. *Phonology Yearbook*, 2, 85–138.

Kiparsky, Paul and Menn, Lise (1977). On the acquisition of phonology. In *Language, Learning and Thought* (ed. J. Macnamara), pp. 47–78. Academic Press, New York.

Kirchner, Robert (1997). Contrastiveness and faithfulness. *Phonology*, 14, 83–111.

Kissock, Madelyn (2002). Do experimental studies inform theoretical research? MS, Oakland University.

Kornfeld, J. R. and Goehl, H. (1974). A new twist to an old observation: kids know more than they say. In *Papers from the Parasession on Natural Phonology* (ed. A. Bruck, R. Fox and M. LaGaly), pp. 210–19. Chicago Linguistic Society.

Kuhl, P. and Iverson, G. K. (1995). Linguistic experience and perceptual magnet effect. In *Speech Perception and Linguistic Experience* (ed. W. Strange), pp. 121–54. York Press, Timonium, MD.

Labov, William (1994). *Principles of Linguistic Change: Internal Factors*. Blackwell, Oxford.

LaCharité, Darlene and Paradis, Carole (1993). The emergence of constraints in generative phonology and a comparison of three current constraint-based models. *Canadian Journal of Linguistics*, **38**, 127–54.

Local, J. and Coleman, J. (1994). The 'no crossing constraint' in autosegmental phonology. *Linguistics and Philosophy*, **14**, 295–338.

Lust, Barbara (2006). *Child Language: Acquisition and Growth*. Cambridge University Press.

Lyons, John (1970). *Chomsky*. Fontana, London.

Macken, Marlys A. (1995). Phonological acquisition. In *The Handbook of Phonological Theory* (ed. J. A. Goldsmith), pp. 671–96. Blackwell, Oxford.

Maddieson, Ian (1984). *Patterns of Sounds*. Cambridge University Press.

Maddieson, Ian and Precoda, K. (1989). Updating UPSID. *Journal of the Acoustical Society of America*, suppl. 1, **86**.

Marantz, Alec (1982). On the acquisition of grammatical relations. *Linguistische Berichte*, **80/82**, 32–69.

Marcus, G. F. (1993). Negative evidence in language acquisition. *Cognition*, **46**, 53–85.

Marlett, S. and Stemberger, J. (1983). Empty consonants in Seri. *Linguistic Inquiry*, **14**, 617–39.

Martin, S. (1954). *Korean Morphophonemics*. Linguistic Society of America, Baltimore, MD.

Masilon, Todd and Ross, Kie (1996). Weak syllable deletion: an Articulatory Phonology account. MS, UCLA, Linguistics Department.

Maye, J., Werker, Janet and Gerken, L. (2002). Infant sensitivity to distributional information can affect phonetic discrimination. *Cognition*, **82**, B101–111.

McCarthy, John (1986). OCP effects: gemination and antigemination. *Linguistic Inquiry*, **17**, 207–63.

McCarthy, John (1988). Feature geometry and dependency: a review. *Phonetica*, **45**, 84–108.

McCarthy, John (1993). A case of surface rule inversion. *Canadian Journal of Linguistics*, **38**, 169–95.

McCarthy, John (1994). The phonetics and phonology of Semitic pharyngeals. In *Phonological Structure and Phonetic Form: Papers in Laboratory Phonology III* (ed. P. Keating), pp. 191–233. Cambridge University Press.

McCarthy, John (1995). Faithfulness in prosodic morphology and phonology: Rotuman revisited. ROA 110-0000.

McCarthy, John (1996). Remarks on phonological opacity in optimality theory. In *Studies in Afroasiatic Grammar: Papers from the Second Conference on Afroasiatic Linguistics, Sophia Antipolis, 1994* (ed. J. Lecarme, J. Lowenstamm and U. Shlonsky), pp. 215–43. Holland Academic Graphics, The Hague.

McCarthy, John (2000). The prosody of phase in Rotuman. *Natural Language and Linguistic Theory*, 18, 147–97.

McCarthy, John (2003a). Sympathy, cumulativity, and the Duke-of-York gambit. In *The Syllable in Optimality Theory* (ed. C. Féry and R. van de Vijver), pp. 23–76. Cambridge University Press.

McCarthy, John (2003b). Richness of the base and the determination of underlying representations. Ms., University of Massachusetts, Amherst.

McCarthy, John (2006). *Hidden Generalizations: Phonological Opacity in Optimality Theory*. Equinox, London.

McCarthy, John and Prince, Alan (1995). Faithfulness and reduplicative identity. In *University of Massachusetts Occasional Papers in Linguistics*, vol. 18 (ed. J. Beckman, L. W. Dickey and S. Urbancyk), pp. 249–384. GLSA, University of Massachusetts at Amherst, Amherst, MA.

Menn, Lise and Mathei, Edward (1992). The two-lexicon approach to child phonology: looking back, looking ahead. In *Phonological Development: Models, Research, Implications* (ed. C. A. Ferguson, L. Menn and C. Stoel-Gammon), pp. 131–63. York Press, Timonium, MD.

Miller, J. L. and Eimas, P. D. (1983). Studies in the categorization of speech by infants. *Cognition*, 13, 135–65.

Mohanan, K. P. (2000). The theoretical substance of optimality formalism. *Linguistic Review*, 17, 143–66.

Odden, David (1986). On the Obligatory Contour Principle. *Language*, 62, 353–83.

Odden, David (1988). Antiantigemination and the OCP. *Linguistic Inquiry*, 19, 451–75.

Ohala, John (1990). The phonetics and phonology of aspects of assimilation. In *Papers in Laboratory Phonology I: Between the Grammar and Physics of Speech* (ed. J. Kingston and M. Beckman), pp. 258–75. Cambridge University Press.

Ohala, John J. (1998). A bibliography of the phonetics of sound change. MS, University of California at Berkeley.

Orgun, C. O. (1997). Sign-based morphology and phonology with special reference to Optimality Theory. Ph.D., University of California at Berkeley.

Paradis, Carole (1988). On constraints and repair strategies. *Linguistic Review*, 6, 71–97.

Pesetsky, David (1982). Paths and Categories. Ph. D., MIT.

Piatellia-Palmarini, M. (1994). *Inevitable Illusions: How Mistakes of Reason Rule Our Minds*. Wiley, New York.

Pierrehumbert, Janet B. (2001). Stochastic phonology. *GLOT International*, 5, 195–207.

Pinker, Steven (1984). *Language Learnability and Language Learning*. Harvard University Press, Cambridge, MA.

Pinker, Steven (1995). *The Language Instinct*. HarperCollins, New York.

Popper, Karl (1962). *The Open Society and Its Enemies*, 2nd edn. Princeton University Press.

Prince, Alan and Smolensky, Paul (1993). Optimality Theory: constraint interaction in generative grammar (Technical Report). Rutgers Center for Cognitive Science, New Brunswick, NJ.

Prince, Alan and Tesar, Bruce (1999). *Learning Phonotactic Distributions; Technical Report TR-54.* Rutgers Center for Cognitive Science, New Brunswick, NJ.

Pulleyblank, Douglas (1997). Optimality Theory and features. In *Optimality Theory: An Overview* (ed. D. Archangeli and D. T. Langendoen), pp. 59–101. Blackwell, Cambridge, MA.

Pylyshyn, Zenon (1973). The role of competence theories in cognitive psychology. *Journal of Psycholinguistic Research*, 2, 21–50.

Pylyshyn, Zenon (1984). *Computation and Cognition.* MIT Press, Cambridge, MA.

Pylyshyn, Zenon (2000). Situating vision in the world. *TRENDS in Cognitive Science*, 4(5), 197–207.

Quine, Willard (1972). Methodological reflections on current linguistic theory. In *Semantics of Natural Language* (ed. G. Harman and D. Davidson), pp. 442–54. Humanities Press, New York.

Reiss, Charles (1995). A theory of assimilation, with special reference to Old Icelandic phonology. Ph.D., Harvard University.

Reiss, Charles (1996). Deriving an implicational universal in a constrained OT grammar. In *Proceedings of the Northeast Linguistics Society* (ed. K. Kusumoto), pp. 303–17. UMass Graduate Linguistics Association, Amherst, MA.

Reiss, Charles (1997). The origin of the *nn/ð* alternation in Old Icelandic. *North West European Language Evolution*, 30, 135–58.

Reiss, Charles (2000). Optimality Theory from a cognitive science perspective. *Linguistic Review*, 3–4, 291–301.

Reiss, Charles (2001). L2 evidence for the stucture of the L1 lexicon. *International Journal of English Studies*, 1, 219–39.

Reiss, Charles (2003a). Quantification in Structural Descriptions: Attested and Unattested Patterns. *Linguistic Review*, 20, 305–38.

Reiss, Charles (2003b). Deriving the feature-filling/feature-changing contrast: an application to Hungarian vowel harmony. *Linguistic Inquiry*, 34, 199–224.

Reiss, Charles (2007). Modularity in the 'sound' domain. In *The Oxford Handbook of Linguistic Interfaces* (ed. G. Ramchand and C. Reiss), pp. 53–80. Oxford University Press.

Rennison, J. (2000). OT and TO. *Linguistic Review*, 17, 135–41.

Rice, Keren and Avery, Peter (1995). Variability in a deterministic model of language acquisition. In *Phonological Acquisition and Phonological Theory* (ed. J. Archibald), pp. 23–42. Erlbaum, Hillsdale, NJ.

Robins, R. H. and Waterson, Natalie (1952). Notes on the phonetics of the Georgian word. *Bulletin of the School of Oriental and African Studies*, 14, 55–72.

Sapir, Edward (1925). Sound patterns in language. *Language*, 1, 37–51.

Sklar, Lawrence (2000). *Theory and Truth: Philosophical Critique within Foundational Science.* Oxford University Press, Oxford.

Smith, A. and Goffman, L. (1998). Stability and patterning of speech movement sequences in children and adults. *Journal of Speech Language Hearing Research*, 41, 18–30.

Smith, N. V. (1973). *The Acquisition of Phonology: A Case Study*. Cambridge University Press.

Smolensky, Paul (1996). On the comprehension/production dilemma in child language. *Linguistic Inquiry*, 27, 720–31.

Sosa, Anna Vogel and Stoel-Gammon, Carol (2006). Patterns of intra-word phonological variability during the second year of life. *Journal of Child Language*, 33, 31–50.

Steriade, Donca (1997). Phonetics in phonology: the case of laryngeal neutralization. Available at: http://www.linguistics.ucla.edu/people/steriade/papers/phoneticsinphonology.pdf

Stevens, K. N., Keyser, S. J. and Kawasaki, H. (1986). Toward a phonetic and phonological investigation of redundant features. In *Symposium on Invariance and Variability of Speech Processes* (ed. J. Perkell and D. H. Klatt), pp. 426–63. Erlbaum, Hillsdale, NJ.

Stoel-Gammon, Carol (2004). Variability in children's speech. Paper presented at Talk: Child Phonology Conference 2004, Arizona State University, Tempe.

Streeter, L. A. (1976). Kikuyu labial and apical stop discrimination. *Journal of Phonetics*, 4, 43–9.

Szabolcsi, Anna (1988). Filters versus combinators. In *Intensional Logic, History of Philosophy, and Methodology* (ed. I. Bodnár, A. Máté and L. Pólos), pp. 91–101. Filozofiai Figyelo, Budapest.

Tesar, Bruce (1997). Multi-recursive constraint demotion. MS, available at Rutgers Optimality Archive (http://roa.rutgers.edu), ROA-197.

Tesar, Bruce and Smolensky, Paul (1993). The learnability of Optimality Theory: an algorithm and some basic complexity results. Computer Science Department, University of Colorado, Boulder.

Tesar, Bruce and Smolensky, Paul (1998). The learnability of Optimality Theory. *Linguistic Inquiry*, 29, 229–68.

Thelen, Esther and Ulrich, Beverly D. (1991). Hidden skills: a dynamic systems analysis of treadmill stepping during the first year. *Monograph of the Society for Research in Child Development*, 56, 1–98.

Titifanua, Mesulama and Churchward, C. M. (1938). *Tales of a Lonely Island*. Oceania Monographs 4, Sydney.

Wegner, Daniel M. (2002). *The Illusion of Conscious Will*. MIT Press, Cambridge, MA.

Wexler, Kenneth and Culicover, Peter (1980). *Formal Principles of Language Acquisition*. MIT Press, Cambridge, MA.

Wexler, Kenneth and Manzini, M. Rita (1987). Parameters and learnability in Binding Theory. In *Parameter Setting* (ed. T. Roeper and E. Williams), pp. 41–76. Reidel, Dordrecht.

Yip, Moira (1988). The Obligatory Contour Principle and phonological rules: a loss of identity. *Linguistic Inquiry*, 19, 65–100.

Index